System and Process
in Southeast Asia

About the Book and Author

Southeast Asia, although not garnering the headlines of ten to twenty years ago, is important in global politics. Vietnam's domination of Indochina, for example, has polarized the region, given the Soviet Union new regional access, and magnified the military threat to Thailand. Insurgency movements supported by the radical Left or Right continue to plague governments. The Strait of Malacca, the major sea-lane through Southeast Asia, provides primary access for the U.S. Pacific fleet to the Indian Ocean and the Middle East and is Japan's oil lifeline. U.S. commercial and military interests remain strong in the Philippines and are expanding in Indonesia, the world's fifth largest country (with a population approaching 170 million people), whereas Thailand, Malaysia, and Singapore are sources for investment, raw materials, and potential markets. Thailand, once closely allied with the United States, has again renewed those ties in the face of Vietnam's expansion.

This comprehensive, up-to-date textbook analyzes Southeast Asia in the context of regional and global political systems, both traditional and contemporary. After looking at the traditional patterns of interstate relations in the region, Professor McCloud shows that Southeast Asia has been and continues to be dependent on the global system. However, he also identifies a "neotraditional current" in contemporary Southeast Asian politics, as elements of traditional beliefs and values reassert themselves in policy and practice, redefine the patterns of interstate behavior in the region, and set the limits to dependence on the global system.

The book is intended as a primary text for courses on the history or politics of Asia or Southeast Asia, regional development and integration, and the role of Southeast Asia in world politics. It will also be useful in survey courses in Asian studies, comparative politics, and Third World development.

Donald G. McCloud is the associate executive director of the Midwest Universities Consortium for International Activities (MUCIA). He also holds an adjunct appointment in the department of political science at the Ohio State University.

In memoriam
Jean G. McCloud

Donald G. McCloud

System and Process in Southeast Asia: The Evolution of a Region

Westview Press • Boulder, Colorado

Frances Pinter (Publishers) • London, England

Copyright © 1986 by Westview Press, Inc.

Published in 1986 in the United States of America by Westview Press,
Inc.; Frederick A. Praeger, Publisher; 5500 Central Avenue, Boulder,
Colorado 80301

Published in Great Britain by Frances Pinter (Publishers) Limited,
25 Floral Street, Covent Garden, London WC2E 9DS

Library of Congress Cataloging in Publication Data
McCloud, Donald G.
    System and process in Southeast Asia
    1. Asia, Southeastern--Politics and government.
2. Regionalism--Asia, Southeastern. I. Title.
DS526.7.M38 1986   959'.05   85-26574
ISBN 0-86531-587-6
ISBN 0-86531-588-4 (pbk.)

British Library Cataloguing in Publication Data
McCloud, Donald G.
    System and process in South East Asia: The
    evolution of a region.
    1. Asia, South Eastern--Politics and government
    I. Title
    320'.959   JQ96.A2
ISBN 0-86187-506-0

Composition for this book was provided by the author.

Printed and bound in the United States of America

The paper used in this publication meets the minimum requirements of the American National Standard for Permanence of
Paper for Printed Library Materials Z39.48-1984.

6   5   4   3   2   1

Contents

Preface

The thoughts and ideas presented in this book have evolved over a long period of time. The process began in the late 1960s during my graduate training and has continued ever since, paralleling the general pattern of thought among other Southeast Asian scholars. The project required such a long period for completion partly because of the slow developments in the field and partly because duties prevented me from focusing fully on research and writing. My approach to the subject was greatly influenced by Richard L. Walker and Donald E. Weatherbee. The intellectual debt that I carry from them and others at the University of South Carolina is enormous and one that I feel I seldom repay. Don Weatherbee also provided valuable criticisms for balancing the material and substance of this work.

The opportunity to participate in the Department of Political Science of The Ohio State University and the encouragement from its members, particularly R. William Liddle and Charles F. Hermann, stimulated my desire to undertake the project. For those resources not available in the libraries at Ohio State, the Southeast Asian Collection at Ohio University proved invaluable and its staff knowledgeable and supportive. The editorial staff at Westview Press has also been extremely supportive and helpful, even at times when it appeared that the manuscript might never be completed.

My deepest appreciation goes to the Midwest Universities Consortium for International Activities (MUCIA), not only for providing for my livelihood but also for giving me the opportunity to travel frequently to Southeast Asia and to become intimately involved in development work there. The demands of program

xii

development and maintenance at MUCIA were often consuming but so too was the insistence of the executive director, William L. Flinn, that the book be finished. Without his friendship and support, as well as that of the consortium's Board of Directors and staff, this task would ultimately have been impossible. Within the executive office of the consortium, Jayne Allison worked tirelessly preparing the early drafts, revisions, and versions using different formats; Mark Simpson assisted greatly with documentation and citations; John Biefeldt carefully edited the first complete version of the manuscript; and Donald R. Walker and Dorothy Shanfeld rescued the entire project when, at the last minute, all of the manuscript had to be retyped into a new word-processing system. Their efforts are sincerely appreciated.

The actual preparation of the manuscript began in 1982, and since that time my family has endured with a husband and father who appeared to be working at two full-time positions. The patience of Carol, Laura, and Grant in listening to the phrase "I'm writing" has kept family life somewhere near normal.

Despite the kindness and efforts of so many on my behalf, clearly the errors and shortcomings of this work are my responsibility.

Donald G. McCloud
Columbus, Ohio

CHAPTER 1

Southeast Asia in
Regional and Global Contexts

Different people think of Southeast Asia in different ways. Mention of Thailand, Indonesia, or the Philippines, for example, often brings to mind an exotic tropical paradise of palm trees, beautiful ocean beaches, and costumed dancers. Monkeys, temples, volcanoes, and terraced rice fields are sometimes added to this travel-poster image, but names other than Bali, Manila, or perhaps Bangkok are difficult to recall. However, this image is not current. Many contrasts--for example, between the airplanes that deliver visitors to Southeast Asia and the plodding water buffalo that travelers see there--exist and confound the mind. The idealized (if not romanticized) view of traditional societies, evoking images of peace, harmony, and quiet stability based on communal village life and mutual social welfare, is now contradicted by intruding Western values of individualism, consumerism, nationalism, and other trappings of the modern world. The stereotypical travel-poster image belies a region that is rich in historical and cultural traditions, complex social structures, vigorous political, economic, and cultural growth, and increasingly confident in its prominent place in global politics.

Other perceptions of Southeast Asia have also obscured the realities of the region. The British, French, Dutch, and other Europeans retain images of a bygone era of white-jacketed colonial administrators and great shaded verandas, too often symbolizing the "white man's burden" among indolent natives. However, this sense of moral obligation, a hallmark of the colonial era, stood side by side with the phenomenal exploitation by the colonial powers of the region's physical and material wealth. The colonial period had been evaluated in great detail from

many perspectives,[1] but the prevalent view today has
shifted the focus of Southeast Asian history away from
indigenous cultures and politics and toward European and
American involvement, thus perpetuating the view that
little of political or economic importance transpired in
Southeast Asia before the arrival of the Europeans.
Histories of Southeast Asia from 1500 to 1940 have been
largely a record of colonial conquests, governors,
policies, and economic developments, with the "natives"
depicted as recipients of colonial largesse in the form of
occasional educational, health, or other reforms. The
result, for the Western world, has been deeply ingrained
perceptions that the Southeast Asians were incapable of
defining or managing their own affairs.[2]

Even after World War II, despite Allied rhetoric of
self-determination and independence,[3] the primary goal
for British, French, and Dutch leaders was apparently to
reestablish their colonial administrations in Southeast
Asia, perhaps under an evolutionary program leading toward
some type of semi-independence or commonwealth status.[4]
The British plan for Burma, for example, was to help Burma
attain, "as fully and completely as may be possible," the
"high position of Dominion status--a position to which
[the British] would not lightly admit outside people
without full consideration of the character of their
Government."[5] At the time (1941), British newspapers
carried letters suggesting that the Burmese were unfit for
early self-rule.[6] This vision of postwar Southeast Asia
demonstrates the Europeans' failure to measure accurately
the vigor of anticolonialism, growing nationalism, and
other radical sentiments in these countries.

For Americans, proud of their role in the Philippines
where U.S. colonial policies had led to independence and
democracy following the acquisition of the Philippines
from the Spanish, there has also been an alter-image of
the tropical paradise of Southeast Asia--the jungle
foliage of Vietnam, with its bamboo spikes, tiger cages,
and death for young U.S. soldiers. Nevertheless, since
the late 1970s Southeast Asia has receded from daily
headlines and (despite the ubiquity of Vietnamese and
Cambodian refugees, continuing concerns about American
MIAs, or the growing turmoil in the Philippines) again has
become for most Americans a faraway, and exotic, if
somewhat tarnished, tropical paradise. Certainly the
Vietnam war did little to educate the American people to
the realities of Vietnam or Southeast Asia. For
Americans, who think of themselves as mentors of freedom

and nationalism, the traumatic experience of Vietnam may have been analogous to the rejection felt by the colonial powers. Vietnam became the site of the collapse of the U.S. policy of containing communism in Asia,[7] but most Americans were unable to grasp sufficiently the political implications of this conflict and were thus unable to judge whether the United States should have intervened in the first place or withdrawn when it did. Ultimately, Americans will remember the Vietnam war for its impact on domestic politics, not because it altered the course of U.S. foreign policy in Asia.

Stereotypes of Southeast Asia sustain the perceptions that Southeast Asia cannot be a competent part of the global political system. In the years since World War II, the former colonial powers have supported policies ranging from vigorous attempts to reestablish colonial control through military means, to benign neglect of former colonies, to the establishment of special commercial, defense, or cultural relations based on and seemingly strengthened by the intense relationships of the colonial past. Facile perceptions of the region have also left policymakers vulnerable to the argument that the threat of global Communist expansion is a legitimizing argument for involvement in Southeast Asia. The domino theory, when applied to Southeast Asia, has magnified that threat. The lack of sensitivity to the social and political environment of Southeast Asia has left the governments of Western Europe and the United States without adequate knowledge to formulate policies that would strengthen local political dynamics. Just as the moral certitude of the "white man's burden" proved insufficient for the reassertion of colonialism, so the moral verve and simplicity of saving people from communism collapsed in the face of the complexities of the Vietnamese revolution. Time and history have made further questions of colonial policy as well as U.S. policy in Vietnam moot; yet they have also made it clear that an understanding of the dynamics of the region is essential for the adequate development of contemporary and future policies.

For the region, many questions remain. Is there a rationale for superpower involvement in Southeast Asia? Where? in Thailand? in Indonesia? What type of involvement? supplies and war material? economic aid? moral support? soldiers? Why should these be provided (or why not)? to stop communism? to protect national interests? to aid "free" people? to legitimate governments? Should special relationships be maintained

with former colonies? Have animosities from both sides
diminished enough to allow this? At what cost are special
relationships maintained, and who bears these costs?

These questions illustrate the need for a better
understanding of Southeast Asia. The travel-poster image
of the region must be replaced with real knowledge of the
Southeast Asian role in the global political and economic
systems. The lack of comprehension throughout the Western
world may be part of a larger inability to grasp the
contemporary realities of global interrelationships; what
transpires in Malaysia (or Botswana or Chile, for that
matter) has little obvious impact on day-to-day life in
Europe or the United States. Their countries' longer
histories of involvement in world politics may offer to
Europeans a greater sense of world history than that
achieved by many Americans, but the average citizen,
whether in Great Britain or the United States or France,
is not cognizant of the economic realities of a highly
integrated global economy. Other issues pervade Western
consciousness: For the United States, there is the
omnipresence of the Soviet Union; for the British and
French, there are struggles in the European Common Market
and the distractions of that generally incomprehensible
ally across the Atlantic, the United States. In the
coming decade, however, Asia in general and Southeast Asia
in particular will probably have the greatest prospects
for growth of any region in the world. A parallel
expansion in Western understanding of Southeast Asia must
take place if conflict is to be minimized and relations
expanded usefully.

REGION OF DIVISIONS

The boundaries of Southeast Asia are relatively easy
to delineate. The region can be outlined by extending a
line from the western tip of China to the northern coast
of Australia, from there to the southern tip of India, and
finally from India back to the first point in China. The
area within this triangle--the Indo-Pacific Peninsula, the
Indonesian archipelago and the Philippine archi-
pelago--roughly corresponds to Southeast Asia.[8] There
are, however, exclusions within this triangle. For
example, Hainan Island is usually included as part of
China. Papua, New Guinea, under Australian control for
many years, also is not generally considered part of
Southeast Asia; however, since attaining independence it

has increasingly developed an Asian focus for its foreign policy.[9] Sri Lanka (Ceylon) and to a lesser extent, Bangladesh, although geographically close to and economically and politically similar to Southeast Asia, are generally linked to South Asia because of their cultural and geographic proximity to India. Even the inclusion of the Philippines as a part of Southeast Asia is sometimes challenged because, despite geographic and ethnic similarities to the region, the intensive Spanish and U.S. colonial impacts on the Philippines have diluted its cultural affinities with the region.

The countries[10] of the region, then, include Burma, Thailand, Laos, Cambodia, Vietnam, Indonesia, the Philippines, Singapore, Malaysia, and Brunei. (See Map 1.1, following.) In addition to being in geographic proximity, these countries are similar, though not identical, in tropical monsoon ecology. They are also similar in that, with the exception of Singapore, they are all economically underdeveloped but culturally extremely sophisticated. Independent governments reemerged in Southeast Asia only following World War II (except Thailand, which had avoided direct colonial control and thus never lost its independence). Before the colonial period, Southeast Asia was part of a world trading system that linked China to the Middle East and Europe, and as a crossroads in this system, experienced various forms of cultural/religious penetration from Hinduism, Buddhism, Islam, and Christianity.[11] As these commonalities mask diverse and complex political, cultural, and economic patterns, an understanding of Southeast Asia must begin with the balancing of these often divergent and overlapping characteristics.

Much of the diversity of Southeast Asia is rooted in its geographic fragmentation. Not only is the area encompassing Southeast Asia quite large, but there is a natural division between the area attached to the Asian landmass (called mainland Southeast Asia) and the insular portion of Southeast Asia. The countries of Burma, Thailand, Laos, Cambodia, and Vietnam are located on the Indo-Pacific Peninsula, which extends directly southward from China. The archipelagic countries include Indonesia, the Philippines, Singapore, Brunei, and Malaysia. Although the inclusion of Malaysia can be disputed because it is attached to the mainland, Malaysia's historical, cultural, ethnic, religious, economic, and political links to Sumatra and the other islands of the archipelago

6

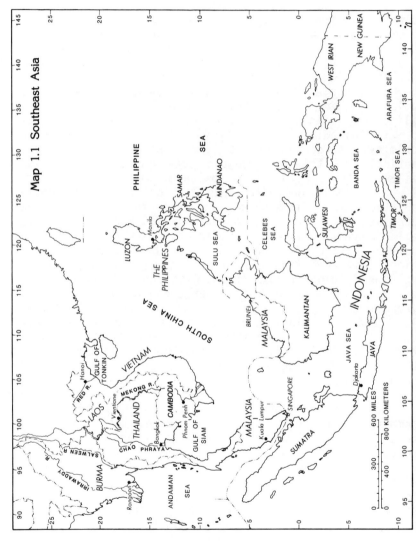

Map 1.1 Southeast Asia

From Ashok K. Dutt, *Southeast Asia: Realm of Contrasts*, 3d rev. ed. (Boulder, CO: Westview Press, 1985), p. 3. Used by permission.

suggest that Malaysia fits more precisely with that group.[12]

This geographic division within Southeast Asia is repeated in its religious base. Most of the mainland countries are Buddhist, although there are resident enclaves of Hindu, Muslim, and Christian minorities, as well as various Chinese religions, such as Taoism and Confucianism. Archipelagic Southeast Asia, by contrast, is predominantly Muslim in Malaysia and Indonesia, with a substantial Muslim minority in the south of the predominantly Christian Philippines. There are exceptions to these generalizations, including the Hindu population on the island of Bali in Indonesia, the Buddhists in Singapore, and the Buddhists and Hindu Indians in Malaysia. Further complicating the religious context is the plethora of animistic, mystical, and other traditional belief systems, which, in intertwining with the major religions, have given a syncretic religious disposition to the region. Although such religions as Islam have large numbers of devout and doctrinally correct adherents, many of the Muslims in Southeast Asia, particularly in Indonesia, also continue to practice a wide range of mystic and other non-Islamic rituals and beliefs.

Ethnic subdivisions of Southeast Asia reflect the geographic and religious subdivisions of the region. The Islamic archipelago is largely inhabited by Malayo-Polynesian peoples commonly known as Malays. Their common ethnic background, however, has not prevented the growth of great cultural and linguistic diversity among various Malay subgroups throughout the archipelago. In Indonesia alone, there are some 25 major languages and 250 or more dialects.[13] On the mainland there are four major ethnic groups--the Sino-Tibetan group, which includes the Burmese and Karens as well as Chinese; the Austroasiatic group, including the Vietnamese and the Khmer; the Thai, including also the Laos and the Shans; and the Malayo-Polynesians, including mostly Chams. These four major population groups have provided the nucleus for the contemporary countries but there are numerous subdivisions within these groups, some of which are ethnically related (e.g., the Anamese of Indochina and the Mon-Khmer of Thailand). There are more than 150 distinct ethnic groups in the mainland of Southeast Asia.[14] Throughout much of Southeast Asia are found mountain peoples and other small ethnic groupings, many of whom inhabited the region before the arrival of the principal ethnic groups of today but were pushed into the more remote regions as the present inhabitants moved into Southeast Asia. Inhabiting the northern part of mainland Southeast Asia, in particular, are mountain peoples, such as the Meos, who are relative newcomers to the region. The size of these groups has substantially declined as they have been absorbed into the dominant group. There remains much debate concerning the migration patterns and movements of peoples into Southeast Asia, which the great historian D.G.E. Hall has described as a veritable "chaos of races and languages."[15]

Non-ethnic factors also divide the peoples of Southeast Asia. The intersections of these factors with the ethnic and geographic patterns already noted have created a mosaic of inlaid and overlaid loyalties, belief systems, and communications patterns. For example, the people in the region can be divided in terms of domicile and agricultural practices into upland and lowland groups. The upland peoples generally practice dryland agriculture, and the lowland peoples generally practice irrigated cultivation. Wet-rice cultivation, which requires a sophisticated system of water management and regulation and returns a significantly higher volume product from each unit of land, was closely tied to the evolution of many of the great land-based kingdoms of traditional Southeast Asia. During various historical periods, the lowland peoples have been divided into agricultural and commercial or agricultural and seafaring populations. The seafaring groups, historically dependent on the regional and world trading systems, monopolized the Southeast Asia segment of that system and were able to amass great wealth and establish strong political units based on control of this trading subsystem. These economic divisions provided the basis for the development of seveal strikingly different types of political units in Southeast Asia.[16]

SOUTHEAST ASIA AS A REGIONAL UNIT

Although the region has been recognized for centuries in political and geographic terms by kings, writers, merchants, and travelers, the term Southeast Asia (also South East Asia and South-East Asia) is relatively new in Western political thought. Occasionally used by European, especially German, writers in the late nineteenth century, it was first brought to general prominence with the establishment of a Southeast Asia military command by the

British during World War II--one of the first attempts to bring together the previously fragmented colonial perspectives of the British, Dutch, French, and Americans.[17]

The ethnocentric views of Southeast Asia as well as the political and economic divisions, established during the colonial era and perpetuated ever since, have made it very difficult for Westerners to perceive or accept Southeast Asia as a viable global unit. The acceptance of the concept of a regional unit has been made more difficult by the social and cultural complexities of the region and by the paucity of available data for historical analysis. In recent years the regional concept has been further obscured by Western scholars, particularly international relations theorists bent on applying culturally biased models and theories of regional systems models to their analyses of the contemporary realities of Southeast Asia.[18] One concerned scholar has been prompted to note that "Southeast Asia, as a conventional term, has become increasing the property of university area specialists," thus possibly limiting and obscuring intellectual "horizons through an over-obsession with a geographical convention."[19]

Yet prior to the colonial period, the region was historically recognized with some clarity by Chinese, Arabic, Egyptian, and even Greek and Roman writers. Such clearly functional recognition was based primarily on the role played by Southeast Asian states in the international trading systems. The Chinese provided for Southeast Asians, as for other barbarians in the theoretical world view of the Middle Kingdom, by dividing the outlying regions according to the points of the compass and in terms of distance. They used the generic terms Nanyang to refer to the region of the Southern Seas and, by the third century B.C., employed the term K'un lun as a referent for islands or states in the Southern Seas. The latter term designated volcanic lands "endowed with marvelous and potent powers" and also denoted ocean-going peoples engaged in international trade.[20] The Chinese later divided the region into Burma, Laos, and Annam while maintaining a "separate and distinct set of relationships" for the rest of Southeast Asia.[21] The Japanese, using a term with a similar meaning, referred to Southeast Asia as Nan yo.[22] The early Arabic term qumr, used as a reference for Southeast Asia, was later replaced by Waq-Waq,[23] which evolved to mean all of the little-known area from Madagascar to Japan.[24] The term Zabag was used by the Arabs to refer to Southeast Asia, and the Indians called the region <u>Suvarnadvipa</u>.[25]

By the end of the seventh century A.D., Arab navigators were sailing with some regularity to Southeast Asia[26] in search of spices and medicines.[27] The region was also known to the Greeks and Romans. International trade by sea is known to have been frequent by the end of the second century A.D.,[28] although the sea routes through Southeast Asia may have been active as early as the middle of the third century B.C., when the land routes across Central Asia and India were blocked.[29] Southeast Asia was recognized, although its geographic limits and location were obscure, as a mysterious region that produced spices and other exotic products and that was peopled by skilled and courageous seafarers.

Implicit in this latter point is that the Southeast Asians themselves were active in the transshipment of cargo in the early centuries A.D. As already noted, they traveled as far west as Madagascar in such numbers and with such frequency that early geographers and navigators often thought of Madagascar as part of Southeast Asia. Thus, from the earliest times, Southeast Asia was an integral part of the evolving world trading system, providing valuable commodities and fulfilling vital functions in linking the Asian and Middle Eastern segments of the system.[30]

Southeast Asia's close association with, if not dependence on, international trade has continued to the modern era. Historically, when overland caravan routes from China through Central Asia to Europe were open, the sea route and concurrently the welfare of Southeast Asia declined; conversely, when the caravan routes were closed, Southeast Asia flourished economically and politically. The Europeans recognized the importance of Southeast Asia when they sought, through colonial expansion, to monopolize international trade by controlling Southeast Asia directly.

The domination by the colonial powers of writing and intellectual thought over a period of three hundred years, as much as the political domination of the region, fragmented the integrity of Southeast Asia as a cultural, political, and economic unit. Although colonial administrators and European businessmen emasculated the indigenous political and economic systems, the national perceptions of British, Dutch, and French writers ensured that the regional history would be perceived as an

appendage of European history and that little comparative
study on a regional basis (across colonial boundaries)
would be undertaken. Ironically, however, it was also
during the colonial period that the details of Southeast
Asia's cultural richness became known to the world. The
rediscovery and repair of the great religious monuments at
places like Angkor in Cambodia and Prambanan and Borobudur
in Indonesia, the beginnings of records of the sociology
of peasant society, and reports of linguistic and cultural
aspects of Southeast Asian societies by early European
scholars provided the foundations for a contemporary
understanding of Southeast Asia.

In recent decades following World War II, Southeast
Asia has been viewed by the scholarly community with
varying degrees of uncertainty. The debate concerning the
validity of Southeast Asia as an "independent" region has
been weighed down by the mass of Chinese and Indian
cultural imprints. Nevertheless, as bits of history have
been uncovered, the concept of Southeast Asia as an entity
unique in its regional nad global contexts has been
strengthened. The process has been evolutionary. Some
have argued that, in fact, Southeast Asia existed only
culturally as a colonial annex of India.[31] There
remains, for example, an organization called the All-India
Kamboj Association, which claims that Indians founded the
"overseas" Kamboja and that "fraternal relations have
existed between the Kamboja or India and the Cambodians
since the time of the Mahabharata when Rana Sudarshan
Kamboj and his followers had established 'blood bonds'
between the two countries."[32] These views have been
restated as a theory of cultural extension and adaptation
in which Southeast Asia developed a civilization of its
own, though of Indian parentage.[33] According to J. C.
van Leur,[34] this indigenous culture, strengthened by
selective borrowings from India and China, provided the
impetus for the growth of a Southeast Asian history, which
is still progressing.[35]

Thus, despite the continued lack of data and the
presence of diversity and contradictions, the region has
increasingly been accepted as a unit. Southeast Asia may
not have lent itself to political analysis as Western
theorists would have it, but by the early 1970s it had
become clear that the region was very much its own
master--despite the continued interest of and intrusion
from global powers. Southeast Asia has emerged in the
modern era as part of a global system predicated on
Western international law, which is markedly different

from that of traditional Southeast Asia. The international relations of the region since independence following World War II have been a history of adjustment and accommodation to this system.

Most of the impetus for this regional "self-assertion" has come, as it must have, from within Southeast Asia, and it has not been without misdirection and false starts. First, the region is the primary field of activity for a political organization, the Association of Southeast Asian Nations (ASEAN), founded by five regional states-- Indonesia, Malaysia, Singapore, Thailand, and the Philippines. There were also several ill-fated attempts at regional cooperation such as MAPHILINDO (Malaysia, the Philippines, and Indonesia) and the Association of Southeast Asia (ASA), which included Malaysia, the Philippines, and Thailand.[36] These compare with earlier externally instigated regional organizations as the Southeast Asia Treaty Organization (SEATO), which had only two regional members and six nonregional state members.[37] In the context of world politics, Southeast Asia has been an area of confrontation and contention among the superpowers. More recently, however, the ASEAN states have proposed that Southeast Asia be made a "zone of neutrality"--a proposal that has received support from many regional countries as well as from larger nations around the world.[38]

This regional view is reflected at the national level as well. In one of the earlier statements on Indonesian foreign policy, Mohammad Hatta, then Indonesia's vice-president, emphasized the need for good relations with Indonesia's immediate neighbors, whose circumstances were very similar to its own, as one of six major goals of Indonesian foreign policy at that time.[39] After several subsequent digressions into regional conflict, Indonesia has recently returned to this position. Because regional events have a direct bearing on its own national development, Indonesia has come to see a very close relationship between its own future and that of Southeast Asia.[40] The regional focus has been stressed by other Indonesian officials, who have urged that Southeast Asia be given increased consideration: "Without neglecting the relations with the communities of wider score . . . Indonesia's attention should be centered on the common interest of Southeast Asian countries associated in ASEAN."[41] Thailand has always sought a strong regional structure as a counterweight to its American alliance,[42] whereas Malaysia has looked for regional support as

Britain has expanded its European relationships at the expense of its Commonwealth. Singapore has sought regional cooperation to stabilize its regional economic role, and the Philippines has used regional linkages to strengthen its Asian self-image.

Several studies by Western scholars have attempted to capture this Southeast Asian view of a political unit or system. One such study discussed a "subordinate state system" in Southern Asia consisting of three "fields"-- South Asia, Southeast Asia, and China. Although this study suggested that weakness and tendencies toward disintegration were among the more important and predominant features of the system, the author concluded that "for all states but India and China, the Subordinate System is the primary, if not exclusive, framework for their foreign policy."[43] Elsewhere, Sheldon Simon has described the complexities of Asia as "not one system, but a series of overlapping groups of states interacting in the political, economic, or military issue areas,"[44] and ASEAN as the most institutionalized political system in Southeast Asia (although the author potentially includes a future neutralized Southeast Asian system as well as other possible configurations led by Indonesia, Vietnam, or Thailand in the same category).[45] Several recent studies have attempted to integrate the Southeast Asian subsystem with the global system by focusing on security issues and the strategic position of Southeast Asia within global politics.[46]

The present study accepts the existence of Southeast Asia as a regional unit and applies the concepts of a political system throughout, including the principal systems vocabulary (e.g., actors, boundaries, environment, and interaction). The systems model provides an organizing framework for comparing patterns in foreign policy behavior and regional interaction within and among the traditional and contemporary systems of Southeast Asia. The model also helps clarify the elements of historical continuity.

The systems framework is ideal for regional analyses because it allows for shifts in the level of analysis above and below the regional unit. The value of shifting from the regional unit upward to the global system or downward to the actor (state) or substate level is found in an understanding of the linkages among various systems and subsystems. For example, the relationship between governors and the governed is essential in understanding state behavior. At the same time, state behavior in traditional Southeast Asia was also conditioned by relationships with China, India, and other states outside the regional system. The interrelatedness of these levels can best be conceptualized in a systems model. Within the boundaries of the system, specified parts--states, or actors--exhibit certain behaviors that are sustained and repeated over time, and these actors will interact with one another and perhaps with external systems or actors outside the immediate system. The systems framework also provides for interaction between individually equal systems that exist in unequal or subordinate relation to other independent systems.[47] Key distinctions among political systems, or within the same system at different times, can be made on the basis of modernity, distribution or political skills and resources, patterns of cleavage and cohesion, severity of conflict, and the institutional use of power.[48]

There is, however, a certain danger that the use of a systems framework will force the premature conclusion that such a system actually exists.[49] This is an important issue in the case of Southeast Asia, as there are analysts who reject the region as any type of homogenous unit. A second concern is that the systems framework can create a perception of a system moving toward some ideal and perhaps highly integrated form. Hence the systems framework is applied rather cautiously here in an effort to avoid these problems. Although the system in question is not presented as static (i.e., change is accepted as constant), tendencies toward disintegration are treated as similar to integrative tendencies to the extent that both explain the functioning of the system. There is no value judgment attached to either of these extremes. The focus will be on the subsystem or region, as the principal area for discussing of Southeast Asia, whereas the global system will constitute the "environment."

Two historical periods will be considered.[50] The analysis will focus on a discrete regional unit functioning with varying degrees of efficiency in a general environment of global and extraregional states. Although their forms and practices were very different from those of their Western counterparts, large political units (the traditional states) have existed in Southeast Asia at least since the beginning of the Christian era. Scattered throughout the region, many of these states have been lost to recorded history; a few, however, are sufficiently well known to allow some generalizations about the nature of such units in traditional Southeast

Asia. The traditional state will be analyzed by constructing a model to clarify the social relationships between government and the mass of society. Such a model will also reveal the strengths and weaknesses of the traditional state as the principal actor in the regional system. This model state is based in part on archaeological and other historical sources and in part on extrapolations from contemporary anthropological and social science data, as many social practices in the region's present rural villages differ little from those of the last millenium.[51]

A secondary focus of analysis will be the adaptation of traditional Southeast Asian states to a global system increasingly shaped by principles of European international law, given that their experience and understanding of international politics is grounded in another more traditional system of interstate relations. The concept of two competing systems--the traditional Asian system of international politics and the Western system as manifested by the intruding colonial powers--provides insight into the reasons for the successful penetration of Southeast Asia by the European powers. It will also serve to clarify the unique character of traditional Southeast Asia.

Elements of the traditional system have important explanatory value in relation to contemporary politics in Southeast Asia. For example, the process of "neotraditionalization" of political leadership has been described in the following terms: "Traditional, indigenous elements of belief and behavior become reinvigorated within the modern organizations . . . increasing the influence of indigenous and particularistic rather than modern, rational criteria on the way in which public officials fulfill their prescribed roles."[52] Neotraditional values have been offered as an alternative to Western ideologies in that they provide structural models for organization of the state and explain the behavior of political leaders and bureaucrats. The impact of traditional political philosophy and practice on contemporary regional politics has rarely been considered.[53] Accordingly, this study transfers the concepts of neotraditional behavior to the regional system.

Although their forms and practices were very different from those of their Western counterparts, large political units have existed in Southeast Asia at least since the beginning of the Christian era. Scattered throughout the region, many of these states have been lost to recorded

history; a few, however, are sufficiently well known to
allow some generalizations about the nature of such units
in traditional Southeast Asia. By drawing together
existing evidence from those known states, one can
construct an overview of the traditional interstate system.

After a relatively brief period in the immediate
postindependence years, when certain Southeast Asian
political leaders sought vigorously to reshape the global
system, a more stable system emerged in the region. This
system has increasingly shown many of the "traditional,
indigenous elements" of bureaucratic politics. It has
become clear that Southeast Asia--from its political
leaders to its general populace--is a product of the
totality of its history and cultural experiences. The
colonial experience did not erase the past for the
Southeast Asians, although the experience may have
obscured their past and temporarily deflected Southeast
Asians from the evolution of a modern system based on
their own cultural and political heritage. Whatever
Southeast Asians may have absorbed from the colonial
experience, or from the West in general, has been
conditioned and legitimized by their own cultural and
historical perceptions and experiences. By definition,
this process has been one of interpretation of Western
principles through indigenous eyes. In the realm of
regional and international politics, too, Western patterns
of behavior have been adopted, but we must analyze the
traditional system of Southeast Asia in order to see that
traditional indigenous practices are evident today.

NOTES

1. See, for example, D.J.M. Tate, The Making of
South-East Asia (London and Kuala Lumpur: Oxford
University Press, 1979): The European Conquest, vol. 1,
and The Western Impact: Economic and Social Change,
vol. 2.

2. To gain a sense of the enormity of the perceptual
gap between Western and indigenous views of the colonial
period, compare, for example, Paul H. Kartoska, ed.,
Honorable Intentions: Talks on the British Empire in
South-East Asia Delivered at the Royal Colonial Institute,
1874-1928 (Singapore: Oxford University Press, 1983) and
Syed Hussein Alatas, The Myth of the Lazy Native: A Study
of the Image of the Malays, Filipinos and Javanese from
the 16th Century to the 20th Century and Its Function in

the Ideology of Colonial Capitalism (London: Frank Cass and Company, 1977). For the American perception, see James C. Thomson, et al., Sentimental Imperialists: The American Experience in East Asia (New York: Harper & Row, 1981).

3. Article III of the Atlantic Charter declared the right of all peoples to choose their own form of government.

4. Evelyn Colbert, Southeast Asia in International Politics, 1941-1956 (Ithaca: Cornell University Press, 1977), pp. 33-34.

5. John F. Cady, A History of Modern Burma (Ithaca: Cornell University Press, 1958), p. 431, quoting the official statement issued November 4, 1941, by the British secretary of state for India, Leopold S. Amery.

6. Cady, History of Modern Burma, citing the Times (London) of October 14, 17, and November 4, 1941, as well as the News Chronicle (London) of October 27, 1941.

7. See such volumes as Edwin W. Martin, Southeast Asia and China: The End of Containment (Boulder, Colo.: Westview Press, 1977); and Paul M. Kattenburg, The Vietnam Trauma in American Foreign Policy, 1945-75 (New Brunswick: Transaction Books, 1980).

8. See Charles A. Fisher, South-East Asia: A Social, Economic and Political Geography (London: Methuen, 1964).

9. Far Eastern Economic Review, December 4, 1981. For a detailed analysis see also Donald E. Weatherbee, "Papua New Guinea's Foreign Policy: A Bridge to Indonesian Shores," Contemporary Southeast Asia 4 (December 1982), pp. 330-345.

10. The term country is used here because it carries few implications about the unit in question. Other terms such as nation imply a national homogeneity of peoples within the country that is seldom true in Southeast Asia. Also the term state as understood in contemporary world politics carries an implication of more centralized authority than may have been true especially for the countries of Southeast Asia. The nuances of these concepts are examined in more detail in Chapter 2.

11. Although these are specific religions, their impact on Southeast Asia was as much social, political, and generally cultural as religious.

12. This view is commonly accepted among scholars of Southeast Asia. See, for example, G. Coedes, The Making of South East Asia (Berkeley: University of California Press, 1969), p. v.

13. Fisher, South-East Asia, p. 238.

18

14. See Frank M. Lebar, Gerald C. Hickey, and John K. Musgrave, Ethnic Groups of Mainland Southeast Asia (New Haven, Conn.: Human Relations Area File Press, 1964).

15. D.G.E. Hall, A History of South-East Asia (New York: St. Martin's Press, 1968), p. 5.

16. For an excellent introductory study of the geography of Southeast Asia see Ashok K. Dutt, Southeast Asia: Realm of Contrasts, 3rd rev. ed. (Boulder, Colo.: Westview Press, 1985).

17. See D.G.E. Hall, "The Integrity of Southeast Asian History," Journal of Southeast Asian Studies 4 (September 1973); and Hugh Tinker, "The Search for the History of Southeast Asia," Journal of Southeast Asian Studies 11 (September 1980).

18. Morton Kaplan, System and Process in International Relations (New York: John Wiley & Sons, 1957). Among regional integration theorists, see Philip E. Jacob and James V. Toscano, eds., The Integration of Political Communities (New York: J. B. Lippincott, 1964); Joseph S. Nye, Jr., ed., International Regionalism (Boston: Little, Brown, 1968); and Louis J. Cantor and Steven L. Spiegel, The International Politics of Regions (Englewood Cliffs, N.J.: Prentice Hall, 1970).

19. Michael Leifer, "Trends in Regional Association in Southeast Asia," Asian Studies 2 (August 1964), p. 198.

20. Keith Taylor, "Madagascar in the Ancient Malayo-Polynesian Myths," in Explorations in Early Southeast Asian History: The Origins of Southeast Asian Statecraft, edited by Kenneth R. Hall and John K. Whitmore (Ann Arbor: Michigan Papers on South and Southeast Asia, 1976), p. 33, and Gabriel Ferrand cited within.

21. Wang Gungwu, "China and South-East Asia, 1402-1424," in Studies in the Social History of China and South-East Asia: Essays in Memory of Victor Purcell, edited by Jerome Ch'en and Nicolas Tarling (Cambridge: Cambridge University Press, 1970), p. 389.

22. Fisher, South-East Asia, p. 7, fn. 9.

23. Taylor, "Madagascar in the Ancient Malayo-Polynesian Myths," pp. 33-38.

24. J. V. Mills, "Arabic and Chinese Navigators in Malaysian Waters in About A.D. 1500," Journal of the Malaysian Branch of the Royal Asiatic Society 47 (December 1974). The confusion of Madagascar with the islands of Southeast Asia may be related to the fact that Malay sailors frequently traveled there, leaving a cultural imprint that masked the geographic distance in the very early centuries of the Christian era.

25. Tate, The Making of South-East Asia, vol. 1, p. 8. See also W. J. van der Meulen, "Suvaradvipa and the Chryse Chersonesos," Indonesia, no. 18 (October 1974), pp. 1-40.

26. G. R. Tibbetts, Arab Navigation in the Indian Ocean Before the Coming of the Portuguese (London: Royal Asiatic Society of Great Britain and Ireland, 1971), pp. 472-503.

27. G. R. Tibbetts, A Study of the Arabic Texts Containing Materials on South-East Asia (Leiden: 1979), p. 3.

28. Tibbetts, A Study of Arabic Texts; and C.G.F. Simkin, The Traditional Trade of Asia (London: Oxford University Press, 1968).

29. Joseph Desomogyi, History of Oriental Trade (Hildesheim, FRG: Georg Olms Verlagsbuch-handlung, 1968), p. 24.

30. For an analysis of the major components of this historical system, see Adda B. Boseman, Politics and Culture in International History (Princeton, N.J.: Princeton University Press, 1960); Jeremy A. Sabloff and C. C. Lamber-Karlovsky, Ancient Civilization and Trade (Albuquerque: University of New Mexico Press, 1975); K. N. Chaudhuri, Trade and Civilisation in the Indian Ocean: An Economic History from the Rise of Islam to 1750 (Cambridge: Cambridge University Press, 1985); and Immanuel Wallerstein, The Modern World System: Capitalist Agriculture and the Origins of the European World Economy in the Sixteenth Century (New York: Academic Press, 1974).

31. K. M. Panikker, R. Mookeriji, and R. C. Majumbar were among the protagonists of this view. See Hall, A History of South-East Asia, p. 16.

32. B. R. Chatterji, "A Current Tradition Among the Kamboja or North India Relating to the Khmers of Cambodia," Artibus Asiae 24 (1961), pp. 253-254.

33. See George Coedes, Les Etats Hindouises d'Indochine et d'Indonesia (Paris: E. de Boccard, 1948) or the English translation entitled The Indianized States of Southeast Asia (Honolulu: East-West Center Press, 1968).

34. J. C. van Leur, Indonesian Trade and Society (The Hague: W. van Hoeve, 1955).

35. For two summary reviews of the progression of thought on Southeast Asian history, see Hall, "The Integrity of Southeast Asian History," and Tinker, "The Search for the History of Southeast Asia." See also Donald K. Emmerson, "Southeast Asia: What's in a Name?"

Journal of Southeast Asian Studies 15 (March 1984), pp. 1-21.

36. A summary of the context surrounding the formation of these organizations is found in Bernard K. Gordon, The Dimensions of Conflict in Southeast Asia (Englewood Cliffs, N.J.: Prentice-Hall, 1966).

37. The regional members were Thailand and the Philippines. Nonregional members were Pakistan, New Zealand, Australia, France, Britain, and the United States.

38. See the "Kuala Lumpur Declaration of the Foreign Ministers of the ASEAN States" (agreed upon 27 November 1971), reprinted in the Indonesian Quarterly 1 (January 1973), pp. 76-77.

39. Mohammad Hatta, "Indonesia's Foreign Policy," Foreign Policy 31 (April 1953), p. 352.

40. Adam Malik, "Indonesia's Foreign Policy," Indonesian Quarterly 1 (October 1972), p. 29.

41. Sumitro Djojohadikusumo, "Foreign Economic Relations--Some Trade Aspects," Indonesian Quarterly 1 (January 1973), p. 18. Emphasis added.

42. Russell H. Fifield, National and Regional Interests in ASEAN: Competition and Co-operation in International Politics (Singapore: Institute of Southeast Asian Studies, Occasional Paper No. 57, 1979), p. 8.

43. Michael Brecher, The New States of Asia (London: Oxford University Press, 1963), p. 105.

44. Sheldon W. Simon, "East Asia," in World Politics, edited by James N. Rosenau, Kenneth Thompson, and Gavin Boyd (New York: Free Press, 1976), p. 550.

45. Ibid., pp. 528-551.

46. See, for example, S. Chawla, Melvin Gurtov, and A. G. Marsat, eds., Southeast Asia Under the New Balance of Power (New York: Praeger Publishers, 1974); Lim Joo-jock, Geo-Strategy and the South China Sea Basin (Singapore: University of Singapore Press, 1979); and Wu Yuan-li, The Strategic Land Ridge: Peking's Relations with Thailand, Malaysia, Singapore and Indonesia (Stanford, Calif.: Hoover Institution Press, 1975).

47. See James E. Dougherty, "The Study of the Global System," in Rosenau, et al., World Politics, pp. 597-624; and W. Ladd Hollist and James N. Rosenau, "World System Debates," International Studies Quarterly 25 (March 1981), pp. 5-17.

48. Robert Dahl, Modern Political Analysis, 2nd ed. (Englewood Cliffs, N.J.: Prentice-Hall, 1970), pp. 47-58.

49. See Emmerson, "Southeast Asia: What's in a Name?" in which the author observes that "some names, like

'rose,' acknowledge what exists. Others, like 'unicorn,' create what otherwise would not exist. In between lie names that simultaneously describe and invent reality. 'Southeast Asia' is one of these."

50. The main body of the analysis is divided into two periods: (1) the traditional, or precolonial period, and (2) the modern era of independent states, with colonial and Japanese periods considered to be transitional antecedents to this latter period.

51. See Stanley O'Connor's review of R. B. Smith and W. Watson, eds., Early Southeast Asia: Essays in Archaeology, History, and Historical Geography (London: Oxford University Press, 1979), in the Journal of Southeast Asian History 15 (1981).

52. Ann Ruther Wilner, "The Neotraditional Accommodation to Political Independence: The Case of Indonesia," in Cases in Comparative Politics, edited by Lucian Pye (Boston: Little, Brown, 1970), pp. 242-244.

53. For a study specifically focused on Indonesia see John Rienhardt, Foreign Policy and National Integration: The Case of Indonesia (New Haven, Conn.: Yale University, Southeast Asian Studies, 1971).

CHAPTER 2

An Overview
of Early Southeast Asia

This chapter presents a summary of the early history of Southeast Asia, illustrating some major historical features and providing an overview of the region's general political, economic, and cultural evolution.[1] Knowledge of Southeast Asian history is, even today, expanding at a rapid rate because of growth in anthropological and archaeological interest in the region, particularly among indigenous Southeast Asian scholars. Although new studies are pushing further into the past, our present understanding of the history of region before A.D. 800 is still sketchy, and our knowledge of the region before A.D. 200 is obscure and fragmentary.[2] However, as more and more historical data have become available, additional room has developed for an interpretive history of Southeast Asia as a unit.[3]

It is difficult to select a point of departure for an overview of the interstate history of Southeast Asia.[4] Funan, generally recognized as one of the oldest states in the region, enters the historical records, primarily through Chinese sources, as early as the second century A.D., and Ptolemy's Geographic provides additional place names thought to have been located in Southeast Asia in even earlier times.[5] However, the soundness of the sources reporting Funan's existence as a single political entity is not beyond question.[6] Archaeological records give evidence of earlier societies, but so little is known of their political organization that it is presumed that most of them were largely kinship groups.[7] As knowledge is expanded, the records of political organizations within these societies may be discovered.[8]

As noted in Chapter 1, there must be some caution about the concept of "state" when applied to early Southeast

22

Asia. Extrapolation from contemporary Western concepts of the state in terms of organization, authority, and domain, is not appropriate for early Southeast Asian states and must be avoided.[9] In many respects, the period before the intervention of the European powers in Southeast Asia can be characterized as one of chiefdom/agricultural systems, in which transitory elite groups provided organizational leadership but lacked sufficient economic and political strength for their areas of domain to be labeled states. Webb called such areas conditional states because

> the success of the society would depend upon the exact balance of favorable circumstances beyond its control to a much greater extent than is true for states, with their greater capacity for unified and innovative policy making. . . . The transition from chiefdom to state therefore represents a complete transformation in the bases of social control . . . [so that] the point in the archaelogical record at which one begins to refer to evolving polities as "states" (without qualification) is not, perhaps, solely a semantic issue.[10]

The early Southeast Asian state had a tenuous institutional base and was often as fleeting as passing leaders or the arrival of challenges to authority. Wolters described early Southeast Asian leaders in terms of their prowess, saying that a leader's "spiritual identity and capacity for leadership were established when his fellows could recognize his endowment and knew that being associated with him was to their advantage not only because his entourage could expect to enjoy material rewards but also, perhaps, because their own spiritual substance would participate in and share his."[11]

EARLY SOUTHEAST ASIAN STATES

Funan was established in Indochina sometime during the first or second century A.D., the precise date of its founding remains uncertain. However, it is known that early Funan leaders were able to capitalize on the growing maritime trade from China to the Middle East and Europe. At the time of Funan's establishment, the major sea routes still followed the coastline because navigational skills and vessels were not sufficient for direct transoceanic travel. As the volume of this coastal trade grew, the barrier of the Malay peninsula remained the terminus for the first westward segment of the trade route leaving China. Funan's port city of Oc-eo prospered because it was located approximately halfway between Southern China and the Malay peninsula, had a safe harbor, and, with its excellent agricultural hinterland already stabilized and unified by early Funan leaders, was a good site for reprovisioning.[12] Capitalizing on its strategic location in this trading system, Funan applied the additional revenues derived from maritime traffic to further expand its inland control of rice-producing territories. Funan also appears to have increased its agricultural productivity by draining mangrove swamps and and introducing irrigated agriculture.[13]

The process of political organization extended over several centuries, proceeding from kinship groups led by a variety of chieftains and/or elders. These groups expanded the limited kinship capacities for common action with varying combinations of skillful leadership and expanding resources, which were necessary to congeal the fragmented population into one larger unit resembling what today might be thought of as a confederation or state. Chinese records of the third century A.D. refer to the many vassal states of Funan that had previously had their own chiefs.[14]

The identity of Funan's earliest rulers is unknown, but we know from Chinese sources that during the latter part of the second century, Hun P'an-huang, a descendant of the original ruler, expanded his control by stimulating strife among local leaders, using his army to bring order, and then installing his sons as governors of the conquered areas.[15] Funan continued to expand through the fifth century A.D., until, as Hall pointed out, the patterns of international trade shifted away from Funan toward the Strait of Malacca. As shipbuilding and navigational skills evolved, coastal sailing was replaced by direct routes across the South China Sea, thus reducing the revenues available to Funan from entrepot activities.[16] This decline in revenue from trade forced Funan's leaders to develop a broader agricultural base and stimulated a parallel adoption of Hindu trappings of state, which provided the stronger legitimizing paraphernalia, ritual, and legal codes required by an agrarian state.[17] Funan, bereft of a major source of income from international trade, and despite its turn to a more extensive irrigated agriculture, was by the end of the sixth century, weakened and divided by the Chams, who took control of the Mekong Delta, and the Khmers, who controlled the expanding agricultural area around Tonle Sap in modern-day Cambodia.

Funan's history provides a perspective on several factors in the ebb and flow of the commercial political economy of Southeast Asia up to the colonial period. The movement of international commercial trade was the critical factor in shaping the history of the region because it provided the source of and mechanism for the accumulation of capital beyond that extractable from domestic agricultural production. Thus state organization and power ascended to a stronger level when an agricultural chiefdom was able to gain increased economic resources through international trade. There was also a close inverse relationship between the well-being of the leading maritime states of Southeast Asia and the stability and peace along the overland caravan routes through Central Asia. As early as the fourth century B.C., after Alexander the Great had conquered much of the Middle East, there emerged an "age of ascendancy of the overland route over the sea route, of the pack animal over the ship."[18] Toward the end of the third century B.C., however, the land routes were blocked by the Parthians, and trade shifted to the sea routes through Southeast Asia.[19] In the early centuries of the Christian era, the overland routes, as arduous as they were, again became preferable relative to the extremely problematic sea routes from China through Southeast Asia to India and the Middle East before reaching the Mediterranean and Europe. Nevertheless, the Romans built a canal to the Red Sea to serve the sea routes until the end of the sixth century A.D.[20] When the land route was not accessible, the sea-lanes through Southeast Asia were used, and it was the impact of the increased revenues from this international trade system on various states in Southeast Asia that ensured their rise and sustained their power in the region.

Certain states are known to have been contemporaries of Funan. For example, the state of Langkasuka on the northeastern coast of the Malay peninsula was located at the point where most of the international trade moved overland across the isthmus. The Kra isthmus, farther north, was also used for overland transshipping, but, because of the lack of agricultural support in the area, it was less important than Langkasuka. This state, like Funan, developed because of the flow of international trade; also like Funan, it suffered when shipping was developed sufficiently to use the deep water routes through the Strait of Malacca, bypassing Langkasuka.

At least two other states are thought to have existed on either side of Funan--Dvaravati to the west in present-day Thailand and Burma, and Champa in the central regions of present day Vietnam. Champa may earlier have been known as Lin-yi, which according to Chinese records was established in the year A.D. 192.[21] Much of what is known of Lin-yi comes from Chinese descriptions of its attempts at territorial expansion, especially into lands previously controlled by the Chinese themselves.

The early political history in the area of present-day Thailand remains obscure.[22] Dvaravati, the first empire to consolidate much of the central area of Thailand, appears to have been formed in the seventh century but seems not to have been successful in its efforts to expand from the area of lower Manam River to the fringes of the Tenasserim range on the west and southward into the Malay peninsula.[23] It is possible that Dvaravati was active in the transisthmus portage near Kra, but if this was the case, increased revenues from trade did not appear to aid Dvaravati's expansion, as was the case for Funan. Nevertheless, as a result of its long contacts with Sri Lanka (Ceylon), Dvaravati may have been one of the first avenues for Hinduism and Hindu cultural practices in Southeast Asia.

The Pyu peoples of Burma may also have been organized into a state to compete with Funan. Although the accepted founding date of Srikshetra, the capital of the Pyu kingdom, is A.D. 638, earlier records indicate that trade groups traveled up the Irrawaddy to meet caravan traders enroute to and from China. It is unlikely that such complex trading linkages could have been maintained without some effective governmental control.

Little is know of the states in Southeast Asia's archipelago during the early centuries of the Christian Era.[24] The first records are inscriptions from Kalimantan (Borneo) and Java near Jakarta dated approximately A.D. 400 or later. Presumably, there was little impetus for state formation until the international shipping routes shifted southward (although a lack of records may be the limiting factor in this case).

Not only did the early Southeast Asian states try to control the flow of international trade in an entrepot sense, but they also produced agricultural, forest, and other products that entered the system.[25] The product lists varied from time to time and port to port but included pepper, rice, timber, camphor, tin, spices, resins, precious metals, and medicines. Before the fourteenth century A.D., Southeast Asian commodities in the international commercial network were primarily "gathered" products such as camphor, birds' nests, perfumes, pearls, aromatic woods, and gold; after that, however, cultivated crops such as pepper, nutmeg, cloves, and rice commanded a greater portion of the trade,[26] although rice usually remained within the region to feed growing urban populations.

The decline of Funan began when the importance of its geographic position as the last major stopping point on the coastal route between Canton and the portage across the Malay peninsula diminished because of shipbuilding and navigational skills that let traders travel directly to the Strait of Malacca. The records of such travel are found in the diaries of Fa-Hsien, a Chinese Buddhist who visited India via the Straits early in the fifth century A.D.[27] After this time, Chinese records of the tributary states also contain many references to Javanese and Sumatran emissaries, whereas previously most recorded tributary missions from Southeast Asian states had been from Funan.[28]

MARITIME OR COMMERCIAL KINGDOMS

The longer-term impact of this shift in the trade routes away from the coastal route and directly to the Strait of Malacca was the rise of the new and larger maritime kingdoms in the archipelago of Southeast Asia around the Strait. The first of these larger kingdoms appears to have been Srivijaya, located at Palembang in Sumatra. The shift of power did not, of course, proceed directly from one state, Funan, to a second Srivijaya. Other states such as Langkasuka in Malaya, Dvaravati in Thailand, and Champa in Vietnam, as well as numerous smaller consolidated political units of the Pyu and Mon peoples in Burma and petty states around the Kra isthmus were contemporaries of Funan, whereas the state of Malayu and the port state of Tan-t'o-li preceded the rise of Srivijaya in the archipelago. However, Srivijaya apparently succeeded in controlling the maritime commercial traffic in the archipelago, establishing in the process an extensive empire. Srivijaya is thought to have controlled the Strait of Malacca from the seventh through the twelfth centuries A.D.

Although questions remain concerning both the duration of Srivijaya's ascendancy and the geographic extent of its authority, the available evidence suggests that it followed a specific political and economic form based on its relationship to the international trade routes. It has been described as a purely maritime kingdom with virtually no hinterland as a source of manpower, and as having relied on Malay sea nomads as the major source of its power.[29] Srivijaya was a confederation, an alliance system, or perhaps an organization of vassal trading ports under the center at Palembang. As with the earlier Funan, Srivijaya tooks its revenues from passing trade. In return, the state limited piracy in the region (much of the Srivijayan navy may have been composed of subjugated or bribed pirates) and provided harbor facilities for shipbuilding and repair, warehousing, and trade. But Srivijaya's power was not constant. Wolters, researching Chinese records, has shown that during certain periods Srivijaya was the only archipelagic state to send tribute to China, while at other times, missions arrived from many states or ports of the archipelago. He has theorized that when Srivijaya alone sent tribute, its power and control would have been sufficient to stop others. When other emissaries arrived, Srivijaya must have been weaker.[30]

Srivijaya's preoccupation with the maritime world has led most scholars to assume that it had only limited contact with peoples living inland from Palembang and no political control over its hinterland. Recently, however, Hall has suggested that in fact there was substantial trade and communication between the port city of Palembang and the inland villages of Sumatra. He believes that Srivijaya "developed continuing 'treaty' relationships with different groups of people who would have owed each other nothing. Trade transactions became social strategy; reciprocity between representative chiefs of the various peoples became the basis of continued prosperity."[31]

Cady has argued that Srivijaya, while based at the mouth of the Palembang River (South Sumatra), extended over the northeastern half of Sumatra, all of coastal Malaya and smaller parts of Java and Borneo.[32] One of the few descriptions of Srivijaya comes from a Buddhist monk, I-tsing (A.D. 635-713), upon his return trip from India: "After a month we come to the country of Malayu, which has now become Bhoga [Palembang of Srivijaya]; there are many states under it."[33] Another Chinese writer, Chau Ju-kua, described Srivijaya as a "country lying in the ocean and controlling the straits through which the foreigners' sea and land traffic in either direction must pass."[34] Still other Chinese sources list Srivijayan traders in Canton, and regular court appearances were recorded from A.D. 960 until 1178, when several Javanese missions also appeared to ask for Chinese aid against Srivijayan oppression.[35] A few statements about the extent of Srivijaya are found in Arab references to its spectacular military strength.[36]

Hall maintains the lack of fine arts and archaeological records of Srivijaya (as compared with the Khmer Empire, for example) may have been the result of limited cultural values and neglect owing to intense economic interests.[37] Others have argued that such records could easily have been destroyed in the raids by Chola in 1025.[38] Still others, focusing on the lack of supporting archaeological evidence to confirm historical or chronicle records, have suggested that Srivijaya may have been a minor kingdom that existed for less than one hundred years after its founding in A.D. 650, even though its name continued to appear in Chinese records because "the same name might have been borne by one or two later and equally short-lived" kingdoms.[39] The paucity of the archaeological evidence may also be explained by the corresponding lack of information on the coastal and riverine configurations for the east coast of Sumatra during the first millenium A.D.[40]

As a trading center (or set of centers) Srivijaya resembled the later Malacca in the many of its laws and resources worked to encourage trade; virtually all available sources mention Srivijaya in connection with some phase of international trade. There have been few archaeological findings to indicate that any ruler of Srivijaya developed any of the more permanent cultural artifacts. If Hall's thesis about the Hinduization of Funan is correct,[41] it may be that Srivijaya did not transform itself into an inland agricultural kingdom, as Funan did, and simply never developed either the population base or the politico-cultural status system that produced most of the inscriptions, monuments, and temples in other kingdoms.

Elsewhere in the archipelago of Southeast Asia, interisland and international commerce offered the most consistent stimulus to growth as exemplified by the many entrepot city-states that flourished throughout history in places like Ternate, Malacca, Bandjarmasin, Makasar, Palembang, Bantam, Cheribon, and Aceh. The states that developed as commercial kingdoms were often little more than confederations of competing city-states held together by the use of force from a strong center. As the spice trade developed, for example, a state like Ternate in the eastern archipelago of present-day Indonesia emphasized spice production to the point it had to import food, buying most of its rice from Java.[42] At certain times in history, a single city-state was probably able to monopolize this trade while other competing centers languished for lack of strong leadership, organization, and trade revenues; lack of demand for their commodities; or poor geographic position on the maritime trade routes. One city-state for which information is readily available, however, was Malacca, the last great entrepot city-state of Southeast Asia in the traditional period.

Until the beginning of the fifteenth century, Malacca was little more than an obscure fishing village on the Malayan peninsula,[43] probably part of an insignificant, subsistence-oriented, river-delta kingdom. Legend has it that a Sumatran prince named Paramaswera was driven from Palembang to Singapore (then known as Tumasik) and eventually to Malacca. Two factors helped elevate Malacca over a period of relatively few years as an entrepot center: China's need for an ocean trade route because the caravan routes have been closed, and India's desire for a safe route through the Strait of Malacca in order to compete with the Thai-controlled Kra portage.[44]

Malacca began its commercial growth in direct competition with Majapahit on Java and Ayudhya in Siam, both of which had strong trading and commercial interests. The Chinese fleet appeared in 1403, however, and Malacca's future was saved. The greater significance of the Chinese fleet was its dispatch to Southeast Asia to secure the ocean routes for international trade because Tamerlane had closed the caravan routes to the Middle East.[45] However, the Chinese fleet also provided the immediate protected needed for Malacca to expand without risk of invasion from Ayudhya or Majapahit. In a bid to secure the eastbound commercial traffic from India and the Middle East, Paramaswera also transformed Malacca into an Islamic port.

The unique feature of Malacca and other such city-states was their total dependence upon trade: The overall population was preponderantly foreign, the proportion of Malays was small, and there was virtually no indigenous middle class. The government not only maintained a safe harbor but also offered low customs fees, repair facilities, ample warehouse facilities, and many other conveniences to attract international shipping merchants.[46] Entrepot centers such as Malacca depended on international trade for their very existence; consequently, resources were allocated to the maintenance and expansion of the trading system to the neglect of local society. There was little indigenous cultural development, as was possible in the wet-rice kingdoms. Malacca became the greatest of these entrepot centers, truly the crossroads of Asia, and, as such, the first target for control by Europeans when they entered Southeast Asia.

LAND-BASED AGRICULTURAL KINGDOMS

A different type of kingdom, based not on control of international trade routes but on a firm agricultural base, was the Khmer Empire, the mainland agricultural successor to Funan and Chenla. As capabilities in seamanship grew, allowing ships to navigate directly from China to the Strait of Malacca, Funan's importance as a harbor facility declined. As a consequence, Funan drew an ever increasing share of its revenues from agricultural production, turned inward, expanded its irrigation system, and added Hindu rituals to its court and kingship to strengthen its legitimacy among the rural agricultural peasantry.[47] Although Funan was not entirely successful in this transformation and was eventually destroyed (its eastern regions were annexed to another state, Chenla, while the western areas were invaded by Mon armies, conquered, and divided into numerous fiefdoms), the Khmer subsequently inherited much of Funan's territory and its complex irrigation system. They inhabited the same region and controlled the flow of monsoon rain by using grass dams to hold water in natural basins.[48] The Khmer also used Hindu ritual to support their kings' claim to the throne.

During the founding of Angkor in A.D. 802, Jayavarman II used a Brahman who was skilled in magic to perform a ceremony said to make it impossible for Cambodia to pay allegiance to Java. In another ceremony, the Brahman was to fix a curse on all future usurpers.[49] Further, Briggs has pointed to archaeological evidence that indicates the Jayavarman II had built a pyramid-temple, Krus Preah Aram Rong Chen--the first of its kind in Cambodia to be linked to the worship of the royal linga (a phallus, symbol of the Hindu god, Siva, as well as the representation of the king as the center of the world) and the _devaraja_ (god-king). Thus Jayavarman was thought by some to have transformed the long-standing concept of Siva-linga worship by linking it directly to the king who became a god-king (i.e., conceived to be the eternal abstract essence of the king compounded with the divine essence and worshiped in the form of a linga).[50] At the same time, however, a dichotomy developed and was maintained (as ambiguously as possible) in such a way that the concept of god-king could be supplanted by elements of ancestral worship more readily comprehended and accepted by the peasant masses.[51] Adding further to the mystery, the linga was thought to have been received by the king from Siva through the intercession of a Brahman. The meaning of the cult of the _devaraja_ has been widely debated; Kulke, for example, has recently argued that Jayavarman was not consecrated as god-king but that the god Siva as "god who is king" was called to protect Cambodia and especially its king.[52]

The ancestral link, especially for the peasant masses, was critical inasmuch as the "central temple-mountain undoubtedly represented less the _Semeru_ than the symbol of the abode of their ancestors, radiating their force of protection over all the realm."[53] Concepts of supernatural power, the recognition that ancestors and spirits regularly intervened in earthly events, and the concept of the king as the exemplar of his social order became bound together so that the king appeared as a deity. However, the emphasis was not on the deity of the king but on his exalted position, which made him an intermediary to gods and ancestors because "ancestors alone were the source of 'life-power' and were thus comparable to the gods," whereas the king was not a source of "life-power" but more the "bearer and transmitter of that power."[54]

As the Khmer civilization developed, its agriculture and techniques of water management became correspondingly more complex. For example, by A.D. 889, it had constructed an artificial lake by diverting the course of the Siemreap River. This lake measured 1,800 by 7,000 meters and provided water for cities and monasteries in addition to irrigation.[55] The high point of Khmer hydraulic development came about the year A.D. 1000, during the reign of Suryavarman I, who constructed

a marvelous system of waterways, basins, channels, and fountains [in his capital]. These basins, sometimes

> lined with brick, are separated at intervals by
> embankments, but are connected . . . by conduits to
> permit the passage of water. Other basins--more than
> a thousand at Angkor alone . . . depend on rain-water
> . . . [and] are arranged in plans throughout the city,
> . . . Every sanctuary had its own basin.[56]

Undoubtedly the key factor in this development was the
stability of the population and the sociopolitical
structures necessary to ensure smooth operation of the
irrigation systems. Nevertheless, the paddy systems as
well as the political units of traditional Southeast Asia
did not display the rigid authoritarianism of "oriental
despotism," a concept that stresses the regulatory needs
of irrigated agriculture and the development of
authoritarian political structures to ensure that such
regulation is maintained.[57] The same kind of social
stability and organization made it possible to mobilize
resources for cultural and religious developments of which
Angkor Wat, the greatest monument of Khmer civilization,
is an overt manifestation.

There is an unsubstantiated but implied link between
the decline of Funan and the rise of Shailendra rulers in
Java. Both events took place at about the same
time--early in the seventh century--and both kings held
dynastic titles meaning "king of the mountain." It is
often hypothesized that the great Shailendra dynasty ruler
Sanjaya was descended from the exiled princes of
Funan.[58] Shailendra power, like that of earlier Funan
and its successor the Khmer empire, was based on
agricultural production and the control of enough manpower
to maintain that production. A magnificent reminder of
the potential of this controlled manpower was the
construction of the Borobudur temple in Central Java.

The Shailendras also had rather broad regional
interests. It appears that Jayavarman II of the Khmer
Empire was installed on his throne with Shailendra
assistance. There are also records of Shailendra attacks
on Ligor in A.D. 775 and on the Cham capital in A.D. 782.
Perhaps most significant is the Shailendras' increasing
interest in international maritime commerce, which brought
them into conflict with Srivijaya. By the ninth century,
Shailendra rule was established over Srivijaya, perhaps
through royal marriages.

Shailendra rulers are known to have governed Mataram
in Central and East Java after A.D. 732. During this
time, Indian cultural, philosophic, and religious

influence was absorbed throughout Java, first through Mayhayana Buddhism and later through Hinduism. Mataram on Java was an inland agricultural kingdom that used its resource and labor base to produce the finest in Javanese architecture, exhibited in temple construction still evident throughout much of central Java. These temples, built as royal tombs, provide a glimpse in the life of early eighth-century Java: "Gods and Bohisattva kings were everywhere similarly represented; the Brahman priests were bearded, mustachioed foreigners; the monks and hermits were . . . Javanese."[59] Other details give evidence of hairstyles, dress, jewelry, royal accoutrements, chariots, tools and utensils, furniture, and games. By the end of the nine century, Mataram had shifted from Buddhist to Hindu religion, but the vigorous development of temples continued in Central Java, where the Prambanan complex is the best example. Early in the tenth century, the capital of Mataram was moved to East Java, where the present-day Balinese Siva-Buddha had its origins.[60]

About the time of Mataram's decline in Java, there arose a kingdom in Burma, known as Pagan, built as the result of an alliance between the Burmese and the Mons. The Burmese, given their great affinity for spirits and superstitions of all kinds, were culturally less sophisticated than the Mons but provided military and political leadership. Buddhism flourished under Mon instruction and pervaded the legal system as well as education (although spirit worship never died out),[61] and the sangha, the collectivity of Buddhist monks, gained much influence. In the traditional Buddhist kingdoms, religion was linked to kingship in the "karmic concept of 'merit' [Thai: bun; Pali: punnya]. . . . If the king possessed sufficient merit, his kingdom would be peaceful, orderly, and prosperous and the religion of the Buddha would flourish there."[62] Eventually, the monasteries, temples, and other Buddhist centers claimed too much of Pagan's productive capacity and the kingdom declined:

> Although the sangha gave Pagan its culture and "soul," and initially contributed to its economic development, it inadvertently destroyed the state's subsequent basis for survival. Since the wealth that had made Pagan was now in the hands of the sangha as well as the artisan class, the state could no longer maintain its armies nor the loyalty of its aristocracy.[63]

Pagan was not destroyed, however, until Kublai Khan invaded Burma in 1287.

As the Khmer Empire weakened, the Thais developed an independent cultural and political identity in the central regions of mainland Southeast Asia. Multiple centers of political power appear to have existed in the Menam basin until, after the Mongol invasions (1253-1293), a Thai garrison commander led a revolt against the Khmer overlords and established a new kingdom at Sukhothai. Sukhothai's rulers were wise enough to send tribute to the Mongols in Peking, thereby avoiding the vengeance aimed at Pagan, and strong enough to resist Khmer attempts at conquest. By 1350, however, the Thai political center of gravity shifted southward to Ayudhya, eclipsing both Sukhothai and the kingdom of Chiengmai to the north.[64]

CONFUCIAN BUREAUCRATIC KINGDOMS

The northern regions of Vietnam--Tonkin and Annam--were unique because there were controlled by the Chinese from approximately 200 B.C. until A.D. 900. Throughout most of this period, Vietnam was administered as a province of China. Yet, despite these ten centuries of Chinese domination and cultural penetration, Vietnam survived as an entity distinct in culture and driven to protect its independence and identity.

Early in the tenth century, in the wake of the collapse of T'ang China, the Vietnamese gained their independence (A.D. 939). The independent Vietnam immediately faced threats not only from China to the north but also from the Hindu Cham kingdom to the south.[65] Eventually, however, Vietnam gained strength and moved aggressively against the Chams. At the time of Vietnam's independence, Indian-Buddhism expanded somewhat at the local level as a result of the suspicion directed against Chinese Buddhists, but the political relationship between Hinduism and kingship never developed in Vietnam as it had elsewhere in Southeast Asia.[66] Although maintaining its independence from China, Vietnam modeled its kingship and administrative structures after the Chinese state.

The Vietnamese expansion southward was slow but constant, beginning with the Li dynasty around A.D. 1009.[67] The first historical record of this southward movement came in 1069 when the Cham kingdom was defeated and forced to cede two northern provinces to Vietnam.[68] This occurrence marked the beginning of approximately 500 years of southward pressures by the Vietnamese, until the Cham kingdom disappeared from Chinese records in 1543.

As Vietnamese strength was consolidated along the eastern coast of Indochina, the present-day territories of Laos and Cambodia became buffers between the Thais to the west and the Vietnamese to the east. The three centuries between the mid-1500s and the arrival of the French were a turbulent time in Vietnam as palace coups and dynastic rivalries alternated with military moves against the Cambodians or Laotians. The significance of this time for Southeast Asian history was the emergence of a pattern of southward movement and annexations by the Vietnamese.[69] The southward drift of Vietnamese peasants was motivated by instability resulting from dynastic conflicts, war, religious persecution, and colonial domination. Until their movements were stopped by the French, these migrating farmers were often encouraged by the court and supported by the army.[70]

The Vietnamese adopted a great many Chinese characteristics, but, as was true in other Southeast Asian cultures, they were selective and adaptive in molding a distinctive culture of their own. Although some Chinese social institutions such as marriage rituals and dress were simply imposed upon the Vietnamese, an indigenous core of Vietnamese culture, though altered by the long experience with the Chinese, survived.[71] The Chinese also strengthened Vietnam's infrastructure with new roads and bridges and introduced new agricultural techniques--notably, the iron plow. Nevertheless, the Vietnamese developed the strongest cultural group in Indochina, overtaking the Chams by the sixteenth century and challenging the Khmers and the Laos until inhibited by the French after 1860. Some have argued that adoption of more sophisticated Chinese management techniques in fact gave the Vietnamese the strength to throw off Chinese domination.[72]

THE HISTORICAL PERSPECTIVE IN SUMMARY

When the Europeans first arrived, Malacca was the principal commercial center in the area of the Strait of Malacca, thus leaving Sumatra under the control of petty states--except at the northern tip, where Aceh was gaining stature. Java was under the control of Majaphit, whose power was increasingly limited by the emergence of many small, north coastal principalities that had adopted

Islam. At the same time (1767), the Thai kingdom of Ayudhya was destroyed by the Burmese and the Chakri dynasty (centered at present-day Bangkok) arose; and Burma was ruled by the Konbaung dynasty. Laos, first united in the fourteenth century, was again divided into three kingdoms, centered, respectively, in Vientiane, Luang Prabang, and Champassak. Cambodia, in decline since the days of the Khmer Empire, was ruled by Ang Doung but acknowledged the suzerainty to both the Thai Chakri Kingdom and Vietnam. Vietnam itself, after the wars of succession, had been reunified for fewer than fifty years, under the Emperor Gia Long, when the French began to extend their control. Finally, the Philippines, though perhaps intermittently influenced by Srivijaya or Majapahit, did not develop recognizable state political units before the Spanish arrived at Manila in 1571. (For a clear view of the history of Southeast Asia up to the arrival of the Europeans, see Figure 2.1.)

In any case, the details of Southeast Asian history are still surfacing. More information is being developed about known states, and new discoveries are being made about previously unknown states. The beginning dates of political organization and state formation are being pushed back. What emerges from this historical overview is an understanding of Southeast Asia as a region that has prospered despite is geographic fragmentation and ethnic diversity. Drawing upon the great cultures of India and China, Southeast Asia formed a cultural and historical unit unique in social, economic, and political structures but close in its linkages to India, China, and the historical world system.

Figure 2.1 Chronological Table

A.D.	Sumatra	Java	Malaya	Burma
100	Kinship groups and pirates		Langkasuka etc.	
200				
300				Pyu and Mon
400			Funan domination	
500	Malayu and Srivijaya			
600				
700			Langkasuka etc.	
800				832
		Mataram		Nanchao domination in North
900	Srivijaya			Mon Kingdom in South
1000		1049	Srivijayan domination	1044
1100		Kediri		Pagan
1200		1222		
		Singosari		
1300		1293	Thai domination	1287
				Shan penetration
				1364
1400		Majapahit	1402	Shan Ava and Mon Pegu
			Malacca	
1500			1511	
		1520		c. 1555
	Petty states	trading	Portuguese Malacca	
1600		1619		
			1641	Toungoo
		Batavia and Dutch expansion	Dutch Malacca	
1700				1752
1800	1825		1796	Konbaungset
				1826
	Dutch		British expansion	
1900	expansion			

From C.G.F. Simkin, *The Traditional Trade of Asia* (Oxford: Oxford University Press, 1968), p. 384. Used by permission.

Thailand	Laos	Cambodia	Vietnam	Philippines
Dvaravati	Cham domination		Champa and Annam	Kinship groups and pirates
		Funan		
Funan	domination			
Haripunjaya and Dyaravati		Chenla		
		802		
			939	Srivijayan influence
	Angkor domination	Angkor	Champa and Nam Viet or Dai Viet	
Angkor domination 1238				
Sukhothai etc.	Thai penetration			
1350	1353			
		1432		Majapahit influence
			1471	
Ayudhya	Lan Xang	Post-Angkor	Kingdom of Annam	1571
	1712		1673	Spanish Colony
1782			Trinh and Nguyen 1802	
Chakri	Three Kingdoms 1893	1863	Nguyen	
		French expansion		1898
				U.S. rule

40

NOTES

1. For detailed histories of Southeast Asia, see D.G.E. Hall, A History of South-East Asia (New York: St. Martin's Press, 1968); and John F. Cady, Southeast Asia: Its Historical Development (New York: McGraw-Hill, 1964). For a more concise study, see Brian Harrison, South-East Asia: A Short History, third ed. (New York: St. Martin's Press, 1968).

2. See "Part I: The Later Prehistory of South East Asia," in Early South East Asia, edited by R. B. Smith and W. Watson (London: Oxford University Press, 1973), pp. 3-254.

3. See Donald K. Emmerson, "Issues in Southeast Asian History: Room for Interpretation," Journal of Asian Studies 40 (November 1980), pp. 55-68. See also Paul Wheatley, "Presidential Address: India Beyond the Ganges--Desultory Reflections on the Origins of Civilization in Southeast Asia," Journal of Asian Studies 42 (November 1982).

4. See Bennet Bronson, "The Late Prehistory and Early History of Central Thailand," in Smith and Watson, Early South East Asia, for an example of current analysis that tries to push back the dates for recognizing early states.

5. See Hall, A History of South-East Asia, pp. 24-25. See also J. W. van der Meulen, "Suvarnadvipa and the Chrysse Chersonesos," Indonesia, no. 18 (October 1974), p. 1.

6. Claude Jaques, "Funan, Zenla: The Reality Concealed by These Chinese Views of Indochina," in Smith and Watson, Early South East Asia, pp. 371-379.

7. Wheatley, for instance, notes that a "chiefdom degree of centralization" existed in the area of present-day northern Vietnam before the beginning of the Christian era. See Paul Wheatley, Nagara and Commandery: The Origins of Southeast Asian Urban Traditions (Chicago: Research Papers Nos. 207-208 of the Department of Geography, University of Chicago, 1983), p. 91.

8. J. Kennedy, "From State to Development in Prehistoric Thailand: An Exploration of the Origins of Growth, Exchange, and Variability in Southeast Asia," in Economic Exchange and Social Interaction in Southeast Asia: Perspectives from Prehistory, History and Ethnography, edited by Karl L. Hutter (Ann Arbor, Michigan: Papers on South and Southeast Asia, No. 13, 1977).

9. See Fred W. Riggs, Thailand: The Modernization of a Bureaucratic Polity (Honolulu: East-West Center Press, 1966), for a critique of analyses that apply Western values to Thailand's governmental organization.

10. Malcolm C. Webb, "The Flag Follows Trade: An Essay on the Necessary Interaction of Military and Commercial Factors in State Formation," in Ancient Civilization and Trade, edited by Jeremy A. Sabloff and Clifford C. Lamberg-Karlovsky (Albuquerque: University of New Mexico Press, 1975), pp. 164-165. (Emphasis original.) Webb summarized a number of other terms that might capture some further limitations on the transfer of the concept of the state to early Southeast Asian polities; these include kinship state, voluntary state, primitive state, proto-state, nascent state, or segmentary state.

11. O. W. Wolters, "Culture, History, and Region in Southeast Asian Perspectives," in ASEAN: Identity, Development and Culture, edited by R. P. Anand and Purificacion V. Quisumbing (Quezon City and Honolulu: University of the Philippines Law Center and the East-West Center Culture Learning Institute, 1981), p. 5.

12. Kenneth R. Hall, "The 'Indianization' of Funan: An Economic History of Southeast Asia's First State," Journal of Southeast Asian Studies 13 (March 1982), p. 82 and passim.

13. Ibid., p. 82.

14. O. W. Wolters, "Khmer 'Hinduism' in the Seventh Century," in Smith and Watson, Early South East Asia, p. 428.

15. Hall, "The 'Indianization' of Funan," p. 91.

16. Ibid., pp. 97-103.

17. Ibid., pp. 104-106.

18. Joseph Desomogyi, A History of Oriental Trade (Hildesheim: Georg Olms Verlagsbuch-handling, 1968), p. 24.

19. Ibid.

20. Ibid.

21. Hall, A History of South-East Asia, p. 28.

22. H.H.E. Loofs, "Problems on Continuity Between the Pre-Buddhist and Buddhist Periods in Central Thailand, with Special Reference to U-Thong," in Smith and Watson, Early South East Asia, pp. 342-351.

23. Elizabeth Lyons, "Dvaravati: A Consideration of its Formative Period," in Smith and Watson, Early South East Asia, p. 352.

42

24. For an interesting description of primitive culture in part of the archipelago, see F. M. Schnitger, Forgotten Kingdoms in Sumatra (Leiden: E. J. Brill, 1964; first published in 1938).

25. O. W. Wolters, Early Indonesian Commerce: A Study of the Origins of Srivijaya (Ithaca: Cornell University Press, 1967), passim.

26. Anthony Reid, "The Structure of Cities in Southeast Asia, Fifteenth to Seventeenth Centuries," Journal of Southeast Asian Studies 11 (September 1980), p. 236.

27. Fa-Hsien, "A Record of the Buddhist Countries," translated by Li Yung-hsi (Peking: Chinese Buddhist Association, 1957), in The World of Southeast Asia, edited by Harry J. Benda and John A. Larkin (New York: Harper & Row, 1967).

28. Hall, "The 'Indianization' of Funan," pp. 100-103.

29. O. W. Wolters, The Fall of Srivijaya in Malay History (Ithaca: Cornell University Press, 1971), pp. 1-7.

30. Wolters, Early Indonesian Commerce, pp. 229-253.

31. Kenneth R. Hall, "State and Statecraft in Early Srivijaya," in Explorations in Early Southeast Asian History, edited by Kenneth R. Hall and John K. Whitmore (Ann Arbor: Michigan Papers on South and Southeast Asia, 1976), p. 93.

32. Cady, Southeast Asia, p. 69.

33. I-tsing, "A Record of the Buddhist Religion as Practiced in India and the Malay Archipelago," translated by J. Takakusu, in Benda and Larkin, The World of Southeast Asia, pp. 5-6.

34. Chau Ju-Kua, His Work on the Chinese and Arab Trade in the Twelfth and Thirteenth Centuries, entitled Chu-fan-chi, translated by by F. Hirth and V. Rockhill (Taipei: Literature House, Ltd., 1965; reprint of a 1911 St. Petersburg edition), p. 62.

35. Hall, A History of South-East Asia, p. 57.

36. G. Coedes, The Indianized States of Southeast Asia, edited by Walter F. Vella and translated from French by Susan B. Cowing (Honolulu: East-West Center Press, 1968), p. 130.

37. Hall, A History of South-East Asia, p. 55. See also Bennet Bronson, "The Archaeology of Sumatra and the Problem of Srivijaya," in Smith and Watson, Early South East Asia, pp. 394-405; and M. C. Subhadradis Diskul, The Art of Srivijaya (Paris and Kuala Lumpur: UNESCO and Oxford University Press, 1980).

38. Hall, A History of South-East Asia, p. 56.

39. Bronson, "The Archaeology of Sumatra and the Problem of Srivijaya," in Smith and Watson, Early South East Asia, p. 403.

40. See John N. Miksic, "Archaeology and Palaeogeography in the Straits of Malacca," in Hutter, Economic Exchange and Social Interaction, pp. 155-175; O. W. Wolters, "Landfall on the Palembang Coast in Medieval Times," Indonesia, no. 20 (October 1975), pp. 1-58.

41. Hall, "The 'Indianization' of Funan."

42. D.J.M. Tate, The Making of South-East Asia (London and Kuala Lumpur: Oxford University Press, 1979): The European Conquest, vol. 1, p. 55.

43. J. Kennedy, A History of Malaya, 1400-1959 (New York: St. Martin's Press, 1967), p. 1.

44. Cady, Southeast Asia, p. 155.

45. Michael Prawdin, The Mongol Empire: Its Rise and Legacy, 2nd ed. (London: Allen and Unwin, 1961), pp. 411-421.

46. Cady, Southeast Asia, pp. 157-166.

47. Hall, "The 'Indianization' of Funan," pp. 104-105.

48. Hall, A History of South-East Asia, p. 133.

49. Lawrence Palmer Briggs, The Ancient Khmer Empire. Transactions of the American Philosophical Society (Philadelphia: American Philosophical Society, 1951), p. 89.

50. Ibid., p. 90.

51. I. W. Mabbett, "Devaraja," Journal of Southeast Asian History 10 (1969), pp. 202-223.

52. Hermann Kulke, The Devaraja Cult, translated from the German by I. W. Mabbett (Cornell: Southeast Asia Program, Data Paper No. 108, 1978), p. 37.

53. Nidhi Aeusrivongse, "The Devaraja Cult and Khmer Kingship in Angkor," in Hall and Whitmore, Explorations in Early Southeast Asian History, p. 121.

54. Ibid., p. 126.

55. Briggs, The Ancient Khmer Empire, p. 106.

56. Ibid., p. 165.

57. Karl Wittfogel, Oriental Despotism, and Comparative Study of Total Power (New Haven, Conn.: Yale University Press, 1957). See also Karl A. Wittfogel, "Results and Problems of the Study of Oriental Despotism," Journal of Asian Studies 28 (February 1969), pp. 357-374.

58. Bernard H. M. Vlekke, Nusantara: A History of Indonesia (The Hague: W. van Hoeve, Ltd., 1965), pp. 28-30.

59. Cady, Southeast Asia, p. 77.

44

60. Boechari, "Some Considerations on the Problem of the Shift of Mataram's Centre of Government from Central to East Java in the 10th Century," in Smith and Watson, Early South East Asia, pp. 373-491.

61. John Brohm, "Buddhism and Animism in a Burmese Village," Journal of Asian Studies 22 (February 1963), pp. 155-167. Also reprinted in Southeast Asia: The Politics of National Integration, edited by John McAlister (New York: Random House, 1975).

62. Lorraine Gesick, "The Rise and Fall of King Taksin: A Drama of Buddhist Kingship," in Centers, Symbols, and Hierarchies: Essays on the Classical States of Southeast Asia, edited by Lorraine Gesick (New Haven, Conn.: Yale University Southeast Asia Studies, Monograph Series, No. 26, 1983), p. 89.

63. Michael Aung-Thwin, "Kingship, the Sangha, and Society in Pagan," in Hall and Whitmore, Explorations in Early Southeast Asian History, pp. 234-235.

64. Charnvit Kasetsiri, The Rise of Ayudhya: A History of Siam in the Fourteenth and Fifteenth Centuries (Kuala Lumpur: Oxford University Press, 1976), pp. 51-92.

65. Keith W. Taylor, The Birth of Vietnam (Berkeley: University of Oxford Press, 1983), p. 269.

66. Cady, Southeast Asia, p. 104.

67. Hall, A History of South-East Asia, p. 200.

68. Jerry M. Silverman, "Historic National Rivalries and Interstate Conflict in Mainland Southeast Asia," in Conflict and Stability in Southeast Asia, edited by Mark W. Zacher and R. Stephen Milne (Garden City, N.Y.: Anchor Books, 1974), p. 55.

69. Gerald C. Hickey, Village in Vietnam (New Haven, Conn.: Yale University Press, 1964), p. 6.

70. Ronald Provencher, Mainland Southeast Asia: An Anthropological Perspective (Pacific Palisades, Calif.: Goodyear Publishing Company, 1975), p. 41.

71. Taylor, The Birth of Vietnam, pp. xviii-xxi.

72. Hicker, Village in Vietnam, p. 6, citing Le Thanh Khoi, Le Viet Nam--Histoire et Civilisation: Le Milieu et l'Histoire (Paris: Les Editions de Minuit, 1955); and H. Maspero, "Etudes d'histoire d'Annam," Bulletin de l'Ecole Francaise d'Extreme Orient 18 (1918).

CHAPTER 3

Bases for Political Community in Traditional Southeast Asia

To understand the structures of state power and control in traditional Southeast Asia, we must also understand the underlying principles of social organization. In recent years, there has been a concerted effort among Southeast Asian scholars to learn "more about the character and persistence of indigenous value systems, about the changing nature of the relationship between political center and periphery, and about how ordinary people perceived and experienced their world."[1] Unfortunately, few direct records providing data on the structure of the historical rural community in Southeast Asia are still in existence. Historians must glean whatever fragmentary information they can from the traditional histories written in the sixteenth and seventeenth centuries, from temple carvings that have survived, from the records of early travelers, mainly from China, who visited Southeast Asia, and from descriptions provided by early Portuguese writers and later colonial administrators.

Another hindrance to an understanding of the traditional social base is that most of the formal histories of Southeast Asia that do exist are concerned with matters of state as embodied in the activities of kings and courts. Information about the villages and peasant populations is available only in relatively recent work by sociologists, anthropologists, and economists who, moreover, have recognized that change has taken place only very slowly within the village community. Much of the material gathered in the twentieth century, some of it in the last thirty years, describes the traditional patterns of village organization, behavior, and needs. This material, although modern, can be used to construct a model

45

of the social structure of the traditional village because
little had changed in that structure until very recent
times.   According to O'Connor, "as early as the fourth
millenium B.C. in parts of mainland Southeast Asia . . .
[were found] the established competencies and disciplines
required to sustain a settled existence not markedly
different than [that] encountered in rural villagers
today."[2]
     What follows in this chapter, then, is a composite of
traditional village society drawn from contemporary
literature. It is important to grasp the context of the
village community in order to understand its role in the
formation and development of the traditional state in
Southeast Asia.   Although the picture of the village
presented cannot be historical, it is the only substantive
composite that can be drawn from the records that exist
today.

THE VILLAGE COMMUNITY

     Redfield has noted four characteristics of village
communities that can apply here: the village community is
distinctive in terms of its inhabitants as well as its
geographic locale; it is small enough in size   that
acquaintance among its members is possible; it is
homogeneous so that activities, roles, and states of mind
are well understood, accepted, and slow to change; and it
is self-sufficient, providing for nearly all of the
activities and needs of its members.[3]
     Traditional Southeast Asian society was divided into
two groups--the village sphere and the court sphere. At
times, as much as one-third of the peasant village
population may have been slaves, although the distinction
between slaves and peasants does not appear to have been
great.[4] Michael Aung-Thwin has recently shown that in
Burma, the master-slave relationship, as understood in the
West in the seventeenth and eighteenth centuries, never
existed, but various "bonded" relationships were common in
which an individual could, voluntarily or involuntarily,
be tied to the state, the church, or another individual in
a legally contracted sense.[5] In Cambodia, the concept
of slaves was obscured because many commoners were
"slaves" of the gods and "property" of the temple, a
condition yet not fully understood.[6] In Vietnam, the
law code of the fifteenth century distinguished levels
among the lower classes--freemen, those in bond, slaves,

and those in servitude to the state.[7] The court group, on the other hand, included not only the aristocracy but artisans, clerics, warriors, wealthy merchants and businessmen, and others who supported the royal and governmental structures. The two segments of society were linked by an overall metaphysical view of the world and of the individual's role within that world. The result was a socioeconomic system that maximized the autonomy of the village community while assuring it a modicum of security against external threat. All this was legitimized through the metaphysical view of the world as variously labeled from Hindu, Buddhist, or Islamic terminologies. Traditionally, Western perceptions focused on the urban centers, as McAlister and Mus have noted in the case of post-World War II Vietnam: "The authentic life of the country has been that of its villages. However, the representatives of the French tended to think of Viet Nam in terms of urban centers."[8] Beyond such basic principles as common language, geographic proximity, and ethnic similarities, it was the social linkages of the peasant societies of Southeast Asia that provided the basis for state organization as well as the ultimate limits on the development of states within the region. According to Reid and Castles, "the village community forms the basic unit of social organization, of land management, and of conflict resolution. Whether we look at the Batak huta, or the gaukang community of Bone . . . it is the little community with which we must begin an analysis of the historical rise of states."[9]

The bulk of the peasant population resided in village communities in traditional Southeast Asia. The village comprised not only dwellings (including courtyards, gardens, and religious and community buildings) but also all agricultural lands in production and fallow, grazing lands, and certain forest areas used for fuel cutting or hunting.[10] The village was a closed community in that most members were blood relatives, of greater or lesser degree depending on the overall size of the village, and outsiders were seldom accepted permanently within the village. Foreigners actually did reside within some villages but retained only very low social status and were subject to some discrimination, including the required payment of certain taxes apparently not required of native residents.[11]

The traditional villages varied in size and form. In some areas, they were walled enclosures; in others, they constituted numerous scattered hamlets in which only a few families lived. But, in general,

> villages [had] two basic designs, the linear and the cluster. The former [were] found along water-courses, roads or pathways; the latter [became] established around some focal point such as a source of water, temple, or the homes of original settlers or village leaders. Many villages [were] composed of discrete hamlets, separated from one another by their fields; more rarely individual houses may [have been] separated from their nearest neighbours in a scattered formation.[12]

In addition, site selection was determined by topography, material convenience, proximity to kin, social distinctions, domestic water, defense, stream transport, privacy, and supernatural beliefs regarding auspicious directions and forces,[13] as well as by the village economic base.[14]

As the center of economic (agricultural) and social life, the village developed basic patterns of organization that not only governed day-to-day activities but also had a major impact upon the general community. The village was a corporate unit, maintaining a clear definition of citizenship based on kinship or occasionally ritual admission. It regulated economic activities primarily through the control of land and land use, and imposed discipline directly through enforcement of judgments by elders or indirectly through social sanctions.

The origins of the corporate village are obscure. Some have argued that it evolved as part of the communal nature of peasant society,[15] while others have viewed it as a component of the evolution of complex political structures, perhaps as a unit for taxation.[16] The village, as a self-contained social unit, came under extreme pressure as of the twentieth century when colonial policies were enacted that drew villagers increasingly into the cash economy and made them more dependent on colonial administrators or other outsiders for welfare support. Previously, its social mores withstood nearly every outside influence: "After a millennium of Sinization . . . Chinese culture had not penetrated into the masses of the Vietnamese."[17] The ability of the village community to maintain its basic organization, and the tenacity of its controlling social powers despite many diffuse influences from without qualify it as a logical beginning for an analysis of social organization.

The Economic Base. Historically, as the populace in Southeast Asia moved from the gathering stage to a more sedentary existence, more stable village communities emerged. Modes of agricultural production influenced these village structures and their concomitant stability. In areas where slash-and-burn agriculture was practiced--where fields were defoliated through the cutting of brush and burning of the residue on the field for added nutrients--villages moved every few years to be close to new fields while previously used fields were left fallow. Fallow periods varied with general soil and ecological conditions and, more important, with population pressure. Reports show that some fields were not ready for recultivation after twenty years; more recently in northern Thailand, however, fallow periods have lasted from three to ten years, although the original foliage had not returned and soil fertility was generally sufficient to sustain only a single cropping cycle.[18]

The ecological balance of slash-and-burn agriculture is such that only sparse populations could be sustained in these areas. Population growth stimulated by colonial improvements in health care had very negative impacts on slash-and-burn agriculture, although this growth had not been an acute problem before the colonial period. Estimates of sustainable population vary from twenty to fifty persons per square kilometer for this form of agriculture. The variations are attributable to natural ecological differences across Southeast Asia and to the use of slightly different agricultural techniques in different areas.[19]

The stability of location of the slash-and-burn villages varied throughout the region. Some groups were nomadic, moving all belongings with them while traveling over wide areas, whereas others maintained permanent communities in which nonproductive members remained. Still other villages were permanent and maintained extensive agricultural lands around the village, only a portion of which were under cultivation at any one time. The size of any given slash-and-burn village was related to the amount and productivity of available agricultural lands, and permanence was often a function of the value of the village location for purposes of marketing, religion, or transportation.[20]

Among the more stable or permanent villages in Southeast Asia, most depended on some form of flooding or irrigation to provide the soil with nutrients that slash-and-burn farming obtained through the fallow and the burning processes. In certain areas, principally the broad floodplains of primary and secondary river systems, unrestricted flood waters provided the rejuvenating nutrients for the soil, and rice seed was sown in a broadcast manner. The irrigation was not controlled as it was on the mountainside terraces, but monsoon weather and flooding were sufficiently regular to allow for stable agricultural production and the evolution of a sedentary agricultural existence.[21]

Controlled flow irrigation was the most intensive form of agricultural production in Southeast Asia.[22] Ranging from simple dikes built to retain flood waters to the complex and highly interdependent water-distribution systems of paddy fields or the terraces on hillsides with reservoirs or streams flowing from above, this type of agriculture not only provided the highest yield potentials for rice but also increased the chance for multiple crop cycles in each year, because water was more readily and predictably available.[23]

In relatively stable production areas, villages took on greater permanence, particularly if they were able to fulfill secondary functions astride major waterways or roads, or if they were hosts for some type of religious temple or monastic complex. Whether the physical structure of the village followed the more common pattern of centrally clustered households and common buildings or the linear pattern with buildings strung along rivers, roadways, or irrigation canals, each villager's relationships resembled a series of mutually inclusive, concentric circles, beginning with the immediate family and extending outward from genealogical clan and ethnic bases and to territorial groupings. The last circle, in this case, would connote the outside world beyond the perimeter of the village.[24]

The areas of Southeast Asia that supported the more advanced agricultural technologies corresponded roughly to those where larger and more complex political organizations were established. Such parallel developments were, undoubtedly, mutually reinforcing.[25] Peddler trade was probably sufficient to satisfy various village needs but never enough to foster the development of a middle-class commercial or merchant population.[26] The result was a self-sufficient village that saw only a small outflow of surplus food and occasional corvee-labor for tax purposes, as well as a minimal exchange of goods with external peoples.

The social distance between agricultural functions and commercial functions was great. Peasant agriculturalists composed the bulk of the village population, whereas economic contact with the outside world occurred largely through the market. The local market had a distinct and separate physical location near but not usually in the village and often at convenient intersections of roads leading to several villages;[27] at the same time, its operators and inhabitants were generally excluded from the village group. That the traders were not part of the village structure is exemplified in the Javanese word for trader, dagang, which also means "foreigner" or "wanderer." The market was a cultural unit separate from the village with a "status in the wider society [which] has been ambiguous at best, pariah-like at worst."[28] Local peddlers, in addition to Chinese who had settled in Southeast Asia, traveled between China and Southeast Asia, with so little capital that they were often indentured for the price of passage.[29] The peddlers traveled overland throughout the region, but their movements were governed by the monsoon as well as by the cycle of acquiring goods at one end of the trade route to be sold at the other.

Landholding and Land Use. Landholding, of course, was closely related to the mode of production in the village. Slash-and-burn agricultural villages held much greater areas of land than did wet-rice villages supporting populations of comparable size. In most cases, the village itself held "ownership" of the land, and use of these lands was determined by complex social and economic relationships within the village. Even in those cases in which parcels of land were held by an individual, the villages frequently placed restrictions on the disposal of that land. But in all types of villages in Southeast Asia, Western concepts of landownership and private property were not recognizable.

Whyte has identified four types of landholders in the Asian village: (1) individuals who held large blocks of land, such that they could not handle it alone and rented some portion of the land, usually on a share-cropping basis; (2) individuals who held blocks of land that could be farmed by the owner but only with additional hired labor at planting and/or harvest time; (3) individuals who farmed their own land and/or some sharecropped land, usually one to five acres in total, but were unable to generate any stable surplus; and (4) the landless or almost landless laborers who depended primarily on wage employment.[30] This last class was small in the traditional village but grew enormously during the colonial period as the internal dynamics of the village were disrupted by external forces. In Southeast Asia today, it is likely that the first two groups have increased their hold on the land, while many in the third and previously largest group have entered the landless class.

Other factors, as well, determined patterns of landholding. For example, the most important lands were the rice lands; other productive lands, whether they produced secondary crops, forests, or fuel, were considered less desirable. Distribution of communally held lands of these types was determined by status, right, or heredity within the village. Communal lands were further divided between those over which the sultan or other nonvillage officials exercised control and those controlled by the village.[31] Family lands, too, were divided between these two categories and were maintained to protect the ancestral ritual obligations of the family as well as to ensure continued productive use of the lands. The village as a unit, however, exercised considerable weight in determining how these lands could be distributed or redistributed when available.

Kinship and Communal Relationships. An integral part of village self-sufficiency was its traditional emphasis on communalism, which reached beyond common labor on communal lands. No doubt enhanced by the complexities of wet-rice cultivation, in which the many people involved in paddy activity depended for their own success on the work of others and the sharing of resources (such as water) at the right time, corporate action eventually permeated all of village life. A large part of the cooperation within the village was probably attributable to the strong influence of the headmen and the intense pressures of closed village society. The slametan feast as practiced in Java symbolized the communal force within the village such that "Friends, neighbors, fellow workers, relatives . . . all [got] bound, by virtue of their commensality, into a defined social group pledged to mutual support and cooperation."[32] Communal obligations were so extensive that landed peasant farmers were expected to hire day laborers at planting and harvest times, even if the farmer could do the work alone. The communal feature of village life was not only religious in nature, but also expressive of the larger social and economic interdependence of the villagers.

In traditional Southeast Asia, as now, kinship probably formed the basis for interpersonal relationships and strongly communal links. Hickey found that as recently as the late 1950s, nearly three-quarters of the households in a Vietnam village were blood relatives.[33] Kinship provided the security of the familiar as well as a link between the world of the living and the supernatural world of the dead and the unborn.[34] The Balinese extended kinship concepts to include the supernatural, as implied by the term kaiket, which means tied to an array of people, places, things, organizations, temples, interpersonal duties and obligations, as well as to the very earth, where the individual was born.[35] This view of humankind as only one of many components and not the master of the environment, so pervasive in traditional Southeast Asian culture, is an anathema to Western thought, which has stressed individualism, freedom of action, and manipulation of the environment to maximize gain.

Kinship bonds reinforced the closed nature of the village and its parochial view of the world. Wessing has shown how the closed kinship system was maintained among three hamlets in Banten in western Java.[36] Men and women sought marriage partners in "opposing" directions: Women from Cibeo, for example, married men from Cikeusik, whereas men from Cibeo tended to marry women from Cikartawana. A similar pattern of out-marriage operated in Cikeusik and Cikartawana. In actuality, outsiders did enter the system to preserve a male-female balance but within the village hierarchy the system was maintained.

Kinship bonds not only made it difficult for outsiders to become part of the village, but, when extended to the ethnic group level, they also provided (and still do provide) the greatest extent of community ascribed to by most Southeast Asians. Kinship was sometimes extended to a large ethnic group, as among the Bataks of North and Central Sumatra, for instance, there was "a consciousness of themselves as a people and a genealogical system, [as] the descendants of their eponymous ancestor Si Raja Batak . . . [although] seeing Batakdom as one huge family had to await the conditions of colonial rule. . . . In any case there was never the remotest question of political action at the all-Batak level."[37]

Custom and Law. A third factor important to village structure was the syncretic nature of its customary law. In this connection, two traits of Southeast Asian society--the flexible capacity to absorb outside influences and the continuous mutation of custom and habit--can be lumped together. At any rate, customary law provided a further measure of village autonomy. There is a Vietnamese saying that the law of the emperor yields to the customs of the village.[38] However, it was also true that customary law had the ability to absorb new influences while maintaining a high degree of continuity with the past. Customary law formed the sum total of rules, customs, and beliefs that defined acceptable behavior within the village. It was the single most important control over village members, governing, as it did, the family, the fields, and virtually all aspects of the village life--with the result that radically new concepts associated with Hinduism, Buddhism, and Islam were accepted, once they had been rationalized in terms of customary law.

Mysticism and World View. Another important feature of village life was the emphasis on harmony, in part drawn from the communal rather than individualistic social organization of the village, but also linked to the concepts of the human being's relationship to nature:

> Seen as an ecosystem, man is no longer the measure of all things nor the master of nature. He is bound intimately to the grain [rice] he would grow, for without his sensitive observation of wilting and flourishing, these plants might have dwindled to extinction. Like the haiku poets who converse with a still pond, they believe that man, properly trained, develops sensitivity to the voices of plants, and plants can hear men's entreaties.[39]

The concept of harmony with nature was extended to harmony with the cosmic whole. Cosmic power existed in all entities. Balance and harmony had to be maintained because the cosmos was regarded not "as the undifferentiated sum of the entities but rather as the unity of various categories of entities in differing degrees of opposition to each other."[40] Cosmic harmony was maintained through orientation of village buildings and temples using numerology, the points of the compass, and nearby natural landmarks that were believed to be residences for forces of evil.[41] Evidence of geomancy, defined by Wheatley as the "analysis of the morphological and spatial expressions of chi'i [cosmic breath] in the surface features of the earth" similar to those found in Chinese belief systems,[42] has also been found in Vietnam and elsewhere in Southeast Asia.[43] These patterns, "in addition to placating spirits . . . enable the individual to interpret the portents of nature and thereby so orient himself toward his physical surroundings as to attract favorable cosmological influences."[44] Describing Sundanese society, Wessing has noted that

a major feature of the Sundanese belief system is the conviction that life is influenced by various supernatural forces, both beneficent and deleterious. It is important therefore in the conduct of daily affairs to determine where the positive and negative influences are located since these forces are not stationary. . . . If a Sundanese wants to conduct some business in a given place he must ask in which direction his objective is located relative to himself. He then consults his paririmbon [divining books] in order to find out where the evil influence is located on that particular day. If the evil is located in a direction other than the one he must take, he may set out directly toward his goal. Should his goal and the evil coincide, however, it would be best not to go at all. If one must go then it is best to start by heading in the direction opposite to the one in which the evil influence is located and only later curve toward one's objective.[45]

It is the interplay of these variables of village life--an agricultural economy in juxtaposition with commercial, market, or peddler activities; communal interdependence and the social pressures of a closed system; the intuitive aspects of law and behavior that embodied generations of behavior and belief; and the preoccupation with natural and cosmological harmony--that provided the basis for the evolution of political units approximately equivalent to the state. The maintenance of harmony or balance in all things found expression at three levels in traditional Southeast Asia--the level of the village, the state, and the universe. But it was the village level upon which the others rested: "At the very foundation of Vietnamese society, the rice fields have throughout history supplied this society with a reason for being. The fields have provided the basis for a stable social structure, a discipline for work, and a rhythm of communal celebrations--in short, a contract between the society itself, the soil and the sky."[46]

Although village social structures varied in details from place to place and over time, the traditional Southeast Asian village had several common characteristics: (1) Kinship, particularly at the family level and to some degree at the extended family levels, was a major force for social organization. (2) Most of the labor or productivity of the village was agricultural, such that handicrafts, peddling, and other trades were given secondary importance and status, and were often handled in transitory fashion by outsiders. (3) A sense of communal cooperation, extending beyond the immediate family, became an important means of attaining common goals and meeting local needs. And (4) this communalism enveloped or produced a set of cultural values and mores in which individualism was met with suspicion, whereas commitment to and sacrifice for the common good were more esteemed.

THE KINSHIP AND ETHNIC GROUPS

Above the village level, the common base for political organization within early Southeast Asian society was the kinship group, which often provided a measure of geographic continuity as well. Isolated groups were able to coalesce into larger ethnic groups by extending the kinship bond for a common cause, such as meeting an external threat. These extended ethnic groupings were often ad hoc or task specific and tended to revert to smaller or more local organizations when the common problem was eliminated.[47] Neither the kinship group nor the ethnic group represented intermediate or transition stages in state formation, and, in some situations, both groups seem even to have inhibited such state-building. Nevertheless, the kinship group was a key management unit for much of the geographic area of Southeast Asia through much of its history. The state structures and interstate relations in traditional Southeast Asia can be comprehended if we envision the region as divided among rather amorphous kinship groups rather than clearly demarcated in terms of geographic segments or discrete political units.

Records of Batak and Minangkabau societies, although not written until early in the colonial era, provide a glimpse into the common core of Southeast Asian societies at the beginning of the Christian era or earlier. The clan or ethnic group was the widest grouping to which the individual gave allegiance. Beyond that level, common language, customary law, and/or extended ethnic ties made cooperation possible for some adjudicatory as well as religious or other ceremonial purposes and occasionally for common defense against some external threat. But interclan warfare and strife were, in all probability, more common than interclan cooperation and tended to reinforce the fragmentation that limited state-building. In the Toba-Batak areas, for example, a clearly defined political unit above the village or kinship group level never developed. The Bataks had a strong genealogical sense of themselves as a people, and the concepts of clans and related subclan or extended clan units were widely recognized.[48] Yet these ethnic and genealogical ties were rarely translated into political linkages. There were numerous examples of institutions organized above the village and clan levels, including judicial structures, market organizations, and land and water management groups. Even the famous Singamangaraja, despite its god-king title, "was not a major factor in the Batak political system in normal times though it became so in the final stages of the destruction of that system by the Dutch."[49] Contradicting the generally held view that the Singamangaraja was a royal political dynasty, Castles has concluded that

the Bataks of the interior left to their own devices were able to solve their problems without the need of a central authority. . . . Certainly there was constant rivalry and frequent disputes leading to wars. But the ferocity of the wars was limited by tabus, and resources for arbitration were abundant. The small scale of external trade meant that no chief or community could make the monopolisation of it a basis of power. The notion that the clan owned the land was very strongly entrenched. Only rarely did one clan displace another from a territory it had occupied. There was thus no room for the state or ruler as an outsider demanding part of the produce of the tiller.[50]

There are no known instances in which the whole of the Batak populace or even one of its major genealogical or dialetical divisions acted as a political unit, even in the face of external threat.[51]

The same is true for another Sumatran people, the Minangkabau, for whom the concept of the Minangkabau world was nearly global, as in "Western world" or "modern world," although it did not have political connotations. Clan groups of the Minangkabau often included place names, although these referred not to territorial units but rather to kinship groups or lineages of several extended families following matrilineal ties. Local village units--which did have contiguous territorial bases--were sometimes federated into larger units, but even these did not adopt the practices common to states. For example, revenues were raised and retained at the village level.

As with the Bataks, the Minangkabau also had other coalition groups above the village level that exercised some control over one or more aspects of social organization. Given formal titles and great respect but carrying little effective authority were the chiefs, or distinguished elders: the king of customary law, the king of religion, and the king of the world. The role of these "kings" is not fully understood, but they appear to have been more judicial than political figures, even though they made rather grand claims for their powers.[52]

Still other areas of Southeast Asia relied on the informal kinship group instead of developing centralized political systems. In present-day Bali, the extended kin group called dodia provides a strong focus for the individual as part of a "highly corporate group of people who are convinced, with whatever reason, that they are all descendants of one common ancestor."[53] Much of the area of the present-day Philippines appears to have followed this same sociopolitical structure. Until the beginning of the colonial era in the Philippines, the primary political units were probably small ethnic or kin groups (with some territorial connotations) headed by respected elders or chiefs. At the time of the Spanish arrival, the largest of these communities consisted of approximately one hundred families, usually linked by blood; moreover, although several groups might have been mixed throughout the same geographic area, the several chiefs were considered equals and each kinship acted independently.[54] There is no physical evidence that any larger, integrated political units functioned in the Philippine islands.[55] Although Cebu, Manila, and Vigan developed communities larger in population than most local clans, "only in Manila did the barangay chief have attributes resembling those of a monarchial ruler."[56] The evidence is sketchy, but Bronson has shown that in Thailand before the rise of Dvaravati (about A.D. 600) there may have existed at most a "group of smallish states or proto-states in a formative stage of political development."[57] These probably would have been clan or kinship groups.

Why these peoples did not develop stronger governmental structures above the local level is not known. Their widespread systems of irrigated agriculture would seem to have made authoritarian political organization likely. Yet their weak political organization did not necessarily leave them vulnerable to conquest. They may actually have reinforced their own isolation by not creating a weak state apparatus that could have been dominated from the outside. The few export products of these areas may have held little attractiveness, given, at least in the case of the Bataks, a predilection for cannibalism. The great Sumatran states of early history were maritime states such as Srivijaya, which seemingly had little interest in maintaining control of its own hinterland.[58]

Societies such as these did not proceed in social organization beyond "networking," in which marriage played a role in creating links among villages, but the "closeness or openness of the mesh, the range or scope of the network, the kinds of human interests served by the relationships . . . [and] the stability of the relationships" became the measure of both the expanse and the limits for larger political organization.[59] Mair has argued that state formation can take place in such kinship networks when "privileged kin groups are able to command the services of followers through whom they can impose their will on the rest of the people,"[60] whereas Webb maintains that "chiefdoms apparently represent the natural, inevitable end product, the natural culmination of the agricultural revolution."[61]

The transition from village level kinship groups to larger political units was not simultaneous or linear throughout all parts of Southeast Asia. There is evidence that as Islam moved into the Philippines, new concepts of kingship emerged with it.[62] But in general, the underlying pressure toward state organization arose from the need, at the village level, for some superior form of protection and organization. In Trengganu on the Malay peninsula, there was a community "defined by religion and culture as much as by political ties . . . [having] no single capital, no fixed boundaries, and no encompassing administrative network."[63] It was not a state by Western definition, yet it had many of the attributes of loyalty and support that even the modern Southeast Asian states lack. The kind of state- or nation-building in which people recognize their commonality to the exclusion of all outsiders and, on the basis of that recognition, act to form a political organization to protect their values, way of life, or other unique attributes of their society, did not occur in traditional Southeast Asia. Creation of a higher, more remote authority with control of significantly expanded reserves of manpower met the needs for protection from bandits of the everyday world and from the spirits and evil forces of the supernatural world, but government (such as it was) could not break through kinship and local loyalties in order to refocus them on a "nation." This local focus for political community, coupled with the embodiment of sovereignty in the person of a king rather than in the institutions of a state, meant that the traditional state of Southeast Asia was a very fragile unit at best.

NOTES

1. Ruth T. McVey, "Introduction," in Southeast Asian Transitions: Approaches Through Social History, edited by Ruth T. McVey (New Haven, Conn.: Yale University Press, 1978), p. 3.

2. See Stanley O'Connor's review of R. B. Smith and W. Watson, Early South East Asia: Essays in Archaeology, History and Historical Geography (London: Oxford University Press, 1979), in the Journal of Southeast Asian History 15 (1981).

3. Robert Redfield, The Little Community (Chicago: University of Chicago Press, 1960), p. 4.

4. David A. Wilson, "Thailand," in Governments and Politics of Southeast Asia, edited by George McT. Kahin (Ithaca: Cornell University Press, 1964), p. 7.

5. See Michael Aung-Thwin, "Hierarchy and Order in Pre-Colonial Burma," Journal of Southeast Asian Studies 15 (September 1984), pp. 226-232. See also May Ebihara, "Societal Organization in Sixteenth and Seventeenth Century Cambodia," Journal of Southeast Asian Studies 15

(September 1984), pp. 289-291, for a discussion of the complexities of the position of slaves in Cambodia.

6. J. M. Jacob, "Pre-Angkor Cambodia: Evidence from the Inscriptions in Khmer Concerning the Common People and Their Environment," in Smith and Watson, Early South East Asia, p. 423.

7. John K. Whitmore, "Societal Organization and Confucian Thought in Vietnam," Journal of Southeast Asian Studies 15 (September 1984), p. 302.

8. John T. McAlister and Paul Mus, The Vietnamese and Their Revolution (New York: Harper and Row, 1970), p. 44.

9. "Introduction," in Pre-Colonial State Systems in Southeast Asia, edited by Anthony Reid and Lance Castles (Kuala Lumpur: Malaysian Branch of the Royal Asiatic Society, Monograph No. 6, 1975), p. iii.

10. Robert O. Whyte, The Asian Village (Singapore: Institute of Southeast Asian Studies, 1976), pp. 7-9.

11. Antoinette M. Barrett Jones, Early Tenth Century Java from the Inscriptions (Dordrecht, Holland: Forsi Publications, 1984), pp. 24-25.

12. Whyte, The Asian Village, p. 13.

13. Ibid.

14. Charles A. Fisher, South-East Asia: A Social, Economic and Political Geography (London: Methuen, 1964), p. 72.

15. James C. Scott, The Moral Economy of the Peasant: Rebellion and Subsistence in Southeast Asia (New Haven, Conn.: Yale University Press, 1976), pp. 57-150. Scott argues that the need for a guaranteed minimum of economic output brought about the need for strict patterns of social control and reciprocity.

16. Samuel L. Popkin, The Rational Peasant: The Political Economy of Rural Society in Vietnam (Berkeley: University of California Press, 1979), p. 39.

17. Joseph Buttinger, The Smaller Dragon (New York: Praeger Publishers, 1958), p. 108.

18. Lucien M. Hanks, Rice and Man: Agricultural Ecology in Southeast Asia (Chicago: Aldine-Atherton, 1972), p. 23.

19. Clifford Geertz, Agricultural Involution: The Process of Ecological Change (Berkeley: University of California Press, 1966), p. 26.

20. Whyte, The Asian Village, pp. 13-15.

21. Hanks, Rice and Man, pp. 33-36.

22. Geertz, Agricultural Involution, pp. 28-38.

23. Ibid., pp. 38-46.

62

24. Koentjaraningrat, "The Village in Indonesia Today," in Villages in Indonesia, edited by Koentjaraningrat (Ithaca: Cornell University Press, 1967), p. 389.

25. See D. E. Short and James C. Jackson, "The Origins of an Irrigation Policy in Malaya: A Review of Developments Prior to the Establishment of the Drainage and Irrigation Department," Journal of the Malaysian Branch of the Royal Asiatic Society 44 (1972), pp. 79-81. See also James C. Jackson, "Rice Cultivation in West Malaysia: Relationships Between Cultural History, Customary Practices and Rural Development," Journal of the Malaysian Branch of the Royal Asiatic Society 45 (1972).

26. J. C. van Leur, Indonesian Trade and Society (The Hague: W. van Hoeve, Ltd., 1955), pp. 197-198.

27. John Adams and Nancy Hancock, "Land and Economy in Traditional Vietnam," Journal of Southeast Asian Studies 1 (September 1970), p. 98.

28. Clifford Geertz, Peddlers and Princes: Social Development and Economic Change in Two Indonesian Towns (Chicago: University of Chicago Press, 19630, p. 44.

29. van Leur, Indonesian Trade and Society, pp. 197-200.

30. Whyte, The Asian Village, pp. 33-34.

31. Adams and Hancock, "Land and Economy," pp. 92-95.

32. Clifford Geertz, Religion in Java (New York: Free Press, 1964), p. 11.

33. Gerald C. Hickey, Village in Vietnam (New Haven, Conn.: Yale University Press, 1964), p. 93.

34. Robert Wessing, "Life in the Cosmic Village: Congitive Models in Sundanese Life," in Art, Ritual and Society in Indonesia, edited by E. M. Bruner and J. O. Becker (Athens: Ohio University Papers in International Studies, Southeast Asia Series, No. 53), p. 116.

35. John S. Lansing, Evil in the Morning of the World--Phenomenological Approaches to a Balinese Community (Ann Arbor: Michigan Papers on South and Southeast Asia, No. 6, 1974), p. 1.

36. See Wessing, "Life in the Cosmic Village," p. 114, which draws on two earlier studies of Sundanese society: N.J.C. Geise, Badujs en Moslims in Lebak Parahiang (Leiden: Zuid Banten, 1952) and Louis Berthe, "Aines et Cadets L'a-liance et la Hierarchie chez les Baduj," L'Homme 5 (1965).

37. Lance Castles, "Statelessness and Stateforming Tendencies Among the Batak Before Colonial Rule," in Reid and Castles, Pre-Colonial State Systems, p. 68.

38. Adams and Hancock, "Land and Economy," p. 92.

39. Hanks, Rice and Man, p. 23.

40. Wessing, "Life in the Cosmic Village," p. 1021.

41. John James, "Sacred Geometry on the Island of Bali," Journal of the Royal Asiatic Society, no. 2 (1973).

42. Paul Wheatley, The Pivot of the Four Quarters (Edinburgh and Chicago: Edinburgh University Press and Aldine Publishing Co., 1971), p. 459.

43. Hickey, Village in Vietnam, pp. 39-41.

44. Ibid.

45. Wessing, "Life in the Cosmic Village," pp. 103-104.

46. McAlister and Mus, The Vietnamese and Their Revolution, p. 46.

47. See Castles, "Statelessness and Stateforming Tendencies," in Reid and Castles, Pre-Colonial State Systems, pp. 67-76.

48. Jacob C. Vergouwen, The Social Organization and Customary Law of the Toba-Batak of Northern Sumatra, translated by Jeune Scott-Kemball (The Hague: W. van Hoeve, Ltd., 1964).

49. Castles, "Statelessness and Stateforming Tendencies," in Reid and Castles, Pre-Colonial State Systems, p. 74. Castles' thesis contradicts that of another leading scholar on state organization in Southeast Asia--namely, Robert Heine-Geldern.

50. Ibid., pp. 75-76.

51. Ibid., pp. 68-69.

52. Christine Dobbin, "The Exercise of Authority in Minangkabau in the Late Eighteenth Century," in Reid and Castles, Pre-Colonial State Systems, pp. 77-89.

53. Hildred Geertz and Clifford Geertz, Kinship in Bali (Chicago: University of Chicago Press, 1975), p. 5.

54. D.J.M. Tate, The Making of Modern South-East Asia (London and Kuala Lumpur: Oxford University Press, 1979): The European Conquest, vol. 1, p. 335.

55. Harry J. Benda, "The Structure of Southeast Asian History: Some Preliminary Observations," in Man, State and Society in Contemporary Southeast Asia, edited by Robert O. Tilman (New York: Praeger Publishers, 1969), p. 24.

56. Tate, The Making of Modern South-East Asia, vol. 1, p. 335.

57. Bennet Bronson, "The Late Prehistory and Early History of Central Thailand," in Smith and Watson, Early South East Asia, p. 326.

64

58. Castles, "Statelessness and Stateforming Tendencies," in Reid and Castles, Pre-Colonial State Systems, p. 75.

59. Robert Redfield, Peasant Society and Culture (Chicago: University of Chicago Press, 1956), p. 34.

60. Lucy Mair, Primitive Government (Baltimore: Penguin Books, 1962), p. 13.

61. Malcolm C. Webb, "The Flag Follows Trade," in Ancient Civilization and Trade, edited by Jeremy A. Sabloff and Clifford C. Lamberg-Karlovsky (Albuquerque: University of New Mexico Press, 1975), p. 168.

62. Tate, The Making of South-East Asia, vol. 1, p. 341.

63. Heather Sutherland, "The Taming of the Trenggau Elite," in Southeast Asian Transitions: Approaches Through Social History, edited by Ruth T. McVey (New Haven, Conn.: Yale University Press, 1978), p. 36.

CHAPTER 4

The State in
Traditional Southeast Asia

If Southeast Asian states did not evolve through social and cultural processes in which the governed "joined together" to achieve the greater common good, how were these states created? Some have argued that Indian princes conquered the region and established states there. Another, perhaps more likely, theory is that economic change was brought about by increasing international trade routed through the region. This trade offered creative leaders an opportunity, using newly acquired economic resources, to expand their domains.[1] Yet the presence or possibility of trade did not automatically give rise to greater state organization. Some Sumatran ethnic groups, for example, lived in areas of the greatest commercial traffic but never developed structures of the state.

ORIGINS OF THE STATE

Hall, in analyzing kingship in Funan, has shown how state structures may have evolved. Military force was, in all probability, the key to the first establishment of Funan. Petty competing chieftains, divided among themselves, were conquered individually, and sons, relatives, or other trusted allies were placed over the conquered political units.[2] Each additional unit added more economic surplus to the centralizing state. Webb has pointed to the difficulties in this transition:

The full emergence of the state would appear to require eventually the final overthrow of a previously existing traditional system of authority, social controls, and resource allocation whose inelasticity and whose decentralized and localized organization would indeed have very largely inhibited even the initial concentration of power and resources . . . Despite the areas of continuity, or seeming continuity, between advanced tribal and incipient state systems of governance, the shift from the former to the latter entails a basic and total alteration in the manner in which the authority of the leadership is ultimately enforced and upheld.[3]

Webb has also offered a sequential process of reciprocal factors in the early evolution of the state. Needed, first, was an interjection of additional economic resources accruing to one or more of the petty chieftains within the geographic confines of the incipient state. These new resources provided the opportunity to acquire additional manpower that could be translated into an extension of political authority. New manpower resources then had a further impact on economic consolidation and control. The transition period, which might have extended over generations, was highly unstable because of the widespread use of force in maintaining both economic control and political authority. Limits on the use of force arose only as other factors became extant as a basis for political legitimacy.

In Southeast Asia, the formation of Funan appears to have followed the rise of international commerce and shipping traffic, which found safe harbor along the Indochinese coast in the area that was to become Funan. The revenues from this traffic provided the initial influx of economic resources necessary for state formation. Chinese records say that Hun P'an-huang consolidated his authority by sowing dissension among other petty chiefs in the area and then attacking, conquering, and installing his sons and grandsons in authority there--in a process that follows the steps described by Webb.[4] Wheatley has emphasized the political, religious, and social elements of the evolution of the state, pointing out that "with Hinduism came the concept of divine kingship, a political device especially attractive to village chieftains in situations in which the egalitarian solidarity of the tribal society was proving incapable of extending authority to validate the power required for institutionalization of supra-village rule."[5] Elsewhere, Wheatley has drawn this view to the very core of culture, arguing that those peoples whose religion holds that "human order was brought into being at the creation" (as opposed to those religions established through revelation) tended to model the earth as a "reduced version of the cosmos" and that, in the process, "kingdoms, capitals, temples, and shrines" became the physical and institutional structures so designed.[6] Wheatley perceives this transition as a cultural phenomenon at a specific state in the development of society, not necessarily related, although also not in opposition, to economic models of political development in Asia.

THE PROTOTYPE STATE

At least by the first or second centuries of the Christian era, the consolidation of state structures had spread throughout much of the region: "In the early centuries of the Christian era inter-territorial warfare seems to have been frequent. The location and social structure of the principalities cannot be accurately described, but one can suppose . . . a number of independent centers of territorial authority."[7] A Chinese mission sent to Southeast Asia in A.D. 231 reported visiting about one hundred countries there.[8] Although information for most of these states has been lost, a model can be sketched from Chinese and other descriptions of some of them.

The basic type of Southeast Asian state might be labeled the "subsistence, river delta kingdom."[9] In the rough, densely vegetated terrain of much of Southeast Asia, the river systems offered the best and frequently the only method of reaching inland areas. Each river valley also offered a somewhat protected enclosure in which to organize the state--the mountainous watershed roughly forming the boundaries.[10] Chieftains, having established control over the mouths and main trunks of these river systems by force, sustained themselves and their positions by exacting tolls for goods and persons traveling the waterways. Such subsistence kingdoms were largely self-sufficient in food production and were active in international trade and exchange only to the extent of filling for the population needs that could not be met internally. Referring to the natural drainage basin of intermountain water systems as self-contained geographic units, Bronson hypothesized that control of a river artery or of one or more major tributaries provided opportunities to develop the "lord-subordinate" relationships needed to

expand kinship ties into political units by providing
revenues from controlled commercial and other river
traffic. These revenues were the critical economic
surplus needed for expansion.[11]

This pattern of organization was common to much of
Southeast Asia--a pattern that represented the aggregate
of the minor kingdoms in traditional Southeast Asian
history that covered much of the region's landscape.
Scattered in between these kingdoms were sparsely
populated areas lacking political centers of gravity, such
as parts of Sumatra and the present-day Philippines. The
existence of these small, minimally connected states
accounted for the continual shifting of the centers of
power in Southeast Asia; with the necessary combination of
additional economic resources and skillful political
leadership, any of these states might have ascended to the
top rank of regional powers.[12]

From this basic organization, states that attained
significant geographic size or politico-military power
evolved into either of the two major forms described
below, depending on the size of the economic base
affording the resource surplus that made expansion
possible in the first place. First, in larger river
basins such as the Mekong or the Irrawaddy (also the
smaller Solo and Brantas of Java), an expanded form of the
prototype kingdom developed--namely, highly sophisticated
societies supported by advanced techniques of irrigated
agriculture.[13] In such systems of wet-rice farming,
stability, organization, cooperation, and control were
imperative: "Supply and control of water [was] . . . the
key factor; not merely the gross quantity of water, but
its quality, in terms of the fertilizing substances [as
well as] the timing of the flow."[14] These largely
agricultural states tended to be somewhat introverted,
with the court elite giving very strong emphasis to the
religious aspects of the state and to the regular cycles
of agricultural production. The epitome of this form in
Southeast Asia was the Khmer Empire that developed in the
Mekong region of present-day Cambodia.

Second, in those areas where the land was not so
hospitable for intensive agriculture and where the
international trade routes offered potential for resource
consolidation, states developed that focused entirely on
the flow of international trade. The geography of these
kingdoms was not so much riparian as characterized by
"facing coastal lowlands linked together by their own
ships across a common stretch of sea."[15] Particularly

in the archipelago, both interisland and international trade provided a stimulus to the growth of competing entrepot centers which, because of the lack of interest in the hinterland, as in Malacca, became almost city-states. The external economic impetus of the international trade routes was important in the transition from kinship network to state. As entrepreneurial opportunities appeared, particular kinship groups acquired and controlled surplus resources; as a result, reciprocal exchange was supplanted by a system of allocation of surplus to accomplish the greater goals of the polity.[16] These maritime commercial kingdoms were, of necessity, outward looking and cosmopolitan given their close links to the international trading system.[17]

Benda, who formed a model similar to the prototype for the structure of Southeast Asian political units, noted that small, poorly integrated territorial units covered much of Southeast Asia. He pointed to the development in Annam and Tonkin of Chinese bureaucratic states, and to the emergence in much of the remainder of the region of inland-agrarian or despotic hydraulic kingdoms.[18] He also added to his model the riparian or coastal kingdoms that did not follow the hydraulic despotism model because of their predominant interest in international commerce and because of the presence of "a more cosmopolitan population composed of traders and merchants of various, including indigenous, races, an urban, trading bourgeoisie with substantial financial resources and, consequently, very likely possessing some degree at least of 'countervailing' political power."[19] These maritime-agricultural distinctions were not mutually exclusive. For instance, Hall has noted that Funan evolved toward the inland- agricultural model as navigational skills improved and the maritime traffic bypassed its ports. Most of the Javanese kingdoms provided at least surplus rice for intraregional commerce, and some were strong competitors for international trade. Even Srivijaya may have had more interest in agricultural production, at least for commercial purposes, than scholars had previously believed.

The precise manner in which kingship evolved, and how it acquired much of its ritual as well as administrative character, remains unclear. But even the emergence of kingship did not necessarily signal the rise of the territorial state. Early theorists focused on the influence of Indian and Chinese cultural penetration in the region. Some asserted that India and/or China had "controlled" the region,[20] whereas a less extreme view

was put forward by Coedes, who argued that Indochina
developed a "civilization of its own . . . of Indian
parentage [except Vietnam], which even when it achieved
political independence remained an offshoot of Chinese
civilization."[21] But even in Vietnam, where Indian
Buddhism was influential through the eleventh century and
Chinese Buddhism, which grew from the ninth century on,
penetrated much of society,[22] an independent culture
developed. Studying Javanese culture, van Leur put more
emphasis on the role of indigenous cultural forces,
arguing that Southeast Asians borrowed only those Indian
and Chinese cultural traits that complemented the
indigenous system.[23]

The adoption of cultural traits from India or China
took place over extended periods in conjunction with the
growth of states. The rise of the Southeast Asian state
has been described as a two step process in which the
relationship between cities and hinterland was at first "a
contrast between these indigenous scattered communities
and cosmopolitan trading centers thronged with expatriates
and with local people who, by virtue of living there, had
in large measure cut themselves off from their own
society."[24] In the second step of the process, the
cities and hinterland were integrated and irrigated
agriculture was introduced.[25] Wheatley has pointed out
that the adoption of Hinduism, early urbanization, and
primitive state-building were all linked:

These changes were reflected morphologically in the
conversion of the chief's hut into a palace, the
spirit-house into a temple, the spirit-stone into a
linga that was to become the palladium of the state,
and the boundary spirits into the Lokapalas presiding
over the cardinal directions. In other words, the
village community had become the city-state, the whole
process signifying a transformation from culture to
civilization.[26]

There appears to have been a series of cycles that,
although documented only for Burma,[27] can be loosely
applied throughout Southeast Asia. At the beginning of
each cycle, political power and economic control were
scattered among fortified towns and hamlets ruled by
hereditary chieftains. The second phase began with the
rise of a charismatic leader, who, using military skill
and a band of loyal followers, consolidated authority and
built a centralized polity, complete with capital, court,

administrative structures, and military force. At the peak of the cycle, the monarch controlled a centralized state and its revenues. Within a few generations, however, the court became faction-ridden and weak, administrative control broke down, and military strength diminished. Outlying tributary states then declared their independence, decentralization followed, and the forces of localism returned until another charismatic leader arrived on the scene.

STATE ORGANIZATION

The main pressure underlying state formation--namely, the villages' need for protection from superior outside forces--created the requirement for more centrally controlled manpower. This centralization process established a resource and labor pool that expanded the capacities of the system. Yet the resulting kingdoms were fragile and often distintegrated as readily as they had formed. The process was evolutionary but by no means linear. A chief may have capitalized on an alliance of friendship, kinship, marriage, or conquest to knit together a "state" that fragmented upon his demise.[28] Applying these concepts to Funan, Hall has argued that international commercial patterns induced Funan's chieftains to "mediate these initial commercial transactions as the instigators and organizers of Funan's port."[29] Subsequently, the early chieftains of Funan established a "higher economic order, possessing a dual economic base, which was supportive of a more sophisticated level of political integration than was previously true." In the end, one ruler of Funan, Hun P'an-huang, was able to subordinate "local chiefs to his authority as well as that of his successors," thereby creating a more permanent manpower base.[30]

The Southeast Asian state did not approach the classic structure of oriental despotism.[31] Rather, the irrigation systems in Cambodia, Java, and parts of Vietnam met the three basic economic criteria of a very specific division of labor, intensified techniques of cultivation, and the necessity for cooperation on a large scale. At the same time, however, the traditional Southeast Asian states never fulfilled the necessary "managerial functions" of maintaining "critical hydraulic works" or controlling "major nonhydraulic industrial enterprises."[32] It appears that this level of organization

was not attained in traditional Southeast Asia, despite
the sophistication of construction and water systems, as
in Cambodia.[33]

The traditional state in Southeast Asia was not a
concrete or fixed territorial unit but, instead, was
structured in several concentric zones around the nucleus
of the capital. Moreover, the state was not "constructed
of bureaucratic hierarchies . . . [but] was a collection
of revenue-producing regions, which its ruler allocated to
individual members of the elite, who were linked to each
other by personal ties and derived their status from royal
recognition."[34] Beyond the nucleus were secondary or
closely held village settlements, including villagers who
farmed royal lands. More distant yet from the capital was
the strategic zone in which villages were sometimes
stockaded. At the farthest extension of the kingdom were
the conquered or foreign areas.[35] The maritime kingdom
was also divided into several zones: the nucleus of the
dominant city-state and its immediate coastal areas, the
extended coastal regions under continuous control of the
kingdom, farther coastal regional or port cities under
irregular control, and the hinterland only sporadically
under state control.[36]

The lack of rigid structure lent a quality of
"survivability" to the traditional Southeast Asian state.
For example, when Ayudhya (Thailand) was destroyed in
1767, there was no long-lasting disruption of Thai
political history; indeed, the only new elements at the
beginning of the Bangkok period "were the dynasty and the
construction of the capital city."[37]

LOYALTY AND LEGITIMACY

The organized system of state control was usually
based on patrimonial relationships between the king and
his retainers. Territorial subdivisions were delegated to
royal families in return for specific services, but
loyalty was a continuing concern. Loyalty to the king may
generally have been consensual at the center of the
kingdom, but it was mediated by power at the
periphery.[38] To ensure that obligations were carried
out, minor princes or their families were usually retained
at the central court.[39] Royal genealogies were also an
important means for binding numerous and extended kinship
groups to the court, thus "mobilizing political support
through emphasizing a ramifying network of kinship."[40]

Oaths of all kinds--calling on the gods and promising the
most heinous fates for those who broke such oaths--were
issued by kings and Brahmans.[41] The Malay seamen who
played critical roles in the stability of the great
maritime kingdoms were noted for their loyalty, but they
were also fickle and capable of reverting to piracy
whenever the power of the king appeared to wane.

It is clear that loyalty among the village population
was also a problem. Many discoveries have been made of
inscriptions exhorting pride in "this country called
Arimaddana" or "this country called Pagan" in an attempt
to supersede village and kinship loyalties.[42] Yet local
loyalties were never really broken because, in the view
from the bottom, the individual peasant villager gave
loyalty to his or her immediate chief, then upward through
regional divisions, and finally to the king through the
primary ministers and retainers of state.[43] In Vietnam,
however, there is a history of popular mobilization for
defense against the Chinese, established as early as A.D.
974.[44]

The extractive nature of the traditional political
system must be stressed. The Western concepts of social
responsibility, social welfare, and governmental responsibility for the needs of the population (beyond
protection) were not part of the traditional Southeast
Asian polity. The ministers, as well as lower officials
and staff, did not perceive themselves as public servants;
nor did they see the welfare of the people as the
responsibility of government. Although traditional
political philosophers admonished the king to show concern
for the people,[45] in fact the state served primarily the
needs of the king and court. At the same time, there was
little expectation on the part of the peasant population
that specific services would be forthcoming from the state.

Functional legitimacy of the state was based on the
need to maintain the stability of the kingdom, which in
turn provided protection and service so that village life
could continue largely uninterrupted. The king drew upon
corvee labor to provide for such services as road and dam
building, but when village life was interrupted by
banditry or foreign military incursions, legitimacy was
lost. When the king and his court intervened too
frequently, requiring corvee labor or military support or
levying taxes too heavily, legitimacy was lost and
peasants drifted away.[46] A regime of slightly benign
neglect that allowed the village to operate in an
unfettered way appears to have been nearly ideal, but with

too much neglect the bandits returned and the roads decayed--both traditional signs of the weakening and decline of authority.

Cosmology, Harmony, and Legitimacy. The traditional state was not a popular state--that is, the government did not derive from the will or consent of the population. It was necessary, then, to find some means of securing if not consent, at least tacit acceptance. Force or coercion may have provided this acceptance in some measure, but it was not sufficient to sustain the state indefinitely. The common solution in traditional Southeast Asia was to provide the king with a supernatural justification--a divine right developed to its highest level through borrowed Hindu political concepts that linked the state to the universe and the king to the gods.[47]

The primary legitimizing principle between village and court was an overall view of the world in terms of religion. For example, the capital city was usually located near the geographical center of the kingdom. In the Brahmanical view, the universe revolved around Mt. Meru, which held the city of the gods. The axis of Mt. Meru was important in ordering all Hinduized societies,[48] but even in the sinicized Vietnamese system, "the term 'Dragon's Belly' (Long-do) became synonymous with the capital city; it connoted the realm's spiritual center of gravity."[49] The capital city of any kingdom became analogous with Meru; thus the king was intimately linked to the gods in a symbolic king-god merger that explained the peasants' position in terms of a servant-master relationship.[50] Fate explained the peasants' poor position, but it also gave them at least a faint possibility for change in the future.[51] The circle was completed as the king, interceding with the gods, linked his sovereignty to the soil and fertility, thus returning to the village in a directly meaningful way the full mystic force of nature.[52] In addition, the village was associated with the capital--and thus the universe--in what was conceptualized as a series of concentric circles radiating from the capital, or in terms of geomancy and the four points of the compass.[53] Harmony could be achieved in this world through imitation of the macrocosmic universe. In short, each segment of society had a place in the larger framework of metaphysical thought.

The Southeast Asian metaphysical view of the world--indeed, of existence itself, was developed in terms

that subordinated the state and made it part of the larger
pattern of the universe. For traditional Southeast Asia,
as elsewhere, the cosmological significance of all of life
was based on five principles:

1. Reality was a function of the imitation of a
   celestial archetype.
2. Reality was conferred through participation in
   the "symbolism of the Center;" that is, cities,
   temples, and houses became real by the fact of
   being assimilated to the "center of the world."
3. Every act that had a definite meaning--hunting,
   fishing, agriculture, games, conflicts,
   sexuality--in some way participated in the
   sacred; hence profane activities were those that
   had no mythical meaning.[54]
4. The parallelism between the Macrocosmos and the
   Microcosmos necessitated the practice of ritual
   ceremonies to maintain harmony between the world
   of the gods and the world of humans.
5. The techniques of orientation necessary to define
   sacred territory within the continuum of profane
   space involved an emphasis on the cardinal
   compass directions.[55]

Three aspects of this metaphysical view are particularly
important to an understanding of the society of the
traditional kingdoms: the view of the state as a
microcosmic version of the macrocosmic universe; mysticism
and magic; and the desire for continuity of past and
present.

The manipulation of symbols--primarily spiritual,
mystical, or magical trappings--linked the king and court
directly to the supernatural. The adaptation of
successive titles for the king--maharaja from Indian
political thought and sultan from Middle Eastern Islamic
thought--served to strengthen the king's claim to
authority and power. In addition, the continual rewriting
of histories served the important purpose of connecting
the current king to previously recognized great kings and,
through birth or lineage, to one or another of the
gods.[56]

Actual objects and symbols of magical or supernatural
power surrounded the person of the king.[57] For
instance, Jayavarman II of Khmer, according to stone
inscriptions, selected "a brahman named Hiranyadama,
skilled in magic science . . . to perform a ceremony that

would make it impossible . . . to pay allegiance to Java."[58] In Malaya, the royal regalia, including swords, knives, lances, drums, flutes, pipes, betel boxes, jewels, sceptres, seals of state, and umbrellas, were said to have been protected by a "death-striking" electrical charge of divine power.[59] In Burma and elsewhere white elephants were treasured as magical symbols of good fortune; they also exemplified the syncretic belief in Buddhism, animism, magic, and astrology.[60] It has been suggested that the advent of the process of Hinduization in Southeast Asia took place because many princes saw the Hindu rituals as a more sophisticated way of justifying or sanctifying their position.[61]

Mysticism and magic encompassed both village and court. A striking example of the use of mysticism was that found in traditional dance: The highly costumed and choreographically complex dances were used for incantations and spirit liberation, welfare and fertility rites, or direct communication with the gods.[62] In Vietnam, the emperor assigned to each new settlement a guardian spirit--in effect, a symbolic bond between the village and the emperor.[63] Concern for spirits (called nats) in Burma governed all traditional interactions not only between village and court but also between humans and the environment. Criminal punishments frequently relied on some mystical control over body functions and pain. In the courts, one of the powerful sources of magic was the king's regalia,[64] possession of which was often sufficient to justify a usurper's position on the throne. So pervasive was mysticism and magic in traditional Southeast Asian society that it could not be supplanted by even so strong a force as Islam:

> Beginning their invocations with the orthodox preface: "In the name of God, the merciful, the compassionate," and ending them with an appeal to the Creed: "There is no god but God, and Muhammad is the Apostle of God," they are conscious of no impropriety in addressing the intervening matter to a string of Hindu Divinities, Demons, Ghosts and Nature Spirits, with a few Angels and Prophets thrown in, as the occasion may require.[65]

In short, although the implications of the all-evasive magic and mysticism in the Southeast Asian world view may be difficult to comprehend, they account for a large part of the organizational beliefs of traditional society of Southeast Asia.

The concern for continuity of past and present is apparent at all levels of traditional society. In Java, Geertz described "a pious respect for the dead plus a lively awareness of the necessity of being on good terms with one's deceased father and mother"[66]--a concern that does not constitute outright ancestor worship but does indicate an "active past" in the present. In Cambodia (about A.D. 950), sanctuaries "indicate that a pyramid-temple could be devoted, at least in part, to the cult of ancestor-worship."[67] One of the more obvious examples of the desire to maintain continuity is found in alterations of folk-tales to incorporate a usurper king into accepted genealogies. Traditional Javanese histories, such as the Pararaton, were occasionally rewritten to eliminate competing lines to the throne or to make a new line to the past for the present ruler. They were also rewritten to adjust the cultural past to the present, as when earlier Hindu wordings were replaced by Buddhist phrases.[68]

The Vietnamese, while not following these essentially Hindu concepts, stressed a similar cosmological role for the emperor as the "Son of Heaven." The capital was considered a "repository of benevolent supernatural influences," and the emperor, as the patron of agriculture, "performed a plowing ritual with a gilded plow every spring" to ensure fertility for the cropping cycle.[69] Moreover, the autonomy of the village in Vietnam was similar to that of other villages elsewhere in Southeast Asia, and it required a similar type of state structure.

Problems of Legitimacy. A critical element in the process of legitimacy is that it focused on the person of the king and not on the institutions of kingship or the state. For the modern Western state, "the essence of the concept was always its impersonal nature; the state was never to be wholly identified with the individuals holding power . . . In the European tradition, the state broke the personal identification of the older notion of sovereignty."[70] Although the transition from personalized to institutionalized sovereignty was not evenly successful throughout Europe, it did take place. In traditional Southeast Asia, however, there was no evidence that such a transition had begun or was about to begin by the time of the intervention of the European powers.

Within the ranks of the court elite, kinship ties were not as effective in maintaining harmony as were those ties among the villagers. Blood relations were a factor in aristocratic society, and many positions were hereditary, but the "communal interdependence" that prevailed in the villagers' subsistence efforts was largely replaced by expediency and the desire for riches and power: "Kin relationships helped people to identify who could be considered royalty and who might be enlisted in the king's supporting circle, but kinship in and of itself was no guarantee of loyalty," and, as often happened, "kin who were on losing sides or otherwise incurred the king's disfavor could find themselves [and their families] reduced from royalty to slavery."[71] The struggle from the lower elites to the top (kingship) was often marked by intrigue that countermanded any links with blood relations. One had to struggle upward, as well as to meet threats to a current position. Power was clearly the key to court success. Law was of little use without the ability to apply the necessary force. Burma may have been a partial exception to this predominance of power, inasmuch as the Burmese Book of Law carried strong religious sanctions against unrestrained abuse of power, but Cady has noted that "old Burma was a shut-in state which maintained no windows to the outside world capable of providing . . . a more progressive outlook . . . Burma's kings were too absorbed in crushing potential rivals, in waging predatory warfare . . . in collecting white elephants, and building pagodas to concern themselves with governmental reforms."[72] Yet possession of power was tenuous at best, as indicated by the vague rules of succession, and the king's position was assured only so long as he was able to maintain sufficient power.

Even then, within this framework, the king was able to perform several minimal but necessary political functions. For example, within the limits of available power, the king dealt with foreign affairs--which frequently meant fighting wars of invasion. The system did provide a degree of protection from the vagaries of lawlessness: The presence of bandits was one of the first signs indicating that a king's power was on the decline. As certain minimal service requirements--road building and maintenance, for example--fell to the king, another indication of the decline of the ruler's effectiveness was poor maintenance of the road system.[73] In the final analysis, the king's function (and, consequently, that of the entire court) was primarily to maintain order and ensure that the villages' operations could continue with a minimum of outside interference.

Concepts of legitimacy were designed to support claims of a dominant and all-powerful king and to specify the submission of the realm to the king. Little in the way of nation-building could take place under these terms. In the Malay Annals, written about A.D. 1500, there is a passage in which King Sri Tri Buana agrees to a covenant that in effect delimited his authority over the realm--thus clearly suggesting a contract between the governor and the governed.[74] Whether the Malay Annals could have become a Southeast Asian "Magna Carta" can never be known because the Portuguese soon ended Malacca's independence, and that of the rest of Southeast Asia followed soon after.

The dichotomous society--given that the mass of the population lived as peasants in small villages and payed taxes to an elite that fought for control of the excess village revenues while the village remained largely static in its self-sufficient existence--identifies the principal segments of traditional Southeast Asian society. It also clarifies the basic principles that enabled the two segments to maintain a degree of internal cohesion and implies the interdependency of the two: The village needed organized protection to ensure its survival and the court needed the village revenues on which its survival was based.

BUREAUCRATIC STRUCTURES AND FUNCTIONS

The structures of bureaucracy in traditional Southeast Asia were based on a metaphysical concept of the state. As late as the 1890s, the principal ministers of Thailand were designated to represent the four cardinal points of the compass, with additional ministers given responsibility for the royal court (capital city), fields, and treasury.[75] All royalty and officials were ranked "according to genealogical proximity to the monarch," beginning with the heir apparent, who was "Lord of the Eastern [front] House," while other sons were ordered as Southern, Western, or Northern princes, in that order. The chief queen, who ranked below the princes, was the Southern Queen, followed by Western, Northern, and Eastern Queens (the Eastern Queen in particular, who was unmarried and "reserved" for the heir apparent, was also called the "Princess of the Solitary Post"). Usually present were four chief ministers and numerous subordinate ministers, most of whom were senior in status to ranking military officers, except in time of war. This group constituted "higher officialdom" and resided at court.[76] The minister responsible for a given geographic quadrant of the kingdom accepted responsibility for administrative, regulatory, judicial, and governmental functions in that area. He also played a role in the metaphysical structure of the kingdom, linking the peasantry to the king and ultimately to the divine or universal.[77] The divine prescription for harmony throughout the kingdom as well as between heaven and earth had, at the ministerial level, a more practical meaning: In order for the kingdom to prosper (i.e., for agricultural production in the form of wet-rice cultivation to succeed) the minister had to insure that all members of the village community fulfilled their designated roles so that water would be properly available and applied, transplanting and cultivation could be carried out appropriately, and hands would be available for harvest. The minister did not direct these activities, although in Angkor and other agricultural kingdoms the waterworks reached such a level of complexity as to require central control.[78] In northern Thailand, official authority below the ministers was divided on a decimal system "in groups of ten, with a hierarchy of officials controlling groups of ten, fifty, a hundred, thousand, and ten thousand."[79]

It was the ministers' first responsibility to ensure that an environment was obtained in which this complex production system could operate. In other words, public order had to be maintained and the activities of thieves, bandits, or foreign invaders curtailed. The second responsibility for the minister and court was to ensure that the metaphysical world was equally well ordered, such that each peasant, permeated with a belief system heavily laden with fatalism and the expectation that the best life lay in social harmony and the status quo at the expense of individual freedom and growth, could see and receive through the vehicle of the minister and king some assurance of the greater purposes of life. The establishment of temples and stupas, and the lavishing of support and offerings on temples already in existence were meant to suggest that there was life and meaning beyond the rice paddy. But such symbols also required that the ministers gather resources. Taxes were primarily gathered in kind and in corvee labor for construction as well as military service. Certain transportation taxes, particularly river taxes, are known to have existed, and there is evidence of various types of head taxes. Imported and exported commodities were taxed at a 5 to 15 percent rate, usually collected in kind. Given sufficient volume, this practice had the effect of making the state a major marketing competitor. In Burma, a household tax was levied on each village unit "apportioned roughly according to ability to pay . . . not a levy on property or an income tax as such."[80]

Within the central court, there were other officials who served the necessary functions of administration. Virtually every court had a chief priest, who often doubled as the main adviser to the king, and in many cases, was the king's teacher prior to his ascension. Such an adviser, who was usually very close to the king and controlled the mystical rituals, exercised great power and influence in the kingdom. The maritime kingdoms, however, required several specialized officials, such as a powerful harbor master, who was in charge of admitting the ships and checking all cargo; and special judges to hear complaints from foreign merchants.[81] Also present were many individuals who received one or more titles but carried out no functions with respect to those titles.[82]

When Sultan Mahmud Shah came to the throne in Malacca, his new appointments included a minister for commerce and a chief minister (who were to sit opposite one another in the audience hall) a treasurer, several ministers of state, a chief herald, a mystic to cast curses, a chief admiral, and several nonspecific title holders.[83] As Malacca was a maritime kingdom, three among these appointees had specifically commercial assignments: The minister of commerce was in charge of the harbor and the movement of goods through it; the treasurer had overall responsibility for the revenues of the kingdom, derived mostly from commerce; and the admiral controlled sea traffic through the Strait of Malacca, keeping the seas free of pirates and ensuring that all ships stopped at Malacca. In addition to these specific assignments there were numerous ceremonial or honorary appointments. The position of the mystic clearly reached back to the oldest days of state organization in the region.

The single regional exception to the Hindu concepts of state structure was found in Vietnam, where an essentially Confucian bureaucratic structure controlled the state. In contrast to all other parts of Southeast Asia, the Vietnamese bureaucracy and kingship were separate. Bureaucrats were required to study Confucian writings and

were selected by examination. Yet, despite this
systematic and rational approach to government office
holding, the traditional state in Vietnam provided a
"largely passive style of authoritarianism, which stressed
moral example rather than more dynamic goals."[84] The
Vietnamese bureaucratic system developed not so much a
strong problem-solving elite as a highly compart-
mentalized, elitist structure that, as elsewhere in
Southeast Asia, gave full sway to the autonomy and
isolation of the village.

Neither the bureaucratic system of Vietnam nor the few
known instances of ministers appointed to functionally
defined positions (as in Malacca or Trengganu) signaled a
movement toward rational bureaucratic structures in
traditional Southeast Asia.[85] In a study of commercial
and political development in Aceh, Reid concluded that a
rational system was not on the horizon: "The apparent
arbitrariness of such exactions from merchants, and the
total dependence of officials on royal favor, does not
suggest any substantial development towards
professionalism of the bureaucracy."[86] The state
systems remained highly personalized in administration and
dependent on the mystical for legitimization, yet against
the environmental demands of the time these systems appear
to have worked successfully.

LEADERSHIP AND ADMINISTRATION

Leadership in the traditional kingdoms of Southeast
Asia worked within a narrow framework; indeed, there was
little room for "dynamic" political initiatives of the
type expected from contemporary governments. The
theoretical legal restrictions on a monarch's power rarely
inhibited his authority, especially within the
governmental structures and among his retainers; but, even
more important, the king did not possess unlimited
authority over the village populations, as in many
dry-farming areas particularly, villagers would simply
have left if the ruler's oppression became too
severe.[87] In Burma and throughout most of Southeast
Asia, the court was governed by the Code of Manu,[88]
whereas in Vietnam the Chinese classics guided the emperor
in his rule.[89] Law was adopted from Indian legal
thought, but in Southeast Asia these concepts were blended
with indigenous philosophy to produce a set of "rules of
conduct that ought to be observed by reason of social

condition."[90] But the feudal organization of most states stifled growth of government activity beyond those determined by basic social organization and needs.

Among the maritime commercial kingdoms, trade was closely regulated, although the actual authority of the king remained nearly absolute. Commerce was strictly regulated in Malacca in a well-developed set of written laws.[91] Actual administration was organized within a system of land distribution such that each subregion was relatively autonomous, except for taxes and services due to superiors. These administrative divisions evolved into a complex system of appanage lands, bengkok (villages usually assigned to the support of high government officials or monasteries), free villages, and crown domains,[92] all of which formed a "hierarchical line of separate, self-sufficient and highly autonomous units of power."[93] This autonomy is suggested by the following conversation between Tun Perak, an administrator, and Sri Amarat, a herald of the king, in which Tun Perak stated, "As for the business of us who administer territory, what concern is that of yours? For territory is territory even if it is only the size of a coconut shell. What we think should be done we do, for the Ruler is not concerned with the difficulties we administrators encounter; he only takes account of the good results we achieve."[94] The division of administrative power and the basic principles of society were complementary in that they allowed the smaller units to operate with a minimum of interference, except in cases of extreme emergency.

The class of wealthy merchants (orang kaya in Malaya or thutes in Burma) was so powerful in the economic world of traditional Southeast Asia that it often controlled the political system. Merchants were not part of the royal elite, although some were usurpers, and for the most part were not even indigenous peoples but, instead, consisted of Arabs, Chinese, Indians, and later Europeans. They did, however, often hold appointed positions within government, especially in the maritime kingdoms. In a system that gave primacy to personal wealth and that had few institutional counterbalances, the potential for corruption and influence buying was enormous: "These merchants proved to be a force capable of righting any imbalance in the exercise of power . . . When they were ignored or abused, they lent their assistance to a rival . . . When they were courted, they responded favorably and contributed toward a successful working relationship with the ruler."[95] The arbitrariness of politics could

also work against these wealthy merchants, as it did in
Aceh when, in 1589, the new sultan executed many of the
politically powerful merchants, took their possessions,
and regulated the activities of those remaining.[96]
However, as less forceful rulers came to power, the
merchants reasserted their control.[97]

State formation in the traditional Southeast Asian
system was uneven. States did not evolve in all parts of
the region, and where there were states, most were not
well organized. The state was overlaid on the village
community. Although in some areas the state came to
control considerable resources from maritime trade or
agricultural production, it did not dominate the village
community. In fact, the reverse was the case: The state
developed in response to the peasants' need for
organization and harmony in their world because "the
concern . . . was not tyranny but disorder; the 'abuse' of
power was not reflected by autocracy but by chaos."[98]
Harmony in traditional Southeast Asian culture was
manifested at three levels: at the village level, where
man existed in harmony with the ecosystem and managed (not
manipulated) that system for agricultural production; at
the societal level, where the state controlled banditry
(or piracy) and maintained social stability; and at the
level of the universe, where the king ensured harmony with
the gods on behalf of the village populace. Particularly
in the case of Vietnam there is increasing recognition of
the social tension between the village (given its desire
for harmony) and the court (with its predilection for
neo-Confucian hierarchy). After its independence from the
Chinese, the Vietnamese court at first recognized the need
to draw together all Vietnamese both culturally and
politically; it therefore manifested many Vietnamese
traditions, such as the decision to move the capital city
to the site of the ancient third century B.C. Vietnamese
capital.

In time, however, various Chinese traditions reemerged
and the Vietnamese court lost contact with its
people.[99] Elsewhere in the region, moreover, the
traditional states appear to have more or less effectively
fulfilled their role in maintaining earthly and cosmic
harmony, meeting the requirements of early Southeast Asian
society, and responding to the commercial needs of the
international trading system. The state of traditional
Southeast Asia must be seen as an institutionally fragile
entity, relying on the personal capabilities of its king
to mobilize limited available resources. The states did

not, moreover, prove capable of withstanding the challenge
of the Europeans.

NOTES

1. Robert McC. Adams, "The Emerging Place of Trade in
Civilizational Studies," in Ancient Civilization and
Trade, edited by Jeremy A. Sabloff and Clifford C.
Lamberg-Karlovsky (Albuquerque: University of New Mexico
Press, 1975), pp. 451-465.
2. Kenneth R. Hall, "The 'Indianization' of Funan:
An Economic History of Southeast Asia's First State,"
Journal of Southeast Asian Studies 13 (March 1982), p. 91.
3. Malcolm C. Webb, "The Flag Follows Trade: An
Essay on the Necessary Interaction of Military and
Commercial Factors in State Formation," in Sabloff and
Lamberg-Karlovsky, Ancient Civilization and Trade, p. 157.
4. See Webb, "The Flag Follows Trade," pp. 184-186;
and Hall, "The 'Indianization' of Funan," citing Paul
Pelliot, "Quelques textes chinois concernant L'Indochine
hindouisee," Etudes Asiatiques 2, publiees a l'occasion du
vingt-cinquieme anniversaire de l'Ecole Francaise
d'Extreme Orient (Paris, 1925), pp. 243-263.
5. Paul Wheatley, "Urban Genesis in Mainland South
East Asia," in Early South East Asia: Essays in
Archaeology, History and Historical Geography, edited by
R. B. Smith and W. Watson (London: Oxford University
Press, 1979), p. 295.
6. Paul Wheatley, The Pivot of the Four Quarters
(Edinburgh and Chicago: Edinburgh University Press and
Aldine Publishing Co., 1971), pp. 416-417.
7. O. W. Wolters, "Khmer 'Hinduism' in the Seventh
Century," in Smith and Watson, Early South East Asia, p.
428.
8. Hsu Yun-Ts'iao, "Singapore in the Remote Past,"
Journal of the Malaysian Branch of the Royal Asiatic
Society 45 (1973), p. 5.
9. Donald G. McCloud, "A Systemic Study of
Pre-Colonial Southeast Asia" (unpublished manuscript,
University of South Carolina, 1970), p. 8.
10. J. M. Gullick, Indigenous Political Systems of
Western Malaya (New York: Humanities Press, 1958), p. 4.
11. Bennet Bronson, "Exchange at the Upstream and
Downstream Ends: Notes Toward a Functional Model of the
Coastal State in Southeast Asia," in Economic Exchange and
Social Interaction in Southeast Asia, edited by Karl L.

Hutter (Ann Arbor: Michigan Papers on South and Southeast Asia, No. 13, 1977), pp. 39-52.

12. Bernard H. M. Vlekke, Nusantara: A History of Indonesia (The Hague: W. van Hoeve Ltd., 1965), p. 53.

13. M. Groslier, Angkor et le Cambodge au XVI siede d'apres les sources portugaises et espagnoles, pp. 107-21, cited in D.G.E. Hall, A History of South-East Asia (New York: St. Martin's Press, 1968), p. 133.

14. Clifford Geertz, Agricultural Involution: The Process of Ecological Change (Berkeley: University of California Press, 1966), p. 31.

15. Charles A. Fisher, "Geographical Continuity and Political Change in Southeast Asia," in Conflict and Stability in Southeast Asia, edited by Mark W. Zacher and R. Stephen Milne (Garden City, N.Y.: Anchor Books, 1974), p. 9.

16. Paul Wheatley, "Satyanrta in Suvarnadvipa: From Reciprocity to Redistribution in Ancient Southeast Asia," in Sabloff and Lamberg-Karlovsky, Ancient Civilization and Trade, p. 247.

17. See Chapter 2 for a historical description of the major maritime kingdoms and agricultural states.

18. Harry J. Benda, "The Structure of Southeast Asian History: Some Preliminary Observations," in Man, State and Society in Comtemporary Southeast Asia, edited by Robert O. Tilman (New York: Praeger Publishers, 1969), pp. 24-25.

19. Ibid., p. 25. In a footnote, Benda credits J. C. van Leur for the original analysis of these kingdom types; see J. C. van Leur, Indonesian Trade and Society (The Hague: W. van Hoeve, Ltd., 1955).

20. K. M. Panikkar, R. Mookerji, and R. C. Majumdar were the leading protagonists of the "Greater India" concept. See Hall, A History of South-East Asia, p. 16.

21. G. Coedes, The Making of South East Asia (Berkeley: University of California Press, 1969), p. 218.

22. Gerald C. Hickey, Village in Vietnam (New Haven, Conn.: Yale University Press, 1964), pp. 4-5.

23. van Leur, Indonesian Trade and Society, pp. 89-116.

24. I. W. Mabbett, "The Indianization of Southeast Asia: Reflections on the Prehistoric Sources," Journal of Southeast Asian Studies 8 (March 1977), pp. 13-14.

25. I. W. Mabbett, "The Indianization of Southeast Asia: Reflections on the Historical Sources," Journal of Southeast Asian History 8 (September 1977), p. 155.

26. Wheatley, "Urban Genesis in Mainland South East Asia," in Smith and Watson, Early South East Asia, pp. 296-297.

27. Michael Aung-Thwin, "The Role of Sasana Reform in Burmese History: Economic Dimensions of a Religious Purification," Journal of Asian Studies 38 (August 1979), p. 673.

28. Wolters, "Khmer 'Hinduism' in the Seventh Century," in Smith and Watson, Early South East Asia, p. 429.

29. Hall, "The 'Indianization' of Funan," pp. 85-86.

30. Ibid., p. 91.

31. Karl A. Wittfogel, Oriental Despotism: A Comparative Study of Total Power (New Haven, Conn.: Yale University Press, 1957), p. 22.

32. Ibid., p. 48.

33. See Lawrence Palmer Briggs, The Ancient Khmer Empire. Transactions of the American Philosophical Society (Philadelphia: American Philosophical Society, 1951), pp. 163-170.

34. Heather Sutherland, "The Taming of the Trangganu Elite," in Southeast Asian Transitions: Approaches Through Social History, edited by Ruth T. McVey (New Haven, Conn.: Yale University Press, 1978), p. 34.

35. Michael Aung-Thwin, "Kingship, the Sangha and Society in Pagan," in Explorations in Early Southeast Asian History: The Origins of Southeast Asian Statecraft, edited by Kenneth R. Hall and John K. Whitmore (Ann Arbor: Michigan Papers on South and Southeast Asia, No. 11, 1976), pp. 217-222.

36. Kenneth R. Hall, "State and Statecraft in Early Srivijaya," in Hall and Whitmore, Explorations, p. 63. Hall draws extensively from O. W. Wolters, The Fall of Srivijaya in Malay History (Ithaca: Cornell University Press, 1971), for this analysis.

37. Klaus Wenk, The Restoration of Thailand Under Rama I, 1782-1809, translated by Greeley Stahl (Tucson: University of Arizona Press, 1968), p. 122.

38. D. E. Brown, Principles of Social Structure in Southeast Asia (Boulder, Colo.: Westview Press, 1976), p. 224.

39. Soemarsaid Moertono, State and Statecraft in Old Java: A Study of the Later Mataram Period, 16th to 19th Century (Ithaca: Cornell Modern Indonesia Project, 1968).

40. A. Thomas Kirsch, "Kinship, Genealogical Claims, and Societal Integration in Ancient Khmer Society: An Interpretation," in Southeast Asian History and

88

Historiography: Essays Presented to D.G.E. Hall, edited by C. W. Cowan and O. W. Wolters (Ithaca: Cornell University Press, 1976), p. 201.

41. Briggs, The Ancient Khmer Empire, p. 151.

42. Aung-Thwin, "Kingship, the Sangha and Society in Pagan," in Hall and Whitmore, Explorations, p. 205.

43. Virginia Matheson, "Concepts of State in the Tuhfat Al-Hafis," in Pre-Colonial State Systems in Southeast Asia, edited by Anthony Reid and Lance Castles (Kuala Lumpur: Malaysian Branch of the Royal Asiatic Society, Monograph No. 6, 1975), p. 16.

44. Keith W. Taylor, The Birth of Vietnam (Berkeley: University of California Press, 1983), p. 287.

45. Such traditional narratives as the Malay Annals are full of guidelines for rulers, such as Sultan Mansur Shah's deathbed admonition to his son, Raja Radin: "Upon you is laid the duty of faithfully cherishing those who are subject to you and of liberally forgiving any offences they may commit." See Sejarah Melayu, or Malay Annals, translated by C. C. Brown (London: Oxford University Press, 1970), p. 103.

46. David A. Wilson, "Thailand," in Governments and Politics of Southeast Asia, edited by George McT. Kahin (Ithaca: Cornell University Press, 1964), p. 6.

47. See D. Mackenzie Brown, The White Umbrella: Indian Political Thought from Manu to Gandhi (Berkeley: University of California Press, 1968), pp. 24-48; and John W. Spellman, Political Thought of Ancient India: A Study of Kingship from the Earliest Times to Circa A.D. 300 (London: Oxford University Press, 1964), pp. 211-224.

48. Wheatley, The Pivot of the Four Quarters, p. 417.

49. Taylor, The Birth of Vietnam, p. 253.

50. Robert Heine-Geldern, "Conceptions of State and Kingship in Southeast Asia," Far Eastern Quarterly 2 (November 1942), p. 17.

51. See Moertono, State and Statecraft, pp. 15-16. See also H. L. Shorto, "The Planets, the Days of the Week and the Points of the Compass: Orientation Symbolism in Burma," in Natural Symbols in South East Asia, edited by G. B. Milner (London: School of Oriental and African Studies, 1978), pp. 152-164.

52. O. W. Wolters, The Fall of Srivijaya in Malay History (Ithaca: Cornell University Press, 1971), pp. 99-100.

53. Heine-Geldern, "Conceptions of State and Kingship," p. 19.

54. Mircea Eliade, The Myth of the Eternal Return, or Cosmos and History, translated from the French by Willard R. Trask (Princeton, N.J.: Princeton University Press, 1954), pp. 5, 27-28.

55. Wheatley, The Pivot of the Four Quarters, p. 418.

56. P. E. de Josselin de Jong, "The Character of the Malay Annals," in Malayan and Indonesian Studies: Essays Presented to Sir Richard Winstedt on His Eighty-fifth Birthday, edited by John Bastin and R. Roolvink (Oxford: Clarendon Press, 1964), pp. 235-241.

57. Heine-Geldern, "Conceptions of State and Kingship," pp. 15-31.

58. Briggs, The Ancient Khmer Empire, p. 89.

59. Walter William Skeat, Malay Magic, Being an Introduction to the Folklore and Popular Religion of the Malay Peninsula (New York: Dover Publications, 1967; first published in London by Macmillan, 1900), p. 24.

60. Hla Pe, "Burmese Attitudes to Plants and Animals," in Milner, Natural Symbols in South East Asia, p. 102.

61. See van Leur, Indonesian Trade and Society; and Hall, "The 'Indianization' of Funan."

62. Claire Holt, Art in Indonesia (Ithaca: Cornell University Press, 1967).

63. Hickey, Village in Vietnam, p. 6.

64. Heine-Geldern, "Conceptions of State and Kingship," p. 15-31.

65. Skeat, Malay Magic, pp. xiii-xiv.

66. Clifford Geertz, Religion in Java (New York: Free Press, 1964), p. 76.

67. Briggs, The Ancient Khmer Empire, p. 133.

68. C. C. Berg, "Javanese Historiography--A Synopsis of Its Evolution," in Historians of Southeast Asia, edited by D.G.E. Hall (London: Oxford University Press, 1961).

69. David J. Steinberg, ed., with David K. Wyatt, John R. W. Smail, Alexander Woodside, William R. Roff, and David P. Chandler, In Search of Southeast Asia: A Modern History (New York: Praeger Publishers, 1971), pp. 68, 70.

70. J. P. Nettl, "The State as a Conceptual Variable," World Politics 20 (July 1968), p. 575.

71. May Ebihara, "Societal Organization in Sixteenth and Seventeenth Century Cambodia," Journal of Southeast Asian Studies 15 (September 1984), p. 283.

72. John F. Cady, A History of Modern Burma (Ithaca: Cornell University Press, 1958), pp. 6, 11.

90

73. Christine Dobbin, "The Exercise of Authority in Minàngkabau in the Late Eighteenth Century," in Reid and Castles, Pre-Colonial State Systems, p. 79.
74. Malay Annals, pp. 15-17.
75. Wilson, "Thailand," in Kahin, Governments and Politics, p. 13.
76. Michael Aung-Thwin, "Hierarchy and Order in Pre-Colonial Burma," Journal of Southeast Asian Studies 15 (September 1984), p. 225.
77. Briggs, The Ancient Khmer Empire, pp. 90, 98, and passim.
78. Ibid., pp. 165-166.
79. David K. Wyatt, "Laws and Social Order in Early Thailand: An Introduction to the Mangraisat," Journal of Southeast Asian Studies 15 (September 1984), p. 247. The Mangraisat is an early legal text attributed to King Mangrai of Chiang Mai (1259 to 1317), but the available version is more recent.
80. Cady, A History of Modern Burma, p. 20.
81. J. Kennedy, History of Malaya, 1400-1959 (New York: St. Martin's Press, 1967), p. 8.
82. Antoinette M. Barrett Jones, Early Tenth Century Java from the Inscriptions (Dordrecht, Holland: Forsi Publications, 1984), p. 91 and following for an excellent description of recorded titles.
83. Malay Annals, p. 165.
84. Steinberg, In Search of Southeast Asia, p. 68.
85. Max Weber, The Theory of Social and Economic Organization, translated by A. M. Henderson and Talcott Parsons, edited with an introduction by Talcott Parsons (New York: Free Press, 1964), pp. 324-407. Weber describes three "pure types" of authority and bureaucratic structures: (1) traditional structures based on "a belief in the sanctity of immemorial traditionals and the legitimacy of the status of those exercising authority;" (2) charismatic structures based on "devotion to the specific and exceptional sanctity, heroism or exemplary character of an individual person;" and (3) rational structures based on the "belief in the 'legality' of patterns of normative rules and the right of those elevated to authority under such rules of issue commands."
86. Anthony Reid, "Trade and the Problem of Royal Power in Aceh," in Reid and Castles, Pre-Colonial State Systems, p. 51.
87. George Condominas, "A Few Remarks About Thai Political Systems," in Milner, Natural Symbols in South East Asia, p. 51.

88. John F. Cady, Southeast Asia: Its Historical Development (New York: McGraw-Hill, 1964), p. 45.

89. Jerry M. Silverman, "Historic National Rivalries and Interstate Conflict in Mainland Southeast Asia," in Zacher and Milne, Conflict and Stability, p. 56.

90. M. B. Hooker, "The Indian Derived Texts of Southeast Asia," Journal of Asian Studies 37 (February 1978), p. 201.

91. Sir Richard Winstedt and P. E. de Josselin de Jong, "The Maritime Laws of Malacca," Journal of the Malaysian Branch of the Royal Asiatic Society 29 (August 1956), pp. 22-59.

92. Moertono, State and Statecraft, pp. 110, 117-118. See also Aung-Thwin, "Hierarchy and Order in Pre-colonial Burma," p. 224.

93. Moertono, State and Statecraft, p. 104.

94. Malay Annals, p. 57.

95. Leonard Y. Andaya, "The Structure of Power in Seventeenth Century Johore," in Reid and Castles, Pre-Colonial State Systems, pp. 48-49.

96. Reid, "Trade and the Problem of Royal Power," in Reid and Castles, Pre-Colonial State Systems, pp. 48-49.

97. Ibid., pp. 52-55.

98. Michael Aung-Thwin, "Divinity, Spirit, and Human: Conceptions of Classical Burmese Kingship," in Centers, Symbols, and Hierarchies: Essays on the Classical States of Southeast Asia (New Haven, Conn.: Yale University Southeast Asia Studies, Monograph Series No. 26, 1983), p. 74.

99. Taylor, The Birth of Vietnam, p. 270.

CHAPTER 5

The Traditional Interstate System of Southeast Asia

Until the sixteenth century, the political and economic system spanning the distance from China to Europe was, in reality, only a series of loosely connected subsystems with varying degrees of dependence on one another. China, a system in itself, was largely autonomous and independent. Southeast Asia, on the other hand, although it had much room for autonomous action, depended on China and on other subsystems for support of its own systemic well-being.

Within the system of traditional Southeast Asia, power (defined as the level of available military force) was the determining factor in interstate relations. Although no codified system of international law was developed and the regional states followed practices similar to those adopted in India and to a lesser extent China, patterns of interaction were regularized through ritual and repetition and, especially in the regulation of trade and maritime traffic, were sophisticated and clearly defined.[1] (Even here, however, the whim of the ruler could be extraordinary.) The principal needs for the development of a state have been identified as (1) the need to control conflict; (2) the need for improved resource management as population densities increased; (3) the need to manage growing domestic commerce; and (4) the need for an organized approach to rapidly expanding international trade.[2] Foreign policy was the "sole prerogative of the king,"[3] and its two most general objectives were the aggrandizement of the king and court to reinforce the king's claim to domestic legitimacy, and greater wealth for the kingdom so that the preeminent position of the king in his realm could be bolstered further.[4] Thus, interstate politics in traditional Southeast Asia were carried out to enhance the state's domestic political philosophy, and the division of the state into village and court components, with broadly different purposes and constituencies, had an important impact in foreign policy.

The economic base of the kingdom also had a direct effect on the formation of foreign policy. The commercial kingdoms attempted to establish and maintain monopoly control of various products for international trade from their hinterland or elsewhere. It also sought a monopoly over entrepot services for their area. The land-based agricultural kingdoms, on the other hand, wanted to enrich the royal house; demonstrate the righteousness, sanctity, and legitimacy of the kingship through proper religious activities; and emulate where possible the perception that the kingship was the "center of the world."

Each kingdom, in theory, sought a monopoly of its environment--the commercial kingdom in an effort to control the wealth flowing through the region and the land-based kingdom in an effort to fulfill its own philosophical prospectus. This propensity for monopoly severely limited the options of each state in dealing with its environment and with other states.

It was the power resources of the kingdom, however, that defined the limits of its foreign policy. Although China sometimes attempted to mediate or control regional conflict (as in 1403 when a fleet under the command of Admiral Yin Ching intervened to protect Malacca from Thai invasion), there was, in fact, no recourse beyond the capacities of the state to use its available power for protection or expansion. Such a regional political system, based entirely on the use of force, could achieve a modicum of balance or equilibrium if a group of states developed comparable military capabilities, but there was no institutional structure to maintain the balance. Moreover, given the inherent instability of the states themselves, there was little likelihood that a "balance of power" could be sustained for long periods.

The interstate system of traditional Southeast Asia can be divided functionally into religious, economic, political, and military subsystems. Although these subsystems overlapped in an operational sense, a separate discussion of each will ease our analysis of the ways in which they shaped the politics of the region.

THE CULTURAL AND RELIGIOUS SUBSYSTEMS

Religion and custom were not only critical elements of power retention within the state, linking the village and the court in an all-subsuming metaphysical view of the world; indeed, they also played an very important role in sustaining patterns of interstate conduct.[5] The concept of sovereignty was bound up in the belief that the sovereign was directly linked to the gods. As a group, then, the court elite was set apart from the populace, and the blood ties among royal leaders became, at times, a strong factor in support of regional stability. As sovereignty was linked to blood, the elite found opportunities for contact and communication through marriage and through the need to maintain genealogical links to royalty and the supernatural when no direct heir was left for a throne.

Records of contact are few, but this fact should not be taken as a full measure of this interchange. Early in the ninth century, a Khmer prince spent his childhood in Java.[6] It is probable that other royal exchanges took place, as well; in addition, cultural interchange appears to have been frequent. For instance, the nagari script (an alphabet originally from North India) apparently reached Cambodia by way of Java,[7] and there are records of various kings contributing to the support or building of Buddhist or Hindu temples in neighboring kingdoms.

However, although blood relationships and religious interchanges may have led to some measure of interstate cooperation, two additional factors in the region served to strengthen divisions. First, as kingship evolved, the concept of "god-king" became stronger. The exact meaning of this concept in traditional Southeast Asia is not clear, with most of the disagreement among scholars focusing on the "degree" of godliness embedded in the king. Variations range from the view that the king was himself a god to the more limited concept suggesting that "the king had vassals but no overlord."[8] The supernatural concept of kingship had to be balanced with local spirits, gods, and ancestor worship and, as with most of the cultural borrowings in Southeast Asia, seems to have been adopted with little difficulty. Whatever the degree of embodiment of supernatural power, the various god-king concepts of the region had an important impact on the interstate system because the idea was closely linked to the state itself. The perception of the state as the center of the world was elemental to the system of interstate politics. This philosophy provided, in theory, that only one state could exist, although lesser states in vassal or tributary status were recognized. Thus a multi-state system of sovereign and, theoretically, equal states did not develop in Southeast Asia. Although the theoretical never approached reality, it did limit the possibilities for interstate cooperation and alliances.

THE ECONOMIC SUBSYSTEM

As a goal of foreign policy, material enrichment of the kingdom was promoted by whatever means were available. Foreign trade was actively controlled with expansive naval forces by maritime kingdoms like Srivijaya as they sought power over the flow of traffic through the Strait of Malacca, the primary water route for the China to Europe trade. These kingdoms were further able to control trade by providing harbor facilities and other attractions for merchant fleets. The establishment of such a trade center had the effect of controlling nearby lesser kingdoms because merchants sought out the market of the major centers. Another important aspect of policy among commercial kingdoms was the monopoly of interisland trade. Naval force was used to ensure that smaller kingdoms transshipped their produce through the dominant city-state and did not try to set up an independent trade center.

Another facet of trade control was maintenance of security along the main shipping routes. Pirates, common throughout Southeast Asia, found easy refuge among the many small islands scattered throughout the archipelago. In addition, the distinction between smaller kingdoms and large pirate lairs was more a matter of conjecture than fact. So blurred was the distinction between pirates and legitimate kingdoms that the very naval forces used by the maritime kingdoms, in times of breakdown of authority were, in fact, pirates. The burden of patrolling the sea lanes fell on the major commercial kingdoms of the region, and their success or failure had a direct impact on their revenues.

The land-based kingdoms, although primarily interested in agriculture and especially rice production, controlled foreign trade and exchange through their power over passage on the major river systems. Some kingdoms such as Ayudhya and Mataram played dual roles as both maritime commercial and agricultural kingdoms. Export commodities (e.g., rice, spices, minerals, precious metals, and lumber) were controlled by the state, having been gathered domestically as tax payments. Not only the trade routes but also the commodity trading itself were in the hands of the state, and exchanges were carried out at the state-to-state level or between state officials and merchants from China, India, or the Middle East. Kings maintained monopolies over some export commodities, as in Burma, where production of ivory, silver, amber, rubies, and sapphires were under royal control.[9]

Particularly among the agricultural kingdoms, much of the wealth gained through the control of commodity trading was used for religious purposes linked to the legitimization of the state. Consecration of temples, donations of lands to sustain monasteries, construction of new temple complexes, and pilgrimages to India and later to Mecca were among the court's religious activities that filled a basic redistributive need in the nonmarket economies of early Southeast Asia. In Burma, however, the flow of wealth to the religious community eventually contributed to the decline of the state,[10] and during the late Angkor period of the Khmer Empire "all of the Cambodian peasantry was in the service of the gods."[11]

Wealth, itself an important measure of political legitimacy, was both an outcome and a prerogative of political power: "There was no effective distinction between official and personal revenue" in the traditional state.[12] The Malay Annals record Sultan Mahmud Shah as having said, "If the Sultan Muda has but the sword of kingship, he will have gold as well. That is to say, where there is sovereignty there is gold."[13] The ability of the king to lavish gifts on his clients and retainers was very important in maintaining sovereignty. Conversely, the loss of wealth had grave consequences for any king. The Sultan of Perak--though Perak was never an extremely wealthy trading center--fell from power in part because his chief supporters acquired more wealth than the sultan himself.[14]

THE POLITICAL AND DIPLOMATIC SUBSYSTEMS

The political philosophy of the state, based on the metaphysical view of the kingdom as a microcosmic version of the universe, left little room for the development of a set of relationships that presumed the existence of more than one state. Although in reality there were always many states, and although these states dealt regularly with each other, the dealings themselves were not a routine part of the law of states. To have made them routine would have threatened the legitimacy of the states. In short, the concept of multiple sovereign states enjoying domain over specific territories and interacting as equals was eclipsed by the concept of a universal sovereign.

The exchange of ambassadors and diplomatic missions on a permanent basis was not pursued in southeast Asia, and most capital cities had no facilities for receiving them. When envoys or emissaries were sent from one kingdom to another, they usually were met at a frontier point or a port city, rarely traveling to the capital city at all.[15] The standard mode for diplomacy seems to have been a type of courier system, given the exchange of letters. For instance, the Malay Annals contain an exchange in which the Raja of Pahang sent a letter of "friendship" to Siam; however, the foreign minister of Siam rejected the letter, asking that it be rewritten to express "obeisance" to Siam. Reluctantly, this was done, and the letter was accepted.[16] Letters were also commonly used in exchanges between China and the states of Southeast Asia.[17]

Such exchanges of letters may also have been accompanied by tribute. The tributes to China from the states of Southeast Asia have been widely recognized, but a similar custom probably operated within the region, too, as when "incessant border warfare and threats of warfare may have led the Burmese king to pay tribute to Cambodia."[18] Cambodia under the weak predecessors of Jayavaraman VII also paid tribute to Champa.[19] At another time, Pagan, having conquered Thalon, left it largely intact to be used as a tributary link to the international maritime trade.[20] It is important, however, not to overstress the subordinate status associated with tribute because the Asian system at all levels had the capacity to ignore the implications of inferiority while emphasizing the benefits (usually the exchange of wealth). For example, the Sultanate of Trengganu paid tribute to Siam through the eighteenth century. The British, applying European legal concepts of suzerainty, sought authority over Trengganu through cession from Siam, failing to recognize that tributary status in Southeast Asia could "mean anything from friendship to total subordination, and one of the central characteristics of Southeast Asian state relationships was

the constant reinterpretation of such ties, reflecting the
waxing and waning of relative power."[21]

Political contacts in traditional Southeast Asia in an
age of slow communications were not constant and were
almost certainly a function of geographic distance.
Unilateral imperialistic action was the most common
pattern of interstate action, and force was the diplomatic
tool employed. "It is a defensible hypothesis," says
Bronson, "that a built-in expansive tendency is the most
important of all qualities pertaining to the definition of
the state" in traditional Southeast Asia.[22] Neighboring
states were almost continually under threat of or
threatening attack, and the effective border between any
two neighbors was established at the point where their
opposing power met in equilibrium. The purposes of
expanding territory, increasing the pool of available
manpower, or controlling economic resources appear to have
been the most common reasons for military action.
Violence or the threat of violence was also the principal
means of enforcement of the authority in the kingdom.[23]
There are several factors within the social context that
might explain why this was the case. First, the
metaphysical view of the kingdom justified its expansion
over the maximum possible amount of territory because the
kingdom, as the center and controller of the universe, did
not comprehend theoretically other universal centers or
other kingdoms. Second, the mobility of some segments of
the peasant population limited the probability of high
profits for the king from heavy internal taxes; plunder
from other areas was much more lucrative. Finally, the
political organization of Southeast Asia, with its
numerous minor river-delta societies, offered many targets
for imperialism as well as a multitude of power centers
from which imperialism might grow. Whatever the reason,
war among the traditional states of Southeast Asia was the
arbiter of virtually all interstate disputes and the most
common form of interstate action.

The use of force was, in one important sense, an
extension of political legitimacy. The cosmological
concepts on which kingship was based left little room for
development of a stable system of equal and sovereign
states. Rather, the extension of power and the use of
force worked to establish an unequal system of dominant
and vassal states. Although the state and its legitimacy
were in part ethnically and culturally based, the ultimate
domain of the state was determined by its ability, through
force, to extend its power. Boundaries were not

established at some fixed geographic point but fluctuated throughout the frontier area between two states.[24] As capabilities for using force changed over time, affecting that equilibrium, so too was the boundary affected. Andaya has argued that the concept of distinct borders between states was accepted,[25] although these boundaries may have been areas over which no state had effective control, making them more akin to "no-man's lands" than clearly demarcated lines. In a sense, the frontier areas were beyond the control of any government, and resettlement of loyal peasants (encouraged by the availability of land) at these frontiers was one technique used to bring them under control. Power measured in available military force was the critical element in holding the state together, but it "faded into insignificance with distance from the capital; otherwise the autonomy of local chiefs was nearly complete, and whether the effective boundaries of a major state encompassed a certain area depended on ties of blood and marriage, calculations of alliance, and force of arms."[26]

These inexact boundary concepts were made acceptable through the Indian concept of mandala[27] which in its Indian form connoted an alliance system; in Southeast Asia, on the other hand, the term referred to a "circle of kings" in which "one king, identified with divine and universal authority and defined as the conqueror, claimed personal hegemony over the others, who in theory were bound to be his obedient allies and vassals."[28] The mandala of any kingdom existed in several variations of reality, the first level being that territory over which the kingdom could exercise continuous authority. At the second level were those principalities, city-states, and other centers of power that for one reason or another chose to remain in the tribute system operated from the center. Finally, the third level included those power centers whose submission to control occurred largely in the minds and poems of the court chroniclers, such that only occasionally and in conjunction with the threat or use of force did they actually submit to the center.

The fluid nature of this system meant that kingdoms rose and declined as frequently as kingdoms actually fell. Sacking and razing the capital city of a competing king were effective for breaking the terminal from which power was extended. But once the equilibrium was broken, it did not automatically follow that the victor could sustain the extension of power throughout the territorial domain of the defeated state. Establishment of a vassal state through installation of a pretender in place of the defeated king was often the more realistic alternative.

A direct outgrowth of unilateral imperial action by a kingdom was the allegiance/vassal system of interstate organization. Such maritime kingdoms as Srivijaya were largely conglomerates or confederations of previously independent entrepot centers scattered along the Strait of Malacca. In the case of Srivijaya, the confederation was established and maintained by Srivijaya's navy, and each additional port-city brought under Srivijayan vassalage augmented that navy. But such systems had limited permanence and clearly depended on the power of the center for continued existence. For example, the Khmer Empire once owed allegiance to Java before A.D. 800, but Java was unable to maintain its position after A.D. 802.[29] Likewise, at various times the Khmer Empire demanded allegiance of Champa, Annam, Chenla, Louvo, and parts of the Malay peninsula. Allegiance/vassal systems were established and maintained by the power of the leading state for the benefit of that state and reinforced by a blood-bond to the throne of the conquered states. If the power of the leading state waned or if a new king came to power in the center, its imperial organization also diminished.

Temporary alliances and confederations were common, but few developed significantly deep links among various kingdoms, and beyond their expedient or immediate utility they were of little consequence. Most alliance systems were developed to perform some specific defensive task or to meet some immediate purpose, and were soon dissolved. Briggs notes several references over a long period of time to a confederation of Mon kingdoms on the Mekong-Menam and Irrawaddy-Sittang valleys. This confederation appears to have been a mutual association, perhaps a defensive alliance against the Khmer Empire or Burma, but the very limited information available on the period makes any conclusion difficult.[30] Had Southeast Asian kingdoms been more practiced in cooperation, they might have united against the first arrivals from Europe and driven the Westerners out of the region. This did not happen, however, precisely because of the lack of systemic conventions for such mutual cooperation.

Cooperative ventures were recorded, but these were quite disjointed in nature. For example, not only did Jayavarman II of Khmer live for a time in Java, but he was installed on the Khmer throne by the Javanese army.[31] Almost immediately thereafter, however, hostile relations resumed. Also, during the eleventh century, Kediri (Eastern Java) and Srivijaya tacitly agreed on exclusive trading spheres within the archipelago,[32] but Kediri demonstrated the limits to such an agreement by refusing to aid Srivijaya against the Chola raids. These cooperative ventures apparently were subordinated to expediency or short-term gain on the part of one or the other of the cooperating states at the loss of long-term development. There was little in Southeast Asia's systemic context to suggest that interstate cooperation was a valued goal. Because sovereignty was of a personal rather than an institutional nature in early Southeast Asian states, "foreign relations lacked continuity of obligation, extending from one king to his successor,"[33] and the instability of the system increased enormously with the constant need for building, rebuilding, and anticipating changes in relationships.

THE MILITARY SUBSYSTEM AND WAR

Of course, one assurance of the continued stability of kingship and kingdom was the possession of ample loyal military forces. Only a very sketchy picture of military capabilities in traditional Southeast Asia can be described. The system was rife with conflict, and war often was bloody with heavy loss of life in actual combat and further loss as defeated soldiers often committed suicide rather than be taken captive. On the other hand, the principle of "stand fast until the last man drops" was not given undue credence, and escape from combat into the rough jungle terrain was a widely accepted strategy, even for the bravest warriors. Moreover, ritual war, in which a battle was planned for an appointed hour and continued--at a rather leisurely pace from safe distances--until one side retired from the field, was common in Southeast Asia.[34] Also recognized there was the concept of righteous war,[35] although plunder was usually considered sufficient reason for war, as when the Javanese raided Ligor, Champa, and Tonkin six times over a thirty-five year period.[36] But this is not to say that wars were less than devastating and destructive: Much of the population and local agricultural resources were often carried away, and entire villages, towns, and crop areas could be destroyed, as when the Burmese decimated Ayudhya.

Mysticism and magic, as in all areas of traditional Southeast Asian life, played an important role in the preparations for and execution of war. Dreams were important in forewarning warriors and leaders of impending ill fates. Shells, animal teeth, or pieces of iron or copper were worn as amulets or war talismen to ward off evil spirits. Auspicious days were selected for battle--the first day of the new moon was thought to be particularly good. The route leading to the battle site was prepared with small sacrifices, and all natural phenomena along the way were examined for signs of particularly bad omens. Even the actions of villagers left at home were strictly proscribed; for example, women were forbidden to sew because a pricked finger would signify the certain wounding of their husbands.[37]

Naval Forces. Among all the kingdoms of Southeast Asia, but particularly in the archipelago, there is evidence of shipbuilding and naval activity. Shipbuilding was also especially notable in the Mekong and was long-standing and widespread in all of the major river deltas of Southeast Asia.[38] The maritime kingdoms of Southeast Asia appear to have "built, owned, and operated ocean-going ships of respectable size" as early as the first centuries of the Christian era.[39]

The ships of early Southeast Asia are often supposed to have been similar to the Chinese junk, but evidence suggests otherwise. Manguin has noted the six characteristics of these ships that made them unique: (1) They were large enough to carry 500 to 1,000 people and a cargo of 250 to 1,000 tons; (2) no iron was used in fastenings; (3) hulls were made of two or more layers of planks; (4) the ships used dual quarter rudders as steering-gear; (5) they used multiple masts; and (6) they did not use outrigging.[40] It is difficult to fix a time of origin for the use of these ships in Southeast Asia, but Chinese sources date them as early as the third century A.D. Ships were constructed from several layers of thick planks held together with pegs and cords made from coconut fiber. No nails were used. The largest of these ships required at least six or seven feet of water, were more than sixty meters in length, and used sails because they could not be navigated with oars alone.[41] This description seems to correspond with that of the sixteenth century Portuguese writer, Gaspar Correia: "Because she was very tall . . . our people did not dare board her and our firing did not hurt her at all, for she had four super-imposed layers of planks, and our biggest cannon would not penetrate more than two."[42]

The naval capacities of Southeast Asian states were considerable. Chau Ju-kua, the Chinese scholar, has provided a description of the development of naval skills in Srivijaya: "This country in older times . . . used an iron chain as a barrier to keep the pirates of other countries in check. . . . If a merchant ship passes by without entering their boats go forth to make a combined attack, and all are ready to die in the attempt. This is why the country is a great shipping center."[43] In addition, a stone engraving tells of a Cambodian fleet of 700 ships sent against Annam in A.D. 1128.[44] At sea in 1577, the Portuguese met an Acehnese fleet consisting of 115 to 150 ships and carrying approximately 10,000 fighting men and state-of-the-art artillery.[45]

These descriptions of naval forces suggest that maritime states did not so much "create" a large navy as co-opt the sea peoples of the area (many of whom may have been pirates, others of whom were sailors from vassal states) in an effort to gather enough strength to counter any remaining pirate threat. These naval forces, then, constituted the primary mechanism for maintaining the states' commercial position, not only by controlling pirates but also by subduing other competing entrepot centers and forcing all transient shipping into the main harbor.

Any distinctions among legal commerce (given that no international law was universally accepted), monopoly, breakdowns in monopoly control, and simple piracy were difficult to perceive. By the fifth century the Strait of Malacca was so dangerous that trade, at a greatly reduced flow, found it safer to use the Sunda Strait and to travel along the western coast of Sumatra.[46] The fear of such danger seems to have been well justified:

When the vessels sail to the west sea . . . the natives are quite at ease, but on their return voyage the crew have to put up arrow shelters and curtains, and sharpen their weapons. . . . Two or three hundred boats of the pirates would come silently and fight for several days. It would be fortunate if the traveller could meet a fair wind; otherwise the crew would be butchered and the merchandise would be looted.[47]

Tactics in naval warfare appear to have remained primitive. The primary strategy for naval conflict was to bring opposing naval barges alongside one another where the conflict was completed largely in hand-to-hand combat. Southeast Asian navies do not appear to have developed the mobile tactic of deploying ships to take advantage of their speed and maneuverability. Battle rams, too, were apparently seldom used.[48]

Land Forces. Practices for maintaining armies varied over time and throughout the region. Soldiers were not professional, and most village populations held some obligation for military service when called upon. The system was indirect and in some respects feudal. Ministers of state with administrative responsibilities for given areas were required to organize men for military service from these areas. Chou Ta-kuan, a Chinese writer who visited Cambodia in A.D. 1296, described the army as "both naked and barefooted. . . . In the right hand they hold the lance; in the left, the buckler. . . . And [they] have neither bows nor arrows, neither ballistas nor cannon, neither armor-plate nor helmets. . . . All the people were obliged to fight . . . but have neither tactics nor strategy."[49] Wales, however, has described the Burmese and Siamese armies as organized to include wing groups on either side of the main unit, which also had van- and rear-guard groups. Army divisions were composed of infantry, with elephant support groups and cavalry used largely for reconnaissance. Tactics included surprise attacks, night attacks, guerrilla warfare, false retreat, blockade, and seige, as well as frontal attack.[50]

Reid has compiled figures that show standing armies ranging from a royal guard of 3,000 men in Pasai (about A.D. 1518), 40,000 men in Aceh (A.D. 1620), 30,000 men available in Turban "within 24 hours," and 100,000 men available "within 4 leagues of Malacca" (A.D. 1510).[51] Neighboring states, "free-lance seamen, and warriors from regions in which no states were organized sometimes had an important mercenary role in regional military forces. For example, Bugis seamen intervened in northern Malaya for nearly a century to protect or defeat kings in Perak and Kedah.[52] Raids on other areas were often designed to take slaves for military purposes, and armies, though massive, usually left equipment and provisions to the individual.[53] There were, however, cases in which the king provided the arms and then collected them at the end of the campaign.[54]

The military equipment described by most sources seems to have been more advanced than that described by Chou

Ta-kuan. Most of the mainland kingdoms were skilled in the use of trained war elephants.[55] General military equipment included lances, bows and arrows (sometimes poisoned), darts, and crossbows that were large enough to be effective against elephants.[56] The degree of sophistication in weaponry of this age is captured in the description of a pistol crossbow: "The grip might have been from a modern handgun with mortised wooden bow support, [and] the longitudinal channel . . . [combines] bronze and wood components."[57] A study of early Indian weaponry similar to those used in Southeast Asia lists swords, daggers, clubs, spears, pikes, thunderbolts, axes, bows and arrows, and shields used for protection.[58]

Fortification and Defense. Although some cities of traditional Southeast Asia were protected by moats and brick walls,[59] Reid has noted that most, even capital cities, were not well fortified, having only walls or, in times of war, quickly erected bamboo stockades. He points out that manpower, not territory or even cities themselves, was the sustaining element of power and kingship in Southeast Asia.[60] Andaya, who cites the same principle in the context of Johore, has indicated that "Admiral Verhoeven offered to build a fort for Sultan Alauddin" but he "refused saying that . . . he and his subjects could always flee upriver."[61] She further notes that small islands were not thought to be acceptable as locations for capital cities because they did not provide room for escape.[62] The resilience added to these kingdoms by their willingness to abandon specific terrain is shown by the fact that "only a few months after the Dutch reported 'the complete destruction' of Johor Lama in 1673 and a large booty and numerous prisoners taken, a Johor fleet appeared at the mouth of the Jambi River and threatened the 'victorious' Jambi."[63] Not until European fortifications began to appear were permanent walled enclosures stressed as in Kedah: "Though this castle has such a miserable appearance in the eyes of the Europeans, yet it is sufficient to keep the nations here about in awe, merely because it looks European."[64]

EXTRAREGIONAL POWERS

Arguments about the role of indigenous peoples in state-building are vital for understanding the culture of Southeast Asia, but they could miss an important perspective on the interstate system given that China and India were actors in the system as well. Brecher, although writing of contemporary Southeast Asia, defined the Chinese and Indian impacts as "the presence of relatively powerful peripheral states" whose power gave them "de facto membership" in the system.[65] Historically, too, this view may well describe a situation in which autochthonous factors were dominant whereas India and China interacted in the region but as participants in the global trading system.

The one area of diplomacy that most kingdoms of Southeast Asia meticulously maintained throughout their history pertained to relations with India and China. In many respects (excluding the village setting), the Southeast Asian system was quite open in dealing with foreigners. For example, for purposes of interstate commerce, Malay was accepted as the lingua franca throughout the archipelago by the Arabs and Chinese (and later the Europeans), as well as by all indigenous merchants.[66] Wolters has noted that Srivijaya's goal was to cultivate good trade relations with India and China while attempting to dominate or monopolize the entire Southeast Asian trade route "to protect a privileged trading system."[67] Ayudhya's regular tributes to China prevented the destruction of the kingdom during the invasion of Kublai Khan, and Malacca converted to Islam in order to attract Indian merchants.

Thus there were, in fact, opportunities and mechanisms for kingdoms within Southeast Asia to establish contacts and develop cooperative ventures. However, these ventures did not and probably could not flower within the context of traditional Southeast Asia. Except in Vietnam, much of the interest in India apparently was cultural. Southeast Asian states looked to India for religious and philosophical doctrines believed to be superior to their own. These doctrines were adopted and blended with indigenous thought and belief structures. In Vietnam, but not elsewhere in Southeast Asia, the mandarin system of bureaucratic organization and practice was adopted.

Both India and China made contributions to the political legitimacy of Southeast Asian kingdoms, but in markedly different ways. The uses made by Southeast kings of Hindu rituals and metaphysics have already been described. It is also true that recognition by the Chinese emperor was valuable for enhancing claims to the throne because the emperor provided letters and seals acknowledging authority. The Chinese emperor, by conferring military titles and other honors on Southeast Asian kings,[68] intervened directly to influence the stature of states in Southeast Asia.

Commerce and trade were additional areas in which India and China played important roles. Southeast Asia first offered safe harbor in the international maritime route from China to India. Later, Southeast Asians were themselves active and competitive producers of commodities, such as pepper, for the international market. India provided pepper to China in the early centuries of the Christian era, but by A.D. 800 Sumatran pepper, though inferior to the Indian product, had supplanted the Indian varieties in the China market because of its comparatively lower cost. Trading interests with a number of Indian kingdoms, particularly those on the northeast coast of India, might have influenced the need for organized patterns of interaction. Tributary missions to Imperial China would seem to have contradicted the "center of the world" concept of the Southeast Asian states, but potential economic returns and (at certain periods in history) added security provided by the Chinese navy more than countered the potential humiliation of playing the role of tributary state. No doubt, although written records from Southeast Asia are few, it is equally likely that Southeast Asian potentates were able to rationalize away any perceived inferior status as easily as the Chinese accentuated it.

Cases of military intervention by Indians have been recorded, such as the Chola raids of Srivijaya during the eleventh century,[69] but it seems that India was rarely feared for its military might. China offered a somewhat different case. Chinese armies controlled Vietnam for nearly ten centuries, and Mongol armies occupied part of mainland Southeast Asia in the late thirteenth and early fourteenth centuries, reaching as far as Java in 1292. There is little doubt that the presence of a Chinese navy in Southeast Asian seas prompted indigenous kingdoms to send their missions to China. These missions may have saved them from the wrath of the Chinese, but the Chinese presence also gave many smaller kingdoms a powerful ally against harassment by other Southeast Asian kingdoms. Malacca, for example, was protected from Thai intervention. Moreover, trading interests with China surely stimulated the desire for good relations with that country.

Patterns of interstate relations among the traditional kingdoms of Southeast Asia might thus be characterized as unilateral actions. Although other patterns (such as more or less forced allegiance or mutual alliance) could be found, they were the exception rather than the rule: Unilateral action for territorial expansion or economic gain describes the most common type of interstate action. China and India held the interest of the larger Southeast Asian states for commercial reasons, whereas weaker states looked particularly to China for protection from their stronger neighbors.

CHARACTERISTICS OF THE SYSTEM

The historical interstate system in traditional Southeast Asia has been described in the first five chapters of this book, in what has necessarily been a broad overview built upon bits of information gathered from one or another historical situation. As a relatively broad level of discussion has been maintained, useful generalizations can be developed from the available historical material. Of course, there were differences between the villages in Vietnam and those in Java, or between the kingdoms of the second century and those of the fifteenth century. But the detailed studies on which this work is based have also uncovered the substance of these generalizations.

The principle characteristics of this regional system can be summarized in terms of three components: weak institutions, weak interactions, and patterns of dependence on extraregional powers.

Institutional Strength. The key to the fragile nature of the system was a corresponding fragility in its primary actor--the traditional state. No state built a mass political base at any time before the arrival of the colonial powers, nor is there significant evidence of movement in that direction. The personalized nature of political leadership and its reliance on metaphysical and religious sources for legitimacy seemed to ensure that the gap between the people and government would remain wide. The coming of Islam did not change this situation in any major way.[70] In one of the last Southeast Asian states to give way to colonial domination, Trengganu on the Malay peninsula, the sultan introduced some reforms (courts, police, and written law) and created some functionally oriented governmental positions that were filled on the basis of merit. But more basic reforms of the government were rejected because they were likely to bring religious contamination (following the ways of infidels) while others would have infringed on the sultan's personal financial status.[71]

From another perspective, this lack of institutional integrity meant that the state did not exist--except in its embodiment in the king. Kings were transitory, and the state remained in a permanent condition of dependence on the personality of the king and on minimal bureaucratic organization. In addition, because the state offered little in the way of amenities to the people living within its borders, there was little reason for them to stay if other needs called them away. Although bonds within the village, links to the kinship group, or even the natural draw of a birthplace engulfed in spirits and supernatural meaning could attract an individual to stay in place, the state could not.

The consequence was a state structured in such a way that resources were only sporadically and inefficiently mobilized and the authority of the government remained limited, even within its own territory.

System Interaction. The weakness of actors internally carried over into the interstate system. Of critical importance was the lack of a rationale for the development of a multistate system. Stated simply, the problem arose because claims of legitimacy, developed for domestic purposes in line with Hindu mythology, made the state the center of the world--of which there could be only one. To the extent that other states were recognized, they were located on the periphery and in a "lesser" or "lower" position with respect to the center.

In the interstate context, this type of claim to legitimacy meant that boundaries were poorly defined. Although the myth claiming that all lands should be controlled by the ruler did not match reality, it did preclude the development of a clearly defined set of boundaries among states. In the absence of a rationale for set boundaries, power and its extension to the frontier became the only means of establishing limits. The theoretical construct of the state as the center of the world did make it possible to envision several concentric levels of control moving progressively farther from the center, but there was no theoretical or practical end to these circles. This moving frontier was a "means of gauging and aligning the international equilibrium."[72]

Following from this kind of claim to legitimacy was a system constructed of tributary and vassal states instead of a multistate system of theoretically equal governments. This system introduced the further complication that little could be accomplished among states on an equal footing, even in the way of mutually beneficial actions. With little room for mutual agreement, patterns of interstate cooperation did not develop, and violence became the principal means for resolving disputes.

But violence was more than a way of settling disputes. It was also an important tool for development of the state. Territorial expansion for the control of manpower and maritime expansion for control of sea lanes and commerce were the most common mechanisms for enhancing the state. Raids of plunder between "legally" constituted states were also frequent, with booty including not only gold and gems but slaves as well.

The low level of institutional development and the high incidence of violence within the state structures meant that general lawlessness and banditry were commonplace. Without a doubt the single most important function of the state was to protect the village from bandits. However, the most rampant form of lawlessness throughout the region was piracy. Pirates preyed on coastal communities as well as on local shipping and international trade routes.

System Recognition. Systems theorists point to recognition of system membership by its members as one of the critical ingredients for development of an effective system. By implication, the member states in an interstate system tend to recognize themselves as different from states in the external environment. Although the many terms that Chinese, Indians, and Arabs applied to Southeast Asia suggest external recognition of the region as a discrete unit, there is little evidence that the state leaders in traditional Southeast Asia understood themselves in this context.

Examples such as intermarriage among Southeast Asian royalty suggest some such recognition. It also appears that these states understood the unique position of China vis-a-vis the collectivity of states in Southeast Asia. On the other hand, the very open, commercial nature of much of traditional Southeast Asia, as well as its propensity for absorption of external values and cultural traits, tended to obscure the development of a separate identity.

This weak self-identity was of particular importance at the time of the first arrival of the Europeans. The characterization is, of course, hypothetical. But the fact remains that had the Southeast Asian state leaders developed a stronger sense of self-identity, the states of the region may have been able to recognize more clearly the systemic nature of the threat presented by the Portuguese and more intensely by the Dutch. That this recognition did not develop and, indeed, could not have developed in traditional Southeast Asia was a key weakness of that traditional system.

System Dependence. A third characteristic of the traditional interstate system was its dependence on actors external to the system, especially China and India. In an economic sense, however, the interstate system was largely dependent on the maritime trade routes from China to Europe. There is a clear correlation between the well-being of the states of Southeast Asia and the functioning of this international trading system: "It was the voyage from Indonesia to China alone which made possible the creation of entrepot centres."[73] At those times when China repudiated interest in trade, or when trade followed an overland caravan route, Southeast Asia suffered.

Traditional Southeast Asia reached its peak when the maritime trade routes flourished and the states of the region used their wealth to give expression to Buddhist and Hindu concepts borrowed from India. At this time, dependence seems to have been mostly intellectual in nature. The political and religious thought of the region was shaped primarily by philosophies of Indian origin. However, these same philosophies also set real limits to the capabilities of the interstate system.

Nevertheless, although the traditional Southeast Asian system was dependent on or subordinate to the Chinese and Indian systems for much of its cultural well-being and reliant on the global trading system for much of its economic well-being, these dependencies should not be considered apart from the context of a growing and active regional system. This independence continued over long periods of time as much because it was useful to Southeast Asians themselves as because it was imposed by Chinese or Indian power, given that neither China nor India could intervene at will in the region. The record of conflict with Indian and Chinese military forces in the region is by no means one of unmitigated success for the outsiders, and certainly there is little indication that Southeast Asians conceded, knowingly, to the superiority of these forces. Traditional Southeast Asia cannot be perceived, as Nehru reportedly saw it, as an open area for the inevitable political collision between the greater forces of China and India.[74]

The concept of dependence must be kept in perspective. The traditional system of Southeast Asia stood on its own. It was weak, and by contemporary standards, certainly had many deficiencies. Yet it prospered over a period of approximately one thousand years. Moreover, all of the regional systems--the Chinese system, the Southeast Asian system, the Indian system, the Middle Eastern system, the Mediterranean system, and European system--were dependent on each other from at least the beginning of the Christian era. Although the notion of global interdependence is a modern phenomenon,[75] this analysis of the interaction of regional systems suggests that interdependence is not new. This historical interdependence was limited by lack of knowledge and the technological capacities of the time, but it was constant until the regional systems were destroyed by European colonial expansion.

NOTES

1. R. P. Anand, "Maritime Practices and Customs in Southeast Asia Until 1600 A.D. and the Modern Law of the Sea," in ASEAN Identity, Development and Culture, edited by R. P. Anand and Purificacion V. Quisumbing (Quezon City and Honolulu: University of the Philippines and the East-West Center, Cultural Learning Institute, 1981), pp. 86-107.

2. Bennet Bronson, "The Late Prehistory and Early History of Central Thailand," in Early South East Asia: Essays in Archaeology, History and Historical Geography, edited by R. B. Smith and W. Watson (London: Oxford University Press, 1979), pp. 332-334.

3. David A. Wilson, "Thailand," in Governments and Politics of Southeast Asia, edited by George McT. Kahin (Ithaca: Cornell University Press, 1964), p. 8.

4. O. W. Wolters, The Fall of Srivijaya in Malay History (Ithaca: Cornell University Press, 1971), p. 98.

5. Lyman M. Tondel, Jr., ed., The Southeast Asia Crisis: Background Papers of the Eighth Hammerskjold Forum (Dobbs Ferry, N.Y.: Oceana Publications, 1966), p. 21.

6. Lawrence Palmer Briggs, The Ancient Khmer Empire. Transactions of the American Philosophical Society. (Philadelphia: American Philosophical Society, 1951), pp. 108, 148.

7. This route is suspected because of similar corruptions in the Javanese and later Khmer forms of the script. Supposition has it that Java was at various times a religious center for the entire region. See Ibid., p. 106.

8. Nidhi Aeusrivongse, "The Devaraja Cult and Khmer Kingship at Angkor," in Explorations in Early Southeast Asian History: The Origins of Southeast Asian Statecraft, edited by Kenneth R. Hall and John K. Whitmore (Ann Arbor: Michigan Papers on South and Southeast Asia, no. 11, 1976), p. 110.

9. John F. Cady, A History of Modern Burma (Ithaca: Cornell University Press, 1958), p. 20.

10. Michael Aung-Thwin, "Kingship, the Sangha, and Society in Pagan," in Hall and Whitmore, Explorations in Early Southeast Asian History, pp. 214-219.

11. Louis Finot, "Les grandes epoques de l'Indochine," Bulletin de l'Academie du Var. (Toulon, 1935), pp. 77-78, cited in Briggs, The Ancient Khmer Empire, p. 261.

12. Heather Sutherland, "The Taming of the Trengganu Elite," in Southeast Asian Transitions: Approaches Through Social History, edited by Ruth T. McVey (New Haven, Conn.: Yale University Press, 1978), p. 35.

13. Sejarah Melayu, or The Malay Annals, translated by C. C. Brown (London: Oxford University Press, 1970), p. 182.

14. Barbara Watson Andaya, "The Nature of the State in Eighteenth Century Perak," in Pre-Colonial State Systems in Southeast Asia, edited by Anthony Reid and Lance Castles (Kuala Lumpur: Malaysian Branch of the Royal Asiatic Society, Monograph no. 6, 1975), p. 26.

15. Cady, A History of Modern Burma, p. 8.

16. Sejarah Melayu, translated by C. C. Brown, p. 190.

17. Wolters, The Fall of Srivijaya, p. 70.

18. Briggs, The Ancient Khmer Empire, p. 217.

19. Ibid.

20. Aung-Thwin, "Kingship, the Sangha, and Society in Pagan," in Hall and Whitmore, Explorations in Early Southeast Asian History, p. 231.

21. Sutherland, "The Taming of the Trengganu Elite," in McVey, Southeast Asian Transitions, p. 35.

22. Bronson, "The Late Prehistory and Early History of Central Thailand," in Smith and Watson, Early South East Asia, p. 326. This is not to suggest that no law existed. In fact, detailed laws and regulations were issued by various states. See, for example, Sir Richard

114

Winstedt and P. E. de Josselin de Jong, "The Maritime Laws of Malacca," Journal of the Malaysian Branch of the Royal Asiatic Society 29 (August 1956), pp. 22-59.

23. Wolters, The Fall of Srivijaya, p. 13.

24. Chinese records indicate continued concern because Southeast Asian kingdoms refused to "observe good neighborhood relations, and respect each other's boundaries." See Wolters, The Fall of Srivijaya, pp. 52, 66.

25. Andaya, "The Nature of the State in Eighteenth Century Perak," in Reid and Castles, Pre-Colonial State Systems, p. 27.

26. Sutherland, "The Taming of the Trengganu Elite," in McVey, Southeast Asian Transitions, p. 35.

27. John W. Spellman, Political Theory of Ancient India: A Study of Kingship from the Earliest Times to Circa A.D. 300 (London: Oxford University Press, 1964), pp. 156-158.

28. Wolters, "Culture, History, and Region in Southeast Asian Perspective," in Anand and Quisumbing, Identity, Development and Culture, p. 9. See also Soemarsaid Moertono, State and Statecraft in Old Java: A Study of the Later Mataram Period, 16th to 19th Centuries (Ithaca: Cornell University, Modern Indonesia Project, 1958), p. 71.

29. Briggs, The Ancient Khmer Empire, pp. 88-89.

30. Ibid., p. 159.

31. Ibid., p. 108.

32. D.G.E. Hall, A History of South-East Asia (New York: St. Martin's Press, 1968), p. 225.

33. Cady, A History of Modern Burma, p. 19.

34. Dobbin, "The Exercise of Authority in Minangkabau," in Reid and Castles, Pre-Colonial State Systems, p. 83.

35. Aung-Thwin, "Kingship, the Sangha, and Society in Pagan," in Hall and Whitmore, Explorations in Early Southeast Asian Statecraft, p. 231.

36. John F. Cady, Southeast Asia: Its Historical Development (New York: McGraw-Hill, 1964), p. 74.

37. H. G. Quaritch Wales, Ancient South-East Asian Warfare (London: Bernard Quaritch, Ltd., 1952), pp. 4-11.

38. Paul Johnstone, The Sea-craft of Prehistory (Cambridge, Mass.: Harvard University Press, 1980).

39. Pierre-Yves Manguin, "The Southeast Asian Ship: An Historical Approach," Journal of Southeast Asian Studies 11 (September 1980), p. 267.

40. Ibid., p. 276.

41. Ibid., p. 275.

42. Ibid., p. 267.

43. Chau Ju-kua, His Work on the Chinese and Arab Trade in the Twelfth and Thirteenth Centuries, entitled Chu-fan-chi, translated by F. Hirth and W. Rockhill (Taipei: Literature House, 1965; reprint of the 1911 St. Petersburg edition), pp. 60, 62.

44. Briggs, The Ancient Khmer Empire, p. 190.

45. I. A. MacGregor, "A Sea Fight near Singapore in the 1570s," Journal of the Malaysian Branch of the Royal Asiatic Society 29 (1956), p. 12.

46. Briggs, The Ancient Khmer Empire, p. 23.

47. Hsu Yun-Ts'iao, "Singapore in the Remote Past," Journal of the Malaysian Branch of the Royal Asiatic Society 45 (1973), p. 2.

48. Wales, Ancient South-East Asian Warfare, p. 110.

49. Briggs, The Ancient Khmer Empire, p. 249.

50. Wales, Ancient South-East Asian Warfare, pp. 160, 165-169.

51. Anthony Reid, "The Structure of Cities in Southeast Asia, Fifteenth to Seventeenth Centuries," Journal of Southeast Asian Studies 11 (September 1980), p. 329.

52. Virginia Matheson, "Concepts of State in the Tuhfat Al-Nafis," and Barbara W. Andaya, "The Nature of the State in Eighteenth Century Perak," in Reid and Castles, Pre-Colonial State Systems.

53. Chau Ju-kua, Chinese and Arab Trade, p. 60.

54. Anthony Reid, "Trade and the Problem of Royal Power," in Reid and Castles, Pre-Colonial State Systems, p. 49, citing an early work by Augustin de Beaulieu, "Memoires du voyage aux Indes Orientales," in Melchisedech Thevenot, Relations de divers voyages curieux (Paris: Cramoisy, 1664), p. 109.

55. Briggs, The Ancient Khmer Empire, p. 189.

56. Ibid., p. 207.

57. E. Morton Grosser, "A Further Note on the Chou Dynasty Pistol-Crossbow," Artibus Asiae 23 (1960), p. 210.

58. K. Krishna Murthy, "Weapons of War in the Sculptures of Nagarjunakonda," Artibus Asiae 28 (1966), pp. 211-218.

59. Briggs, The Ancient Khmer Empire, p. 109; also, Chau Ju-kua, Chinese and Arab Trade, p. 60.

60. Reid, "The Structure of Cities in Southeast Asia," p. 243.

61. Andaya, "Seventeenth Century Johor," in Reid and Castles, Pre-Colonial State Systems, p. 3, n. 12.

62. Ibid., pp. 3-4.

63. Ibid., p. 7, citing KA-1185, OB1674, Missive from Governor Bort of Malacca to Batavia, 21 Dec. 1673, file

636. KA denotes the colonial archives of the General State Archives in the Hague.

64. M. Osbeck, A Voyage to China and the East Indies (London: publisher unlisted, 1771), pp. 217-218, cited in Dianne Lewis, "Kedah--The Development of a Malay State in the 18th and 19th Centuries," in Reid and Castles, Pre-Colonial State Systems, p. 39.

65. Michael Brecher, The New States of Asia (London: Oxford University Press, 1963), p. 159.

66. Bernard H. M. Vlekke, Nusantara: A History of Indonesia (The Hague: W. van Hoeve, 1965), p. 81.

67. O. W. Wolters, Early Indonesian Commerce: A Study of the Origins of Srivijaya (Ithaca: Cornell University Press, 1967), p. 241.

68. Wolters, The Fall of Srivijaya, p. 41.

69. See R. C. Majumdar, "The Overseas Expeditions of King Rajendra Cola," Artibus Asiae 24 (1961), pp. 338-342.

70. L. F. Brakel, "State and Statecraft in 17th Century Aceh," in Reid and Castles, Pre-Colonial State Systems, pp. 55-56.

71. Sutherland, "The Taming of the Trengganu Elite," in McVey, Southeast Asian Transitions, p. 49.

72. Robert L. Solomon, "Boundary Concepts and Practices in Southeast Asia," World Politics 23 (October 1970), p. 15.

73. Wolters, Early Indonesian Commerce, p. 32.

74. Nehru apparently felt that the intervention of European powers in Southeast Asia created an "unintentional barrier against the expansionist proclivity of both Indians and Chinese." See Guy J. Pauker, Frank H. Golay, and Cynthia H. Enloe, editors, Diversity and Development in Southeast Asia (New York: McGraw-Hill, 1977), p. 19. Pauker notes that Nehru discussed this matter in 1955 at the Asian-African Conference in Bandung, Indonesia.

75. Edward L. Morse, "Interdependence in World Affairs," in World Politics, edited by James N. Rosenau, Kenneth W. Thompson, and Gavin Boyd (New York: Free Press, 1976), pp. 660-681.

CHAPTER 6

Colonial Interlopers
and System Disjunction

Europeans arrived in Southeast Asia without great fanfare. Although their presence in the region was not commonplace, there were other visitors and travelers from Europe in various cities in China and Southeast Asia both before and after Marco Polo's trip there in 1292-1293, and at least one traveler visited the kingdom of Majapahit in Java.[1] As Southeast Asian commercial cities were open to foreign merchants, the arrival of a new group was ordinarily accepted or even welcomed as offering new opportunities for trade. Even the first Portuguese attack on Malacca was not extraordinary in the eyes of Malacca's competitor trading states, who supported the Portuguese attack.

EUROPEAN INTRUSION AND SYSTEMIC CHANGE

The European powers came to Southeast Asia with a mix of objectives and strategies designed to enhance commercial power and spread Christianity. The strategies of the colonial regimes changed frequently, and at times the major objectives of the colonial power changed as well. Three colonial powers--the Portuguese, Dutch, and British--stand out: the Portuguese because they initiated the colonial pattern of intervention and control, and the Dutch and British because their strategies had long-term impacts on the regional system itself.

The Portuguese. The Southeast Asians did not realize that the Portuguese were going to pursue two goals that would inextricably alter the indigenous system. Motivated by their animosity toward Islam (because of their experience

117

in Europe), the Portuguese linked their aim of securing monopoly control of the commercial spice trade with the religious goal of arresting the expansion of Islam in Asia. These goals became intertwined because, by the sixteenth century, most of the active traders in the South and Southeast Asian sections of the international trading system were already Muslim. The Portuguese plan for control was not a unified venture, and decisions were taken in the field without approval or agreement from Lisbon. After the Portuguese had extended their position around Africa and through India, it only then became apparent that to achieve either of their primary goals it would be necessary to expand into Southeast Asia. European knowledge of Asia and particularly Southeast Asia was fragmentary at the beginning of the sixteenth century. However, European and especially Portuguese navigational skills and equipment were improving rapidly. The Portuguese extended the range of their commercial sea travel in stages. By the latter part of the fifteenth century, Portuguese sailors had rounded the Cape of Good Hope. They reached India (Malabar) just before the close of the century. After establishing themselves in Goa in 1510, the move into Southeast Asia at Malacca was the next logical step in the Portuguese quest to stop the eastward diffusion of Islam and to control the flow of spices and other commodities on the westward route to Europe.

Yet the defeat of Malacca did not alter the basic interstate system of sixteenth century Southeast Asia. Malacca may have been past its zenith as an entrepot center, in any case, and several other ports, notably Aceh, Demak, Ternate, Johore, and Mataram on Java, were strengthened by the commercial shift away from Malacca following the Portuguese takeover there.[2] The Portuguese did have some success in controlling a portion of the spice trade to Europe. They were able to secure their position in Malacca with the assistance of disgruntled elements among the merchant class, but they could not exert the monopoly control that they had sought. Nor were they successful in their missionary activities in spreading Christianity or in curtailing the spread of Islam.

In the religious competition between Islam and Christianity, the Southeast Asians, especially those in the archipelago, seemed to recognize their adversarial positions. The Portuguese introduced Southeast Asia to the previously European and Middle Eastern conflict between Christianity and Islam, but Islam was actually strengthened by the intrusion of the Portuguese because it became a rallying point against them. The Arab and Indian merchants, many of whom were Muslim, knew very well the Portuguese goals from their experiences in South Asia. They were anxious to block Portuguese influence and control but unable to translate these desires into political force. Although Islam arrived in Southeast Asia at least several centuries before the major European push for Christianity, it was slow to penetrate inland until after "the decline of the Maritime states, [when] many of their citizens migrated to the territory of Mataram and other inland areas," thus greatly expediting the Islamization of the countryside.[3]

The Portuguese also maintained contacts with Thailand, Burma, Vietnam, and Cambodia and on several occasions tried to form alliances with Java, but their focus from the base at Malacca was largely on the spice islands of the Moluccas. Meanwhile, most commercial interests in the region were sufficiently flexible to bypass Portuguese control. During the sixteenth century spice production spread to many new areas in Southeast Asia. Although Portuguese vassals (or allies) such as Tidore were required to provide their entire spice production to the Portuguese, in fact the Tidorese simply resorted to smuggling and black-market sales of the crops. Other trading centers expanded rapidly to accept the overflow of merchants leaving the Portuguese controlled Malacca. Aceh in particular benefited from the shift among Muslim merchants leaving Malacca and looking for a new base.

Although the Portuguese were successful in penetrating the Southeast Asian system, they became only one more new competitor in the existing system of political and commercial power.[4] Their failure to dominate the system resulted from their limited manpower, resources, and organization. Their strategy was to establish a fort and warehouse at each port while relying on naval forces to force local shipping into port. The success of this strategy required large numbers of sailors and soldiers as well as colonial administrators, and without them, discipline broke down. Portuguese-led piracy and other forms of adventurism became common. The Portuguese nevertheless demonstrated that the Southeast Asian system was vulnerable to outsiders who could bring sufficient force into the region and manipulate the "rules" of the system to advantage. The Portuguese did not attain their goals, but the Dutch who followed were more successful.

The Dutch. By the time the Dutch arrived in Southeast
Asia, Portuguese fanaticism for Christian missionary
activities (more than their economic intervention) made
the Portuguese vigorously hated. The Southeast Asians,
still seeing no basic threat to their system, welcomed the
Dutch in the hope that they could counter the Portuguese;
this they did, although some Portuguese influence remained
as late as the early 1700s in Cambodia in addition to
their control of Timor.[5]

The movement into the region of the Dutch, who at
first were in league with the English, had been hastened
by the closing of the port at Lisbon to Dutch merchants in
1594; hence the source of pepper and spices that the Dutch
had distributed through northern Europe was cut off. The
Dutch were initially content to fit within the regional
system, and their early successful expeditions focusing on
commerce managed to create good profits as well as good
will among the Bandanese, Ambonese, and others. The
Achenese were more suspicious of Dutch intrusions but sent
two ambassadors to the Netherlands to gain a better
understanding of Europe.[6]

Early in the seventeenth century, the Dutch
consolidated their commercial houses under the Dutch or
(United) East India Company (VOC) and concentrated on both
monopoly control of the region and elimination of
Portuguese influence. The VOC was empowered to "act in
behalf of the States General of the Netherlands and to
exercise all rights of sovereignty."[7] However, the
Dutch at first found it advantageous to follow the rules
of the regional system in trading throughout Sumatra,
where the sultans acted as intermediaries to the
pepper-growers. In the Moluccas, already politically and
economically disrupted by the Portuguese and Spanish, the
Dutch found an opening when Ternate sought their
protection. A similar agreement with Ambon put the Dutch
in a very strong position in the eastern archipelago.
They also established a fort at Sunda Kalapa, sometimes
called Jakarta, in the territorial "no-man's land" between
the kingdoms of Mataram extending from East Java and
Bantam from West Java.[8]

In the early decades of the seventeenth century, the
Dutch company, led by the aggressive Governor-General Jan
Pieterzoon Coen, conceived the plan that struck at the
quick of the traditional Southeast Asian system. Coen and
others recognized that there were limits to the profit
potential of the European spice trade and that smuggling
and overproduction would further reduce the likely

profit. However, if the Dutch could also gain control of trade within Southeast Asia, or between Southeast Asia and China, India, or Syria, a great deal more profit appeared to be possible. The Batavia base was secured with the defeat of a large army from Mataram in 1629, and the Dutch poised for "the first decisive step towards the formation of a new empire, commercial at the outset like Srivijaya and Malacca, but gradually becoming predominantly territorial; yet not in the true line of succession to either, since the centre of control lay thousands of miles away."[9] Not only was the control center far away, but the rules that would govern Dutch conduct in Southeast Asia were also at odds with those of the extant system.

The Dutch captured Malacca in 1641, and by the 1650s the Portuguese were effectively eliminated as a force in Southeast Asia. The Dutch also extended their influence to Ayudhya, assisting the Siamese against the Cambodians and against Patani, after which they established a "factory of solid brick construction" there.[10] They tried with only limited success to extend their contacts throughout Indochina, where they met strong competition from the English.

In effect, the VOC became a new actor in the Southeast Asian system. In the context of the traditional Southeast Asian system, it had enormous resources at its disposal, and it had been granted by its home government the power "to dispense justice, to employ and direct the use of troops, to conclude alliances with native princes, and to conduct diplomatic and commercial relations generally."[11] At the same time it experienced few of the limitations common to indigenous states: It had no general constituency to satisfy, as its shareholders received their dividends irregularly and from capital funds; even the company directors had little control because of the time required for communications.

The Dutch move to displace the Portuguese in Southeast Asia was initiated largely for economic reasons grounded in inter-European commerce. However, political goals within Southeast Asia evolved almost immediately "in support" of these European economic and commercial goals. Progressively, from the formation of the Dutch East India Company in 1602 through the period of direct government control after 1798, the Dutch extended their penetration of Indonesian social and economic activity and expanded their geographic area of control. They also introduced (sometimes unknowingly) social, economic, and political changes that would fundamentally alter Southeast Asia.

For example, under their protection, the role of the Chinese in the economy was greatly expanded. Economic exploitation of agriculture reached phenomenal levels under the Cultivation System, which theoretically required farmers to turn over to the government one-fifth of their land for specified crops. In reality, a much higher percentage was often taken. Success at this level of exploitation required that the "authoritarian content of native society be not only maintained but considerably increased."[12] Even after the Dutch government gave up its monopoly control, the introduction of private capital (after 1877) did not bring a system in which the peasant agriculturalist could participate; compulsory labor was still required, substantial taxes were due periodically, and credit at reasonable rates was not available. The continually strengthened economic position of the Chinese and the new European entrepreneurs further ensured the exploitation and disruption of Indonesian society. In some ways the Dutch colonial government sought to protect Indonesian society from external penetration and exploitation, yet, failing that, the results were disjointed social, economic, and political systems that provided maximum status and reward for a few while stripping other segments of society of all but the barest essentials.

The British. The British were late in developing a major colonial interest in Southeast Asia. They had cooperated with the Dutch in the early challenges to the Portuguese but later retired most of their resources to the development of India. Only late in the eighteenth century were the British, working from their secure Indian base, able to challenge and eventually supplant Dutch control in the region. The Dutch had shifted the colonial focus from China to Europe trade to inter-Asian trade. It was the British, using private capital and vessels, who were able to dominate this inter-Asian trade: "Whereas the Dutch Empire had operated from within Indonesia and had been essentially monopolistic in its character and objectives, that of Britain was based on the enormous resources of the Indian subcontinent and finally functioned virtually on a free-trade basis."[13] This free-trade system, based in Singapore, in some respects harked back to the traditional entrepot centers of Srivijaya (Palembang) and Malacca, although, more important, it was initially managed by the British and later local Chinese--not by indigenous entrepreneurs.

British territorial acquisitions in Southeast Asia followed their general pattern of economic penetration. Penang, an island off the west coast of Malaya, was acquired from the Sultan of Kedah in 1786. Singapore, acquired from the Dutch in 1825, evolved during the remainder of the nineteenth century as a leading entrepot center and became the regional base for British colonial free trade. Control of the coastal regions of Burma came in 1826, following war precipitated by Burmese military activity in India,[14] although upper Burma was not annexed until 1886 as the British responded to fears of renewed French activities in Southeast Asia. The Malay states of Singapore's hinterland were of little interest until instability there threatened the production of tin, much of which was exported through Singapore. Britain developed a protectorate status with the four tin-mining states of Larut, Selangor, Sungai Ujong, and Perak. These were followed by similar agreements with Negri Sembilan (1888), Pahang (1888), and Johore (1895), whereas four other states--Kedah, Perlis, Kelantan, and Trengganu were acquired from Thailand by treaty in 1909.

Along with other colonial empires, the British introduced social, economic, and political changes that left the fabric of indigenous society threadbare and torn. Indigenous political leadership was undermined or destroyed. Foreign ethnic groups and local minority groups were given preferential treatment, particularly in the economic sphere. In Burma, the British took steps to introduce some measure of self-rule, but in Malaya there was little political development prior to World War II. British capital investment was substantial but highly specialized and largely extractive. The net result, as elsewhere, was the creation of a social system that could not survive without that paternal hand of the British colonial government. The disjunction that followed the collapse of the British regime in Burma and Malaya was severe.

OTHER COLONIAL POWERS IN SOUTHEAST ASIA

A second group of states--Spain, France, the United States, and Japan--also played a role during the colonial period, but these roles were not systematic and were restricted, for the most part, to the immediate territory under their control. That is, although their policies disrupted the social and economic structure of that territory, their activities did not directly alter the regional system. Japan is an exception in that it brought an end to the colonial European system while imposing a brief colonial rule of its own. But the traditional Southeast Asian system had already been destroyed before the Japanese intervention took place, and Japanese colonial influence in the region was too short lived to influence the shape of the new system. In a broader sense, however, the Japanese contributed to the reassertion of independence by stimulating the growth of nationalism in Southeast Asia.

The Spanish. The Spanish arrival in the Philippines took nearly forty years to complete following Magellan's visit there in 1521. Blocked by the Portuguese, the Spanish had to travel to Southeast Asia via Mexico and the Pacific, and a successful colony was not established until 1565 after four expeditions had failed. With a very few Spaniards and many local allies, the Spanish soon unified the Philippines. However, the full pacification and unification processes truly began with the Spanish missionary effort. The Filipinos of the sixteenth century seem to have been culturally amenable to outside influences. In those areas in which Islam had arrived ahead of the Spaniards, a new religion had already been accepted. Elsewhere in the Philippines, Christianity, the Spanish language, and other cultural traits were more readily adopted than was the case with any other Southeast Asian area. Moreover, the intensity of the Spanish cultural impact spread into social services and education as well, although some areas in the north were not pacified until the nineteenth century and the conflict with the Muslims of Mindanao was never completely settled.

The Portuguese and later the Dutch prevented Spain from extending its influence into other parts of Southeast Asia. The Spanish tried to establish direct trade links between Manila and China and Japan, but this proved difficult; moreover, the strongest Spanish commercial ties were developed between Manila and New Spain (Mexico), thus leaving the inter-Asian trade in the hands of the Chinese or other Europeans. Spanish galleons brought gold and silver to Manila to be exchanged for silks, rugs, cotton, spices, and aromatic woods. This trade continued until the Spanish lost Mexico, and thereafter Manila reoriented its trade to accept non-Spanish shipping. However, Manila's role as a trading center declined throughout the nineteenth century as more ports were opened in China.

From the beginning, the Spanish had put Filipinos in positions of responsibility, if not authority. They relied heavily on local troops to complete the conquest of the islands. They also created a Filipino constabulary and continued to use local chiefs and elders in the colonial administration. They also created a Filipino clergy. These groups became the foundation for the elite that led the Filipino nationalist movement--the earliest and most sophisticated such movement in Southeast Asia despite the previous lack of political organization and experience in the Philippines.

The French. The French movement into Indochina was not as direct as either the Portuguese or the Dutch intrusions into Southeast Asia. Their initial focus was on missionary activities, and their first target for a base in Southeast Asia was Ayudhya. There the French Catholic missionaries encouraged political linkages between King Narai and France, but Narai died in 1688 before the agreements could be fully implemented. French interest in Southeast Asia then receded to low-level missionary activities through most of the next century, although a small group of Frenchmen were instrumental in returning the Nguyen dynasty to power after the Tay-son rebellions.[15]

It was concern for persecution of Christians and harassment of missionaries that prompted the French to intervene in Vietnam during the 1830s. Their initial foothold around Saigon was not secured until 1863, and the French did not develop a plan for economic exploitation until later, when all of Indochina had come under their control.

The French, having established control in Vietnam, found it necessary to take control in Laos and Cambodia to prevent further Thai penetration in these countries. The French employed some Laotian and Cambodian officials in the colonial administration but brought in large numbers of Vietnamese to handle upper-level bureaucratic functions.[16] The highest levels of colonial administration were controlled by French residents, and although the monarchy was left in place, all acts were approved by the French Resident Superieur. Colonial control was relatively brief in these two countries, beginning in Cambodia in 1864 and in Laos in 1904. Nevertheless, the French continued to place more emphasis on Vietnam, using most of the revenues gained in Laos and Cambodia for programs in Vietnam. Yet the period of colonial domination was not sufficient to settle the many ethnic, dynastic, and other conflicts that had traditionally dominated life in these countries.

The United States. The U.S. acquisition of the Philippines, taken from Spain following the Spanish-American War in 1898, was the last introduction of a Western power to the region. From the beginning, U.S. policies seemed to give credence to the goal of Philippine independence, and plans for Filipino independence were first formalized by congressional action in 1916 and again in 1934. There were signs of a Philippine nationalist movement as early as 1815, and it became stronger during the 1840s and 1850s, when Filipino criticism of the Spanish clergy for racial bigotry became widespread.[17] The image of championing freedom and independence fit nicely into the U.S. mythology, but, at the same time, economic policies were enacted to ensure continued Filipino dependence on the United States no matter what its political status.[18]

The Japanese. The destruction of the European colonial system was accomplished in a time and fashion that could not have been predicted. The Japanese success was a spectacular stimulant for anti-Western sentiment, and nationalist feelings throughout Southeast Asia were strengthened by the call of "Asia for the Asiatics." The Japanese presence deeply stirred nationalist sentiments in places like Java and Burma, and challenged both the older intelligentsia and the "semimilitarized" younger generation to become political forces.[19] Thailand was in a unique position to limit Japanese penetration during World War II to some extent, but even so, as the harsh realities of war and defeat became evident, Thailand's relationship with Japan cooled.[20] As World War II unfolded and the U.S. military challenge increased, Japan's harsh extractive policies in the region as well as its brutality and insensitivity soon turned Southeast Asians against them; yet these people did not "look back" to the colonial powers for assistance. The Japanese also stimulated strongly negative racial feeling, especially among indigenous ethnic groups and against local Chinese and Indians. This was especially true in Malaya[21] but was also the case in Burma and Indonesia. Although the Southeast Asians aligned themselves on both sides in the global conflict, but it was clear that the underlying goal was not assistance to the Japanese or the old colonial powers but advance of local national interests.[22] The expectation that, somehow, the Southeast Asians owed the European colonial powers a measure of loyalty seems a bit ludicrous now: They had done little to engender such loyalty and at the hands of the Japanese the Europeans had "suffered far more than a military defeat; indeed, they lost the prestige and aura of invincibility."[23]

The period of Japan's intervention in Southeast Asia was brief, and its goals were dictated by a war that quickly became a losing proposition. However, while from the beginning of its colonial venture in Southeast Asia Japan may have sought to establish a colonial regime similar to that of the displaced Europeans, the immediate needs for support of the war required a degree and type of human and resource mobilization in Southeast Asia never previously experienced. And as the war progressively worsened, Japan moved to politicize the growing nationalist elements in the region.[24]

THE SOUTHEAST ASIAN RESPONSE

The Portuguese intrusion into Southeast Asia represented the first meeting of two radically different interstate systems: The Portuguese and Southeast Asians were "playing the international game" with differing rules. The states of Southeast Asia responded to the Portuguese in terms of their own perspective on interstate behavior and expected the Portuguese to apply the same perspective. For example, Sultan Mahmud, believing that the Portuguese attack on Malacca would follow the traditional pattern of sack, plunder, and abandon, retired from the conflict expecting to return after the Portuguese had departed. But they did not depart. The sultan could hardly have understood that these European merchants had major political goals in the region. Furthermore, weaker states (e.g., Tidore in the Moluccas), following traditional patterns of behavior, were willing to align with the Portuguese against their stronger regional rivals (e.g., Ternate). Tidore did not recognize that the Portuguese intended to control spice production entirely. Other states, including Johore, Aceh, and Mataram, attacked the Portuguese at Malacca and other strongholds in the Moluccas more than fifteen times during the sixteenth century but were unable to create an alliance with sufficient strength to dislodge the Portguese. Only twice were these attacks coordinated.

The regional system, in fact, proved capable of
absorbing the Portuguese, but the remaining states, while
in some respects stronger, did not adapt to counter
further European intrusion. Islam had been consolidated
in the archipelago, but, despite a common religious
philosophy, the indigenous states still found it difficult
to cooperate. They inherited from the Portuguese new
military techniques, wider use of firearms and cannons,
and alterations in sailing vessels for military purposes;
yet they did not capitalize fully on these new
technologies because "in Asia, unlike Europe, there was no
connection at all between science and technics, which
meant that scientific results were not tested by
experimental technology."[25] More critical still, the
Southeast Asians failed to make the organizational changes
at either the state level or the level of the regional
system that could have led to a different regional
response; in other words, they were unable to make common
cause against the Europeans.

Perhaps it was the indigenous propensity for looking
past reality to explain the success of the Europeans that
prevented the Southeast Asians from recognizing the threat
to their system. For example, in the Babad Tanah Jawi,
the chronicler explained that the army of Mataram was
defeated because King Agung sent his traitorous General
Mandureja to attack Batavia, so that when Mandureja was
killed the Dutch were actually fulfilling Agung's plan.
And in any case, it was said, Agung had sufficient magical
power to destroy the Dutch at any time.[26] Curiously,
the Dutch may have enhanced this view when, following
their defeat of Mataram's army, they determined that it
would be less costly to make peace with Mataram than to
fight another war. The ambassadors from Batavia with
their gifts were recorded in the Babad as recognizing the
overlordship of Mataram.[27] Despite such complacency,
the traditional states of Southeast Asia were, by the end
of the seventeenth century, meeting new actors with more
resources, better organization, singleness of purpose, and
an overriding determination to ignore, undermine, or
destroy the traditional system of the region. The reality
of the traditional system was that the claims of
indigenous states "were often absolute but their
capabilities were usually feeble, and colonial forces at
nearly every stage possessed superior strength and
organizational ability."[28]

THE COLONIAL IMPACT ON THE REGIONAL SYSTEM

The traditional Southeast Asian system eventually proved incapable of responding effectively against the penetration of European power. It was not that the traditional states had insufficient power in a military sense; rather, the individual states often did not have the hierarchial authority structures to respond quickly, nor did they recognize the arrival of the Europeans as a system level threat until it was too late. There are several reasons for this. First, the Southeast Asian system was itself weak in terms of its systemic relationships, particularly given the inability of the regional states to develop and sustain cooperative interactions. This inability to cooperate, of course, was reinforced by a high degree of ethnic separation among the states and by Hindu political philosophies of state structure that inhibited the evolution of a multistate system. Furthermore, the regional states had only a weakly defined sense of themselves as an exclusive grouping. Historically, they had recognized threats from the Chinese and the Indians, but even these threats rarely stimulated joint military defense. The very openness of the region made the arrival of any new group of foreigners commonplace; moreover, the first European arrivals (namely, the Portuguese), not having the capacities to alter the system, did tend to adapt to the existing system.[29] Finally, although the Southeast Asian states recognized the religious challenge posed by the Portuguese, the economic actions of the Portuguese were familiar and unthreatening in terms of the standard systemic behavior of "acquiring tribute and booty."[30] Although the Portuguese were quick to use their naval power, the "display of power was in the last instance a factor of rather limited import for the thousands-of-miles-long trade routes" and "became one thread more in the fabric of the international exchange of goods."[31] The Portuguese did profit handsomely from their Asian intervention, but only because they were able to transfer products out of the system and back to Europe.

It was the Dutch who first seriously disrupted the traditional regional system. They were successful because their military power, initially employed against the Portuguese and Spanish, later became an important tool against the indigenous states. Dutch military power was not only superior to that of the Portuguese; it was also more effectively organized. The "chief aim" for the new

Dutch East India Company was to consolidate Dutch power so as to counter the Portuguese more effectively.[32] After 1610 with the creation of the governor-generalship, the Dutch achieved a centralized authority and decisionmaking power beyond that of the Portuguese.[33]

Although the Dutch gave support to Christian missionary activities, they did not have the fanatical approach of the Portuguese and concentrated more directly on economic control--an endeavor that local states seemed completely unable to check even when economic disputes became overtly political. The typical sequence of the transition to Dutch control began with a contract, usually for monopoly over spice production, between the Dutch and the sultan or regent of a particular island or state. As often as not, the sultan signed the agreement under duress, either because Dutch warships were anchored in the harbor or because the sultan feared the power of another local potentate and needed Dutch protection and assistance.[34] The contract price for the commodity was always significantly below the market value, and local traders and producers invariably turned to smuggling and black market sales of the crop. The Europeans generally failed to recognize (or care) that most of the spice islands were net food importers; the heavy spice production in the Moluccas had made them dependent for basic foods on rice produced in Java, and the commodity exchange between Java and the Moluccas was vigorous because it provided economic advantages to both areas. When the Dutch interrupted this commodity exchange, the traditional states had to use cash for food imports, but the low contract price for spices meant less food and an effective decline in the standard of living.

The results of this unequal economic relationship became increasingly political under the Dutch because they had sufficient military power to act, whereas the Portuguese had not. The essence of the Dutch perspective is summarized in a letter by Coen, then governor-general of the Dutch East India Company, in which he spoke of the nutmeg monopoly contract with the Banda islands: "The contracts have been violated so many times that one cannot hope for anything certain from that nation unless they be once and for all brought under control by warfare."[35]

The power of the Dutch East India Company made it an actor with capabilities previously unknown in Southeast Asia. The Portuguese had used greater striking power and better navigational techniques to gain the upper hand in Malacca and elsewhere,[36] but the Dutch added organizational improvements and unity of purpose to outstrip the local states still further. The charter of the Dutch East India Company gave the company sovereign authority as though it were a state.[37] The company, operating thousands of miles from its board of directors and without the inhibitions of a conservative agriculturally based mass constituency (as in the local states) was the potent new force that put the regional system on the road to demise.

The Dutch East India Company did not accept the adaptive approach of fitting into the locally operating regional system. In fact, it moved to destroy the traditional Southeast Asian system in order to fit the remaining pieces into the European system. The company was able to operate virtually without limitation, except that of available power. The Dutch rejected the concept of state sovereignty in favor of the primacy of conquest and refused to acknowledge legitimate economic interests or needs in their drive for monopoly control.

Having established themselves as the most forceful actor in archipelagic Southeast Asia, the Dutch soon recognized that monopoly control of the Asia-to-Europe spice trade was probably not possible. More important, the spice trade could not generate enough profits to support the growing Dutch establishment in Southeast Asia. It became evident to Governor-General Coen that control of inter-Asian trade was the answer to this problem. Thus, in the second half of the seventeenth century, the Dutch completed the second step in the destruction of the Southeast Asian economic system by intervening in the Java-to-China trade and other commercial routes entirely within the region. By eliminating yet another segment of the indigenous economic system, the Dutch further ensured the fragmentation of political power, especially in the archipelago. As with the Portuguese, however, the Dutch seemed to reach the limit of their managerial capacities without creating new political forms or unity in the area.[38]

During the eighteenth and early nineteenth centuries, Southeast Asia was pulled farther from its traditional systemic economic framework. Such external events as the opening of the Suez Canal and the development of the steamship were critical in wedding Southeast Asia to the evolving global economic system. Materials such as tin and rubber replaced spices as the principal commodities sent from Southeast Asia to the industrializing world, and

Southeast Asia itself became more important as a market for basic consumer goods.

Within the region, the British moved to preeminence in control of the Southeast Asian economy. Although the Dutch built an empire on Java and the other islands under their control and exploited it as fully as possible for their own purposes, they were unable to match the free-trade system fostered by the British from Penang and later Singapore. Banking and investment became important in the region during the nineteenth century as industrialization began.

By the end of the nineteenth century, nearly every component of the regional economic system was controlled by Europeans or their Chinese or Indian surrogates. Important indigenous merchant groups and shipping interests had largely disappeared. In traditional Southeast Asian states, the commercial sector of the economy was very closely linked to the political system, and the domination of the economic sector only ensured the demise of the political sector. "Where there is gold," said the Babad Tanah Jawi, "there is sovereignty." When the gold disappeared, sovereignty fell as well. Although the European interlopers often used the local sultans to control the population while assigning a European "adviser" to direct the sultan's decisionmaking, the people recognized that the power, as well as the gold, now resided with the Europeans.

This chapter has focused on the movement of European colonial powers into the archipelagic region, where the spice trade first attracted the Europeans. The extension of colonial authority on the mainland was at first less intense but in the longer term no less destructive of the social, political, and economic fabric of the states there. The Japanese colonial venture before World War II--its "Greater East Asian Co-Prosperity Sphere"--brought the Western colonial period to an end; although the human disruption and suffering during that time were acute, there was little further disruption of the traditional system itself. The Japanese interregnum also provided a brief and not entirely positive stimulus for national independence.

The European intervention in the region thus effectively destroyed, in steps, the traditional interstate system of Southeast Asia. First, the Southeast Asian segment of the China-to-Europe trading system was disrupted, and the role of the indigenous political leaders and merchants was strangled through the monopoly practices of the Europeans. Then, having lost much of their economic base, the political elites throughout the region were undermined, and, eventually, the state system itself collapsed, as states disintegrated or were conquered, or, at the least, governments were left impotent. Third, the socioeconomic integrity of the subsistence agricultural sector in Southeast Asia, at first only minimally affected by changes in the international commercial sphere, was penetrated through the introduction of forced cultivation, plantation agriculture, the privatization of land, and other colonial production and social policies. Fourth, the colonial powers brought in and established alien groups, notably Chinese and Indians, in positions of economic power throughout the region. And, finally, the colonial powers furthered the overall regional economic and political fragmentation by developing intense economic dependencies on the respective colonial metropole while cutting off virtually all contact with other regional centers.

This, then, is the legacy that the former colonies inherited at independence. During the time since independence, much of this colonial heritage has been shed, at times slowly and painfully. But the emergent regional system, while as in the past adopting certain external elements from the colonial experience and elsewhere, has found its confidence in the recognition that it has a cultural, political, and economic heritage of its own that will ensure a regional identity unique in the global system.

NOTES

1. I. de Rachewiltz, Papal Envoys to the Great Khans (Stanford : Stanford University Press, 1971), pp. 180, 199, describes the trip of John of Marignolli and Odoric.

2. D.J.M. Tate, The Making of South-East Asia (London and Kuala Lumpur: Oxford University Press, 1979): The European Conquest, vol. 1, pp. 43-47.

3. S. Soebardi and C. P. Woodcroft-Lee, "Islam in Indonesia," in The Crescent in the East, edited by Raphael Isreali (London: Curzon Press, 1982), pp. 181, 183.

4. Tate, The Making of South-East Asia, vol. 1, p. 43.

5. John F. Cady, Southeast Asia: Its Historical Development (New York: McGraw-Hill, 1964), pp. 196-199.

134

6. Bernard H. M. Vlekke, Nusantara: A History of Indonesia (The Hague: W. van Hoeve, Ltd., 1965), pp. 113, 116.
7. Ibid., p. 199. (Emphasis added.)
8. Ibid., p. 130.
9. D.G.E. Hall, A History of South-East Asia (New York: St. Martin's Press, 1968), p. 331.
10. Cady, Southeast Asia, p. 213.
11. Ibid., p. 215.
12. George McT. Kahin, Nationalism and Revolution in Indonesia (Ithaca: Cornell University Press, 1952), p. 13.
13. Cady, Southeast Asia, p. 304.
14. John F. Cady, A History of Modern Burma (Ithaca: Cornell University Press, 1958), pp. 68-76.
15. Cady, Southeast Asia, pp. 281-284.
16. Roger M. Smith, "Cambodia," in Governments and Politics of Southeast Asia, edited by George McT. Kahin (Ithaca: Cornell University Press, 1964), p. 602.
17. Cady, Southeast Asia, p. 461.
18. Jan Pluvier, South-East Asia from Colonialism to Independence (Kuala Lumpur: Oxford University Press, 1974), p. 41.
19. Benedict R. O'C. Anderson, "Japan: The Light of Asia," in Southeast Asia in World War II: Four Essays, edited by Josef Silverstein (New Haven, Conn.: Yale University Southeast Asia Studies Monograph Series no. 7, 1966), p. 31.
20. Benjamin A. Batson, "Siam and Japan: The Perils of Independence," in Southeast Asia Under Japanese Occupation, edited by Alfred W. McCoy (New Haven, Conn.: Yale University Southeast Asia Studies Monograph Series no. 22, 1980), pp. 286-287.
21. Cheah Boon Kheng, "The Social Impact of the Japanese Occupation of Malaya (1942-1945)," in McCoy, Southeast Asia Under Japanese Occupation, p. 117.
22. Alfred W. McCoy, "Introduction," in McCoy, Southeast Asia Under Japanese Occupation, p. 7.
23. Jon M. Rienhardt, Foreign Policy and National Integration: The Case of Indonesia (New Haven, Conn.: Yale University Southeast Asia Studies Monograph no. 17, 1971), p. 28.
24. Harry J. Benda, The Crescent and the Rising Sun: Indonesian Islam Under the Japanese Occupation (The Hague: W. van Hoeve, Ltd., 1958), pp. 198-200.
25. M.A.P. Meilink-Roelofsz, Asian Trade and European Influence (The Hague: Martinus Nijhoff, 1962), p. 9.
26. Vlekke, Nusantara, p. 147.

27. Ibid., p. 153.

28. Ruth T. McVey, "Introduction," Southeast Asian Transitions: Approaches Through Social History, edited by Ruth T. McVey (New Haven, Conn.: Yale University Press, 1978), pp. 12-13.

29. For an interesting study in the contrasts between Europe and Asia at the time of the colonial expansion, see Joseph R. Levenson, European Expansion and the Counter-Example of Asia, 1300-1600 (Englewood Cliffs, N.J.: Prentice-Hall, 1967).

30. J. C. van Leur, Indonesian Trade and Society (The Hague: W. van Hoeve, Ltd., 1955), p. 170.

31. Ibid., pp. 164-165.

32. Ibid., p. 180.

33. Ibid., p. 181. Van Leur also notes (p. 170) that "Portuguese power was typically medieval" in that there was no distinction between civil and military administration and that the colonial stations were managed by a conglomeration of nobles and condottieri, each with a private retinue.

34. In systemic terms, it seems that local states were much more likely to seek protection from a European ally than to seek protection among themselves from the Europeans. The Dutch exploited this foible very effectively.

35. van Leur, Trade and Society, p. 183, citing T. H. Colenbrander and W. Ph. Coolhaas, eds., Jan Pietersz Coen: Bescheiden omtrent zijn befrijf in Indie [Jan Pietersz Coen: Documents Concerning His Activities in the Indies] (The Hague: no publisher given, 1919-1953): vol. 4, p. 134.

36. van Leur, Trade and Society, p. 164.

37. van Leur, Trade and Society, p. 177, where the author notes that corporate organizations such as the Dutch VOC were "national political creations . . . characteristic of the growing strength of the northwestern European states in the time."

38. Tate, The Making of Modern South-East Asia, vol. 1, p. 41.

CHAPTER 7

Traditional Values in Western Cloth: The State in the Contemporary Period

Early in the twentieth century, hostility toward Western domination began to surface in Southeast Asia. Fueled in part by increasingly destructive colonial exploitation and its concomitant social disruption, this hostility was circumspectly put in focus by small groups of intellectuals. Other factors, such as Islamic and Buddhist religious revivals, stimulated a more general awakening of anticolonial feelings throughout Asia,[1] and events such as the Japanese defeat of the Russians in 1905 contributed to the breakdown of the sense of European superiority. These hostile feelings resulted in rising expressions of nationalism in Southeast Asia as well as throughout Asia. However, in many countries nationalist feelings were slow to coalesce, inhibited as they were by ethnic and religious divisions and by poor communications. There was little in the experiences from either the traditional or colonial periods that effectively conditioned Southeast Asian society for full participation in the Western-model state.

BASES FOR POLITICAL COMMUNITY

The desire to be rid of colonial powers became widespread in Burma, Vietnam, the Philippines, Indonesia, and other countries, and this common goal sustained the nationalist independence movements in the face of colonial repression before World War II. It also gave the nationalist movements sufficient strength not only to survive the Japanese interregum but also to use it to advantage for pro-independence forces and to confront directly the returning colonial powers at the end of World

War II. With the close of the colonial period and the arrival of independence, however, great divisions and contradictions surfaced, often to the detriment of national development.

When the colonial powers retired, the common enemy that had united most local peoples disappeared, and latent animosities and suspicions resurfaced in regional politics. Guyot has pointed out that "the sudden elimination of the British role so wracked the prevailing role system as to create new and conflicting definitions of ethnic self for both Burmese and Karens."[2] Moreover, colonial divisions and boundaries made little sense in terms of the development of national identities. They divided common groups as often as they brought them together because the Europeans had "ignored local factors and introduced extraneous political considerations and alien concepts in the determination of colonial boundaries."[3] Few of the newly independent states in Southeast Asia were built on a geographically and ethnically homogeneous population. On the contrary, the geographic units inherited from colonial administrations had little historical rationale beyond the boundaries created by the colonial leaders that independence was designed to eliminate.[4] To the extent that traditional cultural and ethnic division crisscrossed or subdivided the new national boundaries, the development of national identity and national cohesion was further inhibited.[5] These crisscrossed loyalties have continued to make political cohesion a difficult problem. Because cultural and ethnic groups overlap so randomly, it has been difficult for any single group to impose its will, totally, on the state.[6]

Ethnicity and National Identity. Opposition to colonial authority had smoothed over many deep-seated differences among various factions in early movements toward independence, and after independence the growth of nationalism in Southeast Asia was even more slow and fragmented. Throughout the region, most of the traditional restrictions on the sense of political community remained muted but intact.[7] Ethnic, geographic, religious, and economic divisions limited the feeling of commonality among most of the peoples of Southeast Asia. The concepts of "national" identity that did emerge were heavily couched in ethnic feelings,[8] and smaller ethnic groups sometimes strongly opposed independence. They fought with colonial armies against independence movements led by different, larger ethnic groups, viewing the colonial authorities as protectors against discrimination or repression by major ethnic groups that would control any independent government. Even in those areas with an ethnic core within the new state--the Burmese in southern Burma, the Vietnamese in north and central Vietnam, and the Javanese in central and east Java of Indonesia--there had been no evolutionary development of a national consciousness linked to a political elite or a set of political institutions. The complex set of historical experiences that forged a national identity among peoples in other parts of the world did not operate in Southeast Asia because the traditional political elite, which might have led the region toward a "crystallization" of national consciousness, was emasculated or eliminated by the colonial powers.[9] It has been noted that availability of Bahasa Indonesian, a lingua franca based on local Malay dialects and formed as the commercial language of the region over several centuries but belonging to no major ethnic group in Indonesia, was of major importance in muting interethnic threats to state unity that might have accompanied the adoption, for example, of Javanese as the national language.[10] In Burma, Burmese is spoken by approximately two-thirds of the population, whereas Karen, Chin, and Kachin are spoken by the remaining third, who have resisted adopting the official Burmese. In the Philippines, the official language, Tagalog, is spoken by about one-quarter of the population while others speak several mutually unintelligible Malayo/Polynesian languages. Burma and the Philippines have been less successful in creating a national language than has Indonesia.[11] The ethnic animosities between the core group and smaller fringe ethnic groups had been insulated but preserved during the colonial era because there were few opportunities under colonial administration for these groups to work together and know each other.[12] What became a national identity for the core group seemed like oppression to minority groups. In Malaysia, for instance, there were few nationalist tendencies among ethnic Malays before World War II.[13]

Thailand is an exception in that its government was not destroyed through the intervention of any colonial power; at the same time, however, it did not experience even the limited growth of national consciousness resulting from opposition to colonial masters. Vietnam, despite the deep ideological divisions between Communist and non-Communist groups, may also be an exception given that its sense of nationalism, "deep-rooted in the xenophobia of the people, arose from recognition of the difference between being Vietnamese and not being Chinese, French, or American." Thus in a simple way, and recognizing that many colloquial feelings remain for the Vietnamese as in other parts of Southeast Asia, "every Vietnamese is a nationalist whatever his politics, social status, or education."[14]

The Village Sphere. The traditional political system, of which the village sphere was the core,[15] had functioned more or less effectively in Southeast Asia for a thousand years or more because it met the basic needs of the largest social group--the peasant population of villagers. Above the village level, the traditional political system was weak and subject to some manipulation and exploitation. Within the village, carefully delineated social norms provided for the social welfare of its members.[16] The social fiber of the village was strong enough that there was little need for a powerful central authority. The traditional political system, though based on mystic and supernatural views of power, provided an internally coherent system for sustaining village autonomy while protecting the village from superior external force.

The traditional social cohesion of the village and its closed economic nature made it an easy target for colonial exploitation. The colonial authorities manipulated, bribed, or otherwise co-opted village chiefs in an effort to achieve colonial production goals. The position and authority of the chief were enhanced in the colonial system but traditional social reciprocity was shattered;[17] consequently, the villages' interlocking social and economic welfare systems broke down.[18] Such economic manipulation was profitable for the colonial powers but devastating for the village population. For example, in Cochin-China under the French, widespread land alienation reduced two-thirds of the farm population to tenancy,[19] whereas in the 1850s Dutch policies resulted in famine in East and Central Java.[20] But the most devastating impact on village society was disjunction and disruption of the set of social norms and balanced social structures.[21]

Colonial intrusions disrupted the structures of village authority, generally strengthening authority in the legal context while weakening its sociological responsibilities. Although the primary social penetration through colonialism was indirect, colonial political disruption and pervasive economic penetration of Southeast Asia's traditional sociopolitical structures changed population patterns and undermined social relations. Despite the coming of independence, the village could not resume fully its traditionally autonomous economic position, nor could it sustain its role as prime social-welfare unit for the rural population. In essence, the colonial powers broke the continuity of the traditional state and provided no philosophical or ideological "whole" in its place. Moreover, by manipulating production goals of the village, they had destroyed the historical balance between the individual, the land, and social welfare.[22]

The Urban Elite. Education, which might have helped to develop common bonds among Southeast Asians through the 300 years of colonial domination, was, under most colonial regimes, reserved for only a very small minority of the indigenous population. The educational experience of many individuals in this elite group awakened their nationalist pride and desire for independence but also separated them from the masses of their own peoples. Many sought Western education as a means of escaping the poverty of rural areas; in the process they also "escaped" contact with the concerns of their potential constituencies. The nationalism that developed under their leadership was an urban, educated, and largely westernized phenomenon that inspired relatively little support among the mass of rural, uneducated, and poor peoples.

The social dichotomy between the court and peasant spheres of the traditional era was replicated in the contemporary period in the division between the urban/westernized sphere and a traditional peasant sphere. The new states of Southeast Asia were urban oriented (especially in relation to the capital city), not unlike the kingdoms of the traditional era, but the new elites had more in common with the former colonial powers than with their rural peasant constituencies: "Elite members tend to look outward for their behavioral models and their guiding values."[23] The new urban elites did not and could not lay claim to the Indianized concepts of authority and legitimacy; as McVey has pointed out, "Western education and ideas had undermined indigenous ones," but the new leaders who did not have traditional claims to rule "were not interested in restoring the old

ideological system."[24] Yet, at the same time, they were
unable to define a national alternative that met the needs
for a modern nation-state while inculcating indigenous
values so as to distinguish the Southeast Asian state (in
a modern Indonesian, Burmese, or other form) from alien,
purely Western models and to draw in the mass of still
highly traditional peasants.

The political leadership that emerged in these
systems, even where democratic institutions functioned,
was not representative in a popular sense but
paternalistic:

> Post colonial experience has, if anything,
> enhanced the attractiveness of strong, paternalistic
> rule. The Westernized elite holds a virtual monopoly
> on the education, technical skills, and experience
> necessary to run a modern state. Furthermore, the
> traditional masses for the most part look to the
> Westernized elites with their knowledge and
> organizational skills for leadership. It is not a
> question of the educated elites usurping the role of
> traditional leaders; popular acceptance of, and
> deference to, the Westernized elites--particularly
> civil servants--is the rule rather than the
> exception.[25]

These national elites, true to their Western
educational values, led their states to independence, and
many adopted various forms of parliamentary democracy.
Vietnam, while not espousing liberal democratic theory,
paradoxically adopted an equally Western but Communist
model. However, as the mass base appeared unable to cope
with the rigorous demands of political participation, the
elite responded by "drawing all political resources to the
top."[26] The timing of this process varied throughout
the region but has generally followed a pattern of
transition from parliamentary government, to charismatic
leadership, to bureaucratic/military government; however,
the elites have been drawn from a shrinking political
base, and leaders of lesser and differing political goals
have been blocked or eliminated. Through all of this,
elite communication with the mass peasant base of the
state has remained limited. Although Western-educated
technocrats have taken the reins of government, their
world remains defined by a population (not unlike the
population of the traditional era) that does not
participate actively in the political system and places

only broad limits on the use of power, which "traditionally has been more personal than public, more symbolic than utilitarian, more reserved than purposeful, and above all more a matter of status than of programs and activity."[27] The contemporary political elites have, with few exceptions, not violated these traditional prescriptions, and even in Vietnam where its ideology provides for mass participation, power has essentially accrued to the party elite in Hanoi.

Legitimacy and National Cohesion. National cohesion has remained difficult to establish because of the lack of political community and the ad hoc geographic nature of these states. Diverse ethnic and religious groups brought together under colonial authority have frequently attempted to reassert their individual identities once the colonial power departed. Political loyalties remained focused on the local clan or ethnic level. The concept of political loyalty to the state, having neither traditional precedent nor colonial model, has been difficult to sustain. In the traditional state such minority groups would not have presented a significant problem, especially if they were located on the fringes of the kingdom. For the new state, however, established on the concepts of complete sovereignty within its borders, such divisiveness and lack of control are unacceptable. The state has been defined in the Western political context of sovereignty, territory, authority, and representation; however, the reality has been a reemergence of local political concepts in which sovereignty and territory are relative to available power, authority is focused on personal leadership at the center of the state, and representation in a popular sense finds little support.

A degree of national cohesion had developed during the revolutionary struggles against the colonial powers, when the urgency of the conflict made it possible to subordinate many differences. However, the mythology, or ideology, of independence was built on unobtainable promises of economic well-being as well as political independence. The failure to achieve the utopian expectations created by independence rhetoric fed the ethnic suspicions that have surfaced during the postindependence years as the enormity of each state's economic and social needs as well as its lack of political capability became apparent.

Much of the confusion in the rhetoric of independence resulted from the gap between the mass of the peasant population and the urban nationalist elite. The village, though its social fabric was damaged by the colonial experience, retained its position as the primary locus of loyalty for the bulk of the Southeast Asian population,[28] and the parochial and uneducated villagers maintained many of their traditional values and goals for life.[29] Above the village level, the clan or ethnic group also remained intact as a focal point for self-identity and loyalty. Tenuous though the traditional, mythical Hindu link between court and village had been, its philosophical underpinnings were broadly understood and accepted. However, the contemporary elite--Western educated and urban oriented as it was--developed no such bond with the village population. The goals and aspirations of this elite group were heavily influenced by their Western educations and their adopted world cultural views.[30] The social and political gap that resulted became increasingly obvious after independence as the new governments defined and implemented policies designed to turn into reality the rhetoric of independence. But this independence rhetoric--employing such concepts as democracy, social welfare, political parties, elections, parliament, public services, and education--often confused rather than enlightened the population because the concepts had little meaning in either the traditional or the colonial experience. Political representation--in which a vote implied a link between the official and the electorate, and the official accepted a measure of responsibility for his constituents--had no precedent in Southeast Asia.[31] The concepts of Western democracy articulated by the elites could not provide a rationale for operating the newly independent states until and unless these concepts became understood, agreed upon, and adapted in a system in which a balance of responsibilities and obligations in a social contract met the basic needs of the people. Nevertheless, the new states of Southeast Asia obtained sovereign status but could not develop the national cohesion to support that status.[32]

THE STATE SINCE INDEPENDENCE

The newly independent states of Southeast Asia were created as successors to colonial territories constructed over three centuries in pursuit of a wide range of economic, religious, and strategic goals essentially established in Europe. This process joined peoples never previously part of one political unit, while in other instances a single people were divided across arbitrary colonial boundaries. The new states of Indonesia, Malaysia, Singapore, and the Philippines had no historical precedent as political units, notwithstanding the eloquence of certain traditional histories and chronicles that implied otherwise.[33] Indonesia and Malaysia combined a number of previously independent or autonomous chiefdoms, sultanates, kingdoms, and peoples. On the other hand, Burma, Thailand, Cambodia, Laos, and Vietnam, although they had long historical traditions as independent polities, found that their postindependence boundaries included areas and ethnic groups not previously within their domain.

The colonial powers broke down the traditional system but were unable to introduce an effective alternative. Initially, they attacked the central authority of the state. In some cases, the king, sultan, or chief and his court were physically eliminated and replaced by a colonial governor. In other cases, the ruler remained in place but was controlled by a colonial "adviser." The effect was the same--the official was no longer subject to the social restraints inherent in the traditional system because his authority was buttressed by the external colonial power.[34]

The colonial authorities introduced more effective uses of coercion than had been common in the traditional system. Their policies and decisions were planned to expand the profits for the metropole, and colonial administrators showed little concern or understanding of the sociopolitical systems under their control. However, the colonial experience also did much to reinforce the traditional view that "government was the center of all life, that its officials were the elite of all society, that its authority was omnipotent, and that there should be no limits to the concerns or interests of those in power."[35] Under the aegis of the colonial powers, new and far more efficient governmental practices were introduced.[36]

The postindependence government leaders faced an impossible task of education and mobilization if, indeed, they were to stimulate and sustain mass participation in the political system. For the most part, this approach was ultimately rejected in favor of a more traditional, center-oriented, bureaucratic style of government. This bureaucratic approach, in fact, had the sanction of both the traditional and the colonial systems, and it came close to allowing the village sphere to retain or return to its traditional autonomy.

The dichotomous division of Southeast Asian society did not change during the transition from the traditional period to the colonial period, nor has it changed in the contemporary period. At the macro level, continuity has been maintained in the layering of the governmental structures on top of the societal base, as contrasted with the polity in which governmental structures grow from within the society itself. Even in Thailand, the governmental reforms of 1932 and earlier essentially made the bureaucracy "the inheritor of royal authority" and ensured the "continuation of the bureaucratic system under its own leaders--senior military officers and civilian officials--rather than under kings and princes."[37] As was noted in a case study of Brunei, "indigenous structural forms persist into the present" but now include many added features; furthermore, the addition of new forms has been accompanied by an "extensive transfer of content from the old forms to the new forms."[38] As a result, authority continues to be derived from above, reinforced by the strong traditional propensity for personalized authority and bureaucratic management. The traditional polity, though mystical in its legitimacy, was bureaucratic in form, and the colonial regimes used effective force and bureaucratic control to dispense with required legitimacy. Contemporary governments, on the other hand, have combined the more effective techniques of the colonial regimes with some traditional forms of legitimation (adding also contemporary national concepts of legitimacy)--the product being a refined bureaucratic governmental structure.

Bureaucracy and the Bureaucratic Polity. Bureaucracy has been variously defined but generally identified as pertaining to institutions made up of public officials, sometimes focusing on the higher levels of policymakers and at other times focusing on the lowest-level village workers.[39] Weber has described the following characteristics associated with the "pure type" of bureaucratic administration:

1. The administrators are personally free and subject to authority only in the sphere of official obligations;
2. Officers are organized in a clearly defined hierarchy;

3. Each office has a defined area of competence and legal responsibility;
4. Offices are filled by free contractual relationship;
5. Officer selection is on the basis of technical competence, and officers are appointed, not elected;
6. Remuneration is fixed on a graded scale and rights of termination are protected;
7. The duties of office are the primary occupation of the incumbent, and this constitutes a career position;
8. The officer works without ownership of the means of administration and without appropriation of appointed positions; and
9. The officer is subject to systematic discipline and control.[40]

The bureaucratic polity has been distinguished from other types of polities "by the degree to which national decisionmaking is insulated from social and political forces outside the highest elite echelons of the capital city."[41] In addition, Riggs has noted that this type of polity is distinguished by the fact that the bureaucracy is not under effective control of any extrabureaucratic institutions.[42]

The governments in Southeast Asia have achieved this level of institutional insulation by relying on the power capacities that were increased by colonial techniques as well as on the inertia of their populations. Factors such as popular deference to authority, reinforced by the educational advantage of the bureacratic elite, have strengthened the position of the bureaucracy in the political system.[43] Furthermore, the Southeast Asian bureaucracies are concerned with protecting and promoting their own values such as social status, hierarchical authority structures, and personal leadership and patronage.[44] Bureaucratic control has been a protector of the status quo in government and society, satisfying, for various reasons, much of the aspiring elite as well as fulfilling the peasants' traditional expectations of typical government behavior. However, bureaucratic administration in Southeast Asia has not followed Weber's pure type in several critical respects:

1. Administrators have not been free from outside authority, as patron-client relations have been and remain critical in gaining and keeping positions;

2-3.   The hierarchy of offices has had little impact on performance, and responsibilities have frequently not been defined;

4-5.   Offices have often been filled with political appointees and relatives of high officials;

6-7.   Remuneration may be fixed, but it has often been so low as to require officers to take additional jobs;

8-9.   Officers have seldom been disciplined and can often use their contacts and influence to circumvent regulations and control.

Education and training over the period since independence have done much to alter the negative consequences of some of these bureaucratic problems. Nevertheless, the processes of "neotraditionalization" rendered the forms and procedures of bureaucratic organization and behavior not so much Weberian as Southeast Asian in character.

Structure and Function in the Bureaucratic System. The structures of the state were among the most obvious legacies of the colonial experience. The traditional structure of kingdoms, based on mythology and cosmology, was replaced by the functional ministries typical of most European states. Thailand began this replacement process well ahead of others in the nineteenth century.[45] Other traditional states, such as Aceh, developed some functional bureaucratic structures, but continued "arbitrariness of such exactions from merchants, and the total dependence of officials on royal favor,"[46] meant that a transition to rational bureaucratic forms had not generally taken place in Southeast Asia at the time of the colonial penetration.

The term functional bureaucratic structures is misleading. As a result of traditional cultural characteristics such as deference to authority, the propensity toward form and status over substance, and certain forms of nepotism, combined with poor training and limited or nonexistent supplies and support systems, these bureaucracies have often become refuges for underemployed officials rather than functional governmental structures.[47] This bureaucratic weakness was more acute in foreign affairs than in other fields: Knowledge and experience were scant; little information was provided by the unpracticed foreign service staff sent abroad; policy positions and personal convictions were often blurred; and officials were highly sensitive to any foreign pressure. Most of the new states opened full embassies in only a few selected states and were forced by lack of staff or funds to accredit their representatives to more than one state.[48] However, even when Western institutions have been overtly adopted, their functioning has been governed by indigenous interpretations of purpose and action.

The bureaucratic nature of government in contemporary Southeast Asia is indicative of the coming together or reemergence and blending of traditional and contemporary political thought and structures. The Southeast Asian regimes have retained elements of traditional, charismatic, or personalistic rule as exemplified, in particular, by the earlier leadership styles of U Nu, Sukarno, and Sihanouk. Although the regimes under these men were not as personalistic as the traditional kingdoms and sultanates, the styles of leadership developed by each of them brought to the fore many traditional patterns of behavior. Yet the bureaucratic limits to such personalistic rule were demonstrated in the ultimate downfall of each of these men. Another clear demonstration of government by bureaucracy has been the management system evolving in Vietnam since the death of Ho Chi Minh. It is the bureaucracy and the maintenance of state power that this system has engendered which defines the contemporary polity in Southeast Asia.[49]

Military/Bureaucratic Systems. As with early experimentations of democratic governmental forms, charismatic leaders such as Sukarno, lacking the Hindu and other religious or mythological bases for legitimacy, were unable to shape politically cohesive polities against the pressures toward fragmentation emanating from ethnic, economic, cultural, and religious cleavages. As the consensus derived from personal leadership dissipated, alternatives had to be found. The civilian political leadership was discredited because it came to represent cultural and economic fragmentation and to symbolize indecision and inaction. There was a propensity in some states to move toward military/bureaucratic alliances. In Thailand, Burma, Cambodia, and Indonesia, the military intervened directly in the political system largely because there was no alternative, short of revolution: "Doubt, division, and opportunism among elites often accompany alterations of national institutions in the absence of an overriding imperative, and . . . the resulting illegitimacy and instability of the government increase the risk of interventions by military officers in the interest of stability, law, and order."[50] Indeed, Some writers have noted an almost inevitable trend over the fixed span of time during which disillusionment with civilian leadership sets in and a military coup of some type follows.[51] Perhaps the most common theme among analysts of military intervention in Third World states has been the argument that such intervention is caused by the inability of the civilian politicians to govern.

The concept of the military as an "interventionist" agent or as an aberration of "normal" civilian politics may grow largely out of the biases of Western writers, who frequently perceive the democratic political model as the ideal type toward which all civilizations strive.[52] Hoadley has argued that military interventions do not take place where governments are "led by a cohesive group of purposeful civilian elites," but that the breakdown among civilian politicians of "either cohesion or purpose leaves a leadership vacuum into which military officers march."[53] Huntington supports this interventionist argument, noting that the principal cause of military intervention in politics is "not the social and organizational characteristics of the military establishment but the political and institutional structure of the society."[54]

In Southeast Asia, however, it is not so much the failure of the postindependence democratic political and institutional structures that ensures the intervention of the military as the lack of a political or institutional history prohibiting such involvement--as compared with the Western polities, in which separation of military and civilian political power and subordination of military authority to civilian governmental authority are institutionalized. In Southeast Asia, there appears to be little difference in outlook between civilian and military elites, as the military elite is closely linked "with the members of the elite's cosmopolitan mainstream."[55] The traditional authority of a king, sultan, or chief in Southeast Asia was directly linked to his personal ability to field a military force, and, although the king's power in reality was inhibited by the weakness of the system, there were no institutionalized taboos against the expansion or this use of power if and when a "better" form of power became available. In this context, the colonial regimes provided the "better mousetrap," introducing new concepts of command structures and organization as well as the concept of the professional military. They did not (or could not) impart the concept of the subordination of the military to civilian authority. The concept of direct military involvement in politics gained additional legitimacy through the various revolutionary experiences against the British, French, and Dutch--in Vietnam, Burma, and Indonesia, especially, the army was the revolution. In Southeast Asia's societal context, given the abandonment of traditional religious bases of legitimacy, claims of participation in the revolution eventually became potent forms of legitimacy, where Western concepts such as representation and civilian predominance in politics were weak. In fact, in countries such as Indonesia and Burma, the military exploits of their revolutions harked back to the romanticized military campaigns described in the traditional chronicles, giving the contemporary governments a legitimacy that could be understood in traditional terms.

The military's involvement in politics was not an aberration; rather, it was tied to the reemergence of political structures basically compatible, or at least not incompatible, with the history and tradition of the region. In this context, the civilian governments of Malaysia, Singapore, and the Philippines are exceptions. Vietnam may also be an exception, but its unique situation of nearly three decades of continuing warfare make it difficult to establish with certainty the primacy of civilian and party rule. It may be that the military preoccupation with war in Vietnam and now Indochina--fighting the French, American, Khmer Rouge, and Cambodian rebels in succession--has distracted the Vietnamese military from any possible involvement in domestic politics.

The distinction between the Western philosophy of appropriate military behavior and that extant in Southeast Asia brings into focus the depth of the cultural difference involved. The perspective of Southeast Asian military officers has been summarized by Sundhaussen, whose views reflect those of Abdul Haris Nasution, one of the leading military thinkers in Indonesia and Southeast Asia: "The army should not be seen as trying to dominate the country, but as a social-political group entitled to play a role as one of the forces determining and executing national policies."[56] Woodside has noted, referring to Vietnam, that "it was in the crucible of the 'people's war' that East Asian tradition and Western political theories finally did complete their joint production of a new kind of populist egalitarianism."[57] But it is by no means clear that populism, even in Vietnam, will determine the nature of military politics in Southeast Asia. The evidence would suggest, instead, that military politics will feature a form of bureaucratic traditionalism that continues the division of society into two groups--a small governmental elite and the uninvolved mass of the population. The direct involvement of the military in the political system has gained its clearest statement from the Indonesian experience in which, following the revolution, the army defined "dual functions" for itself: (1) "military force," as in the traditional role of protecting the state from external (and later also internal) attack, and (2) "social and political force" arising from the need to protect the ideological, political, social, economic, cultural, and religious underpinnings of the revolution.[58]

The growth of military/bureaucratic polities further limits access to decisionmaking in the bureaucratic polity because of the distinctions and restrictions placed on civilian bureaucrats. In Indonesia, the group known as "technocrats" exists largely at the behest of their military patrons, although the latter recognize that these technocrats are necessary in order to satisfy major assistance and donor agencies. In Thailand, by contrast, there is a greater and more recognizable division of labor between military and civilian bureaucracies.[59] Burma's military bureaucrats fill supervisory and oversight roles throughout the bureaucracy. In addition, the military/bureaucratic polity has a propensity to extend its control into commercial and business activities, through partnerships and joint ventures with local or international commercial interests. In Burma, this control has taken the form of nationalization of most commercial establishments and the elimination of Chinese and Indian business interests in the name of developing a socialist program. In other states, private business interests have been co-opted in those instances when the typical partner from the bureaucracy provides contacts and access to the bureaucracy itself, while the partner from the private sector provides the capital and business management expertise. In this way, political power has become a tool for claiming economic power, and economic power becomes a tool for sustaining political power. Moreover, the penetration of the bureaucracy into nongovernmental sectors has eliminated the possibility for autonomous development of major economic/political groups outside the control of the bureaucracy. The bureaucracy, having thus co-opted the economic sector, its primary goal--and that of its business cohorts--becomes the maintenance of its power and interests.[60]

Traditionalism and the State. Other elements of traditional state practices have reemerged in the contemporary period. Although there are exceptions and variations, the states of Southeast Asia are in many respects traditional in both domestic and international outlooks. The capital city is still the locus of political activity, and the new states are primarily resource extractive and nonwelfare oriented. Moreover, the lack of bureaucratic responsiveness to popular demands and needs is sustained, as in South Vietnam but also elsewhere, because "neither the survival of the civil service nor the tenure of its officials is affected by such demands."[61] Although the bureaucratic idea of "public service" is acknowledged, the focus of the service is the government itself and not the general population. This emphasis on service to the government as as end in itself has roots deep in Asian culture: "Asia's peasants . . . have long identified government with the tax collector and the oppressor, friend and protector of money-lender and landlord."[62] Bureaucratic structures and methods established before and during the colonial period and refined since, whether military of civilian, reinforce the traditional extractive nature of the state in Southeast Asia.

Only Singapore has developed policies for a basic welfare state with programs in subsidized housing and other health and social services. But even Singapore has been characterized as an "administrative state" in which the "fusion of professional party leaders with leading elements of the bureaucracy . . . and its 'neo-Confucianist' ethos [are] entirely compatible with bureaucratic values."[63] Vietnam carried out major social reorganizations in the North, but years of war have drained resources, made welfare programs impossible, and preserved the extractive orientation prevalent elsewhere in the region. Burma also embarked on an ideological road that stressed social reorganization, but it provided little in the way of a welfare "return."

At independence, the typical extractive pattern of state organization was evident in Indonesia, Thailand, Malaysia, and the Philippines, where political systems were dominated by ethnic, educational, family, or other elites. Economic systems tended to be controlled by resident Chinese, often with close links to the political elite. Concomitantly, there was little participation by the general populations in either the political or economic systems. Elections were held but the ability of the masses to influence the political system through voting or other means (save occasional violence, perhaps) was limited. Agricultural production--the primary economic activity of all of the states--remained in the hands of the peasants, but their limited access to land, capital and markets guaranteed continued domination of the economic system by outsiders. External capital in the form of foreign investment or development assistance was available, but investments seemed to reinforce the positions of the economic and political elite; development assistance, on the other hand, achieved success only in isolated contexts, with little overall impact on the quality of life among the rural poor.

In both Burma and Vietnam, ideology replaced metaphysics as the basic legitimizing mechanism for the state. Most of the other states in Southeast Asia have relied upon variations of an economic development theme as important elements of legitimization. However, whether Communist ideology or economic development provided the state's philosophical base, the extractive nature of the state throughout Southeast Asia ensured very little change in its urban orientation.

The traditional centrist structure of the state was evident in the actions and policies of the governments. The capital city remained "where the action is." Provincial military and government assignments were often used as political punishments, while ambassadorships to small, distant, unimportant states became a convenient way to "exile" political competitors. Burma has not allowed dependents to accompany diplomats and other travelers abroad--a policy reminiscent of the traditional system of retaining hostages in the capital to ensure the loyalty of retainers and officials.[64]

In the postindependence years, the urban orientation of the elite grew more acute, until, for example, many political parties became essentially urban cliques, having little beyond their revolutionary heritage to offer to rural peasants. The political elites have held only minimal understanding of the peasant agricultural base upon which their systems rest and have often initiated government policies that insulate the rural population from the outside world to the extent possible. The single exception to this trend was the leadership of Communist

parties in Vietnam and elsewhere, as Marxism came to stand
essentially for land reform, and its proponents spoke out
against the corruption and materialism of the westernized
urban elite. In Vietnam, the Viet-Minh worked to ensure
support among the rural population because they were
"convinced of the value of their own cause" and because
they had found a "population which, after decades of
disorientation, was predisposed to change."[65] In a
similar way, the Communist party in Indonesia, before its
destruction in 1965-1966, claimed a membership in excess
of 3 million people in the party and a "web of mass
organizations including 15 million members."[66] Scholars
have warned that the lack of effective representation of
the interests that these parties succeeded in
mobilizing--particularly the interests of the
peasantry--can become a source of serious instability,[67]
but the peasants have endured because their expectations
of responsiveness from the government, drawn from the
still traditional political culture, remain low or
nonexistent.

In the centrist systems just described, the extension
of power from national to international contexts was
blurred. Because the geographic boundaries of each of
these states were established by colonial fiat with little
or no consideration of national identity, the geographic
extension of the states' authority has rarely equaled the
territories shown on maps. The ability of the centrist
states to extend their authority outward from the capital
depends on their military capabilities, the remoteness of
the areas in question, the infrastructural developments,
the loyalties of the local populations, and the capacities
of competing sources of authority. One or more of these
limiting factors was evident in some border region of
every state in Southeast Asia.

Another aspect of the urban orientation that harked
back to traditional Southeast Asia was the direction of
power--from the center toward the borders of the state.
In large part because of the deep ethnic divisions within
each of the newly independent states and also,
coincidentally, because many of these ethnic splinter
groups inhabited border regions, every Southeast Asian
state has had difficulties in maintaining its borders and
its authority throughout its territory. In Burma, for
example, the Shan and Karen areas constitute nearly
separate states in which taxes are collected, law and
order are maintained, and authority is exercised outside
the realm of the government in Rangoon. In Thailand,

Laos, and Cambodia, the Lao peoples on both sides of the Mekong continue to view the river as an artery of communications rather than a border. The Muslim separatists represent a problem for the Philippines, and Indonesia, although relatively stable in recent decades, experienced separatist resistence in Sumatra as well as in the eastern islands. For years, Sihanouk preserved peace and independence for Cambodia by the de facto concession of large parts of Cambodia to Vietnamese control,[68] but by the 1980s the Vietnamese had deposed the Khmer Rouge Communists, who sought to reassert Cambodian control over these border regions, installed a client government in Cambodia, and were rumored to have begun colonization throughout the country.[69]

Because the state is not secure in its own territory, and because most of the territorial claims were subject to challenge on ethnic, ideologic, economic, or other grounds, the concept of sovereignty (coupled with territorial security) of the state remains weak. The contemporary states have all accepted the standard Western concept of fixed and clearly demarcated borders, although they have not always accepted the borders as drawn. However, the traditional concept of fluid frontiers and borders remains extant in many areas of Southeast Asia because the centrist state does not have the capacity to extend its authority fully to the officially recognized border. When this lack of capacity exists at the same time in neighboring states, the frontier may become a buffer zone overlapping the border on both sides. This is commonly the case when a river--in traditional times the central artery for communications--becomes a political dividing line for an ethnic or cultural group living astride that river. When this local ethnic group has sufficient capacity, it may organize its own "polity," with local guerrilla or traditional clan practices filling regulatory needs. In other cases, when one state has more power than its neighbor, the more powerful state may extend its authority beyond the official border.

The lack of ethnic cohesion and the related limits to territorial integrity have a direct impact on the ability of the state to conduct its foreign policy. Enloe has pointed out that among such fragmented states there are clear patterns indicating that these problems (1) induce greater dependence on foreign powers--especially for military and economic assistance; (2) provide opportunities for other powers to interfere in the domestic political arena--especially in the border areas occupied by ethnic splinter groups; and (3) forestall intraregional cooperation because the national leadership is not sufficiently secure within its own political and territorial base.[70]

THE CONTEMPORARY STATE

The states of Southeast Asia (see Map 7.1, following) survived the pains of independence and outlived the disillusionment of unmet expectations. Pre-independence hopes did not come to fruition, but neither did these states collapse upon themselves. Burma has shown that a Southeast Asian state can survive alone; Vietnam has demonstrated that a Southeast Asian state can outlast, if not defeat, a superpower; and Malaysia and Singapore have demonstrated that states can survive without revolutionary fervor.

Now entering their fourth decade of independence, these states exhibit increased confidence. Although their methods and organization may not find approval or understanding in the West, their neotraditional approaches to government are a statement that Southeast Asians have rediscovered and reasserted an indigenous identity. The tenacity of traditional patterns of behavior within the domestic context is visible in the structures and the functioning of government as well as in policy prescriptions. This is not to argue against change, however--for change is everywhere in Southeast Asia. Rather, change has taken place only as new patterns of behavior and institutions have been adopted by Southeast Asians, and this has happened only in the framework of their historical and cultural understandings. With the passage of time, the response to change has more consistently been defined in indigenous terms, even where Western concepts may be applied.

Nor is the emergency of the indigenous an assurance of success. Problems remain, and there is uncertainty over how or whether the governments of Southeast Asia can solve them. They face continuing challenges from population growth and from the continued destruction of precapitalist social formations. The established elites have become more firmly entrenched, despite some expansion of the middle class, and incipient mass protests have been met with greater political repression.[71] The state, while ostensibly lacking many of the finer points of Western political organization, has been redefined in its historical context and must now develop for itself a

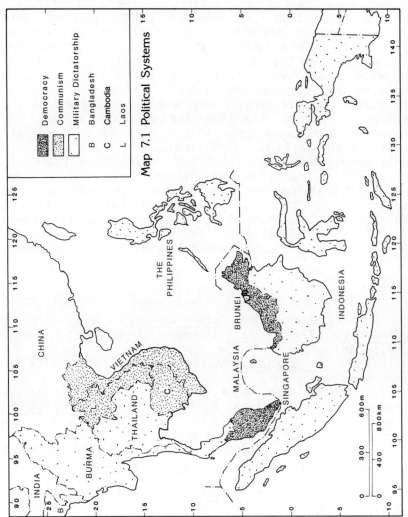

Map 7.1 Political Systems

From Ashok K. Dutt, *Southeast Asia: Realm of Contrasts*, 3d rev. ed. (Boulder, CO: Westview Press, 1985), p. 2. Used by permission.

formula for growth and development that uses this historical context to advantage.

The Southeast Asian tradition tends toward acceptance or acquiescence to the existing governors in the seat of power; popular legitimacy has historically been weak. Currently, as well, most states derive much of their legitimacy through acquiescence, but whether this situation can be sustained indefinitely is not certain. In fact, it appears likely that education, both formal and informal through the global spread of ideas, will continue to erode local identification with the village and clan and turn the attention of the individual more directly to the state. As ever larger numbers of Southeast Asians are exposed to formal education and external values, the challenges confronting the elites will be to integrate these new forces (i.e., both people and ideas) adaptively while maintaining a cultural and political unity.[72] In the short run, education remains largely an elite luxury, and the training reaching broader segments of the population is largely technical in nature. But as education in the more liberal sense penetrates these societies, the elites will find it necessary to broaden the sense of participation and belonging in these systems.

NOTES

1. Jan Romein, The Asian Century: A History of Modern Nationalism in Asia (London: George Allen & Unwin, 1962); and Fred R. von der Mehden, Religion and Nationalism in Southeast Asia (Madison: University of Wisconsin Press, 1968).

2. Dorothy Hess Guyot, "Communal Conflict in the Burma Delta," in Southeast Asian Transitions: Approaches Through Social History, edited by Ruth T. McVey (New Haven, Conn.: Yale University Press, 1978), p. 195.

3. Robert L. Solomon, "Boundary Concepts and Practices in Southeast Asia," World Politics 23 (October 1970), p. 7.

4. Lee Yong Leng, Southeast Asia: Essays in Political Geography (Singapore: Singapore University Press, 1982), pp. 1-32.

5. Cynthia Enloe, "Ethnic Diversity," in Diversity and Development in Southeast Asia, edited by Guy J. Pauker, Frank H. Golay, and Cynthia H. Enloe (New York: McGraw-Hill, 1977).

6. Donald K. Emmerson, Indonesia's Elite: Political Culture and Cultural Politics (Ithaca: Cornell University Press, 1976), p. 223.
7. Guyot, "Communal Conflict in the Burma Delta," in McVey, Southeast Asian Transitions, p. 195.
8. R. K. Dentan, "Ethnics and Ethics in Southeast Asia," in Changing Identities in Modern Southeast Asia, edited by David J. Banks (The Hague: Mouton Publishers, 1976), pp. 70-81.
9. Guy J. Pauker, "National Politics and Regional Powers," in Pauker et al., Diversity and Development in Southeast Asia, p. 20.
10. Emmerson, Indonesia's Elite, pp. 223-224.
11. Peter Lyon, War and Peace in South-East Asia (London: Oxford University Press, 1969), pp. 45, 49.
12. Lee, Southeast Asia: Essays in Political Geography, pp. 123-142.
13. William R. Roff, The Origins of Malay Nationalism (New Haven, Conn.: Yale University Press, 1967).
14. Lyon, War and Peace in South-East Asia, p. 68.
15. See Chapter 3 of this book.
16. James C. Scott, The Moral Economy of the Peasant: Rebellion and Subsistence in Southeast Asia (New Haven, Conn.: Yale University Press, 1976). For a competing view that stresses the individual initiative of the peasant in contrast to the group-cooperative perspective, see Samuel L. Popkin, The Rational Peasant: The Political Economy of Rural Society in Vietnam (Berkeley: University of California Press, 1979).
17. Ruth T. McVey, "Introduction," in McVey, Southeast Asian Transitions, p. 14.
18. Scott, The Moral Economy of the Peasant, p. 7 and passim.
19. D.J.M. Tate, The Making of Modern South-East Asia (London and Kuala Lumpur: Oxford University Press, 1979): The Western Impact: Economic and Social Change, vol. 2, p. 317.
20. John F. Cady, Southeast Asia: Its Historical Development (New York: McGraw-Hill, 1964), p. 364.
21. J. S. Furnivall, Colonial Policy and Practice: A Comparative Study of Burma and Netherlands Indies (New York: New York University Press, 1956), p. 318.
22. Ibid., pp. 468-512.
23. R. William Liddle, Ethnicity, Party, and National Integration (New Haven, Conn.: Yale University Press, 1970), p. 206.

160

24. McVey, "Introduction," in McVey, Southeast Asian Transitions, p. 27.

25. James C. Scott, Political Ideology in Malaysia: Reality and the Beliefs of an Elite (New Haven, Conn.: Yale University Press, 1968), p. 251.

26. McVey, "Introduction," in McVey, Southeast Asian Transitions, p. 27.

27. Karl D. Jackson, "The Political Implications of Structure and Culture in Indonesia," in Political Power and Communications in Indonesia, edited by Karl D. Jackson and Lucian W. Pye (Berkeley: Unniversity of California Press, 1978), p. 42.

28. Koentjaraningrat, "Villages in Indonesia Today," in Villages in Indonesia, edited by Koentjaraningrat (Ithaca: Cornell University Press, 1967), p. 389; see also Gerald C. Hickey, Village in Vietnam (New Haven, Conn.: Yale University Press, 1964), p. 285.

29. Liddle, Ethnicity, Party, and National Integration, p. 207.

30. Ibid. See also Emmerson, Indonesia's Elite.

31. Clark D. Neher, "Political Values and Attitudes," in Thailand: Its People, Its Society, Its Culture, edited by Frank J. Moore (New Haven, Conn.: HRAF Press, 1974), p. 375.

32. Pauker, "National Politics and Regional Powers," in Pauker et al., Diversity and Development in Southeast Asia, p. 20.

33. Every court maintained a chronicle or history such as the Babad Tana Jawi or the Malay Annals sometimes in written form but often only retained in oral form.

34. A dramatic portrayal of the repressive results of this system can be found in the classic polemic by Edward Douwes Dekker, Max Havelaar, or the Coffee Auctions of the Dutch Trading Company (The Hague, 1860). First published under the pseudonym Multatuli, this two-volume novel became widely recognized in the late nineteenth century as an expose on corrupt and oppressive Dutch rule.

35. Lucian W. Pye, Politics, Personality, and Nation Building (New Haven, Conn.: Yale University Press, 1962), p. 83.

36. Scott, The Moral Economy of the Peasant, p. 7.

37. John L. S. Girling, The Bureaucratic Polity in Modernizing Societies: Similarities, Differences, and Prospects in the ASEAN Region (Singapore: Institute of Southeast Asian Studies, Occasional Paper no. 64, 1981), p. 12.

38. D. E. Brown, Principles of Social Structure in Southeast Asia (Boulder, Colo.: Westview Press, 1976), pp. 214-215.

39. Joseph La Palombara, "An Overview of Bureaucracy and Political Developments," in Bureaucracy and Political Development, edited by Joseph La Palombara (Princeton, N.J.: Princeton University Press, 1967), pp. 8-9.

40. Max Weber, The Theory of Social and Economic Organization, translated by A. M. Henderson and Talcott Parsons (New York: Free Press, 1964), pp. 333-334.

41. Karl D. Jackson, "Bureaucratic Polity: A Theoretical Framework for the Analysis of Power and Communications in Indonesia," in Jackson and Pye, Political Power and Communications, p. 4.

42. Fred W. Riggs, Thailand: Modernization of a Bureaucratic Polity (Honolulu: East-West Center Press, 1966), p. 328.

43. Scott, Political Ideology in Malaysia, p. 251.

44. Girling, The Bureaucratic Polity in Modernizing Societies, p. 9.

45. David A. Wilson, Politics in Thailand (Ithaca: Cornell University Press, 1966), p. 3.

46. Anthony Reid, "Trade and the Problem of Royal Power in Aceh," in Pre-Colonial State Systems in Southeast Asia, edited by Anthony Reid and Lance Castles (Kuala Lumpur: Malaysian Branch of the Royal Asiatic Society, Monograph no. 6, 1975), p. 51. See also Heather Sutherland, "The Taming of the Trengganu Elite," in McVey, Southeast Asian Transitions.

47. Ann Ruth Willner, "The Neotraditional Accommodation to Political Independence: The Case of Indonesia," in Cases in Comparative Politics--Asia, edited by Lucian Pye (Boston: Little, Brown, 1970), pp. 244-245.

48. Russell H. Fifield, The Diplomacy of Southeast Asia (New York: Praeger Publishers, 1958), p. 59.

49. Girling, The Bureaucratic Polity in Modernizing Societies, p. 7.

50. J. Stephen Hoadley, Soldiers and Politics in Southeast Asia: Civil-Military Relations in Comparative Perspective (Cambridge, Mass.: Schenkman Publishing Company, 1975), p. 163.

51. Roger Scott, ed., The Politics of New States: A General Analysis with Case Studies from Eastern Asia (London and Sydney: George Allen & Unwin and Australasian Publishing Co., 1970), pp. 39-40.

52. Salim Said, "The Genesis of Power: Civil Military Relations in Indonesia During the Revolution for

Independence, 1945-1949" (Ph.D. dissertation, The Ohio State University, 1985), p. 7.

53. Hoadley, Soldiers and Politics in Southeast Asia, p. 162. See also Edward Shils, "The Military in the Development of the New States," in The Role of the Military in Underdeveloped Countries, edited by John J. Johnson (Princeton, N.J.: Princeton University Press, 1962), p. 40.

54. Samuel P. Huntington, Political Order in Changing Societies (New Haven, Conn.: Yale University Press, 1968), p. 194.

55. Girling, The Bureaucratic Polity in Modernizing Societies, p. 11.

56. Ulf Sundhaussen, "The Military: Structures, Procedures, and Effects on Indonesian Society," in Jackson and Pye, Political Power and Communications, p. 47.

57. Alexander B. Woodside, Community and Revolution in Modern Vietnam (Boston: Houghton Mifflin, 1976), p. 239.

58. Harold Crouch, The Army and Politics in Indonesia (Ithaca: Cornell University Press, 1978), pp. 24-45.

59. Girling, The Bureaucratic Polity in Modernizing Societies, p. 25.

60. Ibid., pp. 31, 53.

61. Allen E. Goodman, Politics in War: The Bases of Political Community in South Vietnam (Cambridge, Mass.: Harvard University Press, 1973), p. 223.

62. Michael Brecher, "The Search for Political Stability," in International Politics of Asia, edited by George P. Jan (Belmont, Calif.: Wadsworth Publishing Co., 1969), p. 45.

63. Girling, The Bureaucratic Polity in Modernizing Societies, p. 12. The concept of the administrative state is taken from Chan Heng Chee, "Politics in an Administrative State: Where Has the Politics Gone?" in Trends in Singapore, edited by Chee Meow (Singapore: Singapore University Press for the Institute of Southeast Asian Studies, 1975).

64. Lyon, War and Peace in South-East Asia, p. 55.

65. Milton Osborne, Region in Revolt: Focus on Southeast Asia (Victoria: Penguin Books Australia, 1971), p. 120.

66. See Ruth T. McVey, The Rise of Indonesian Communism (Ithaca: Cornell University Press, 1965). See also Donald Hindley, The Communist Party of Indonesia, 1951-1963 (Berkeley: University of California Press, 1966); and Donald Hindley, "Political Power and the October 1965 Coup in Indonesia," Journal of Asian Studies 26 (February 1967), p. 237.

67. Daniel S. Lev, "Indonesia 1965: The Year of the Coup," Asian Survey 6 (February 1966), p. 110.

68. Osborne, Region in Revolt, p. 161.

69. See Associated Press, Bangkok, December 31, 1984, and Asia 1984 Yearbook (Hong Kong: Far Eastern Economic Review, 1984), p. 144.

70. Cynthia H. Enloe, "Foreign Policy and Ethnicity in 'Soft States': Prospects for Southeast Asia," in Ethnicity and Nation-Building: Comparative, International, and Historial Perspectives, edited by Wendell Bell and Walter E. Freeman (Beverly Hills: Sage Publications, Inc., 1974), p. 226.

71. Herbert Feith, "South-East Asia and Neo-Colonialism," in Looking North to South-East Asia, edited by Edward P. Wolfers (Honolulu: University Press of Hawaii, 1978).

72. Kusuma Snitwongse, "Internal Problems of the ASEAN States: The Dilemmas of Nation-building," in International Security in the Southeast Asian and Southwest Pacific Region, edited by T. B. Millar (St. Lucia: University of Queensland Press, 1983), pp. 144-166.

CHAPTER 8

Global Powers
and Southeast Asia

In the present international system, some states (actors) are able to extend their power or influence throughout the globe, whereas others can extend power and influence regionally but not beyond. The limits of power apply primarily to offensive or initiative influence as contrasted with the negative or rejecting influence that a weaker (regional) actor may exert locally on a stronger (global) actor. For example, either the United States or the Soviet Union, generally speaking, has the ability to begin foreign policy actions in any part of the globe, whereas a state such as Brazil has the ability to act throughout South America as well as certain abilities to limit the United States or the USSR through rebuff of these countries' initiatives toward Brazil itself or through public criticism of their acts elsewhere. This simple dichotomy of regional and global power is, in actuality, a continuum involving the relative power of each state actor and the issues involved.

The policy problem for any state, then, is to establish a proper "mix" between its global and regional perspectives. In current popular thought, most regions and regional states are seen, at one time or another, as victims of the global or regional policies of the super-powers. Southeast Asia is no exception. Although the various nationalist, revolutionary, and military ventures of the Southeast Asians successfully defeated all of the former colonial powers, they have been less successful in limiting later interventions in the region as actors in the global political system sought political or other advantages in the area. Moreover, regional policy initiatives taken on the basis of global objectives have often had serious and unforeseen consequences at regional and/or

global levels. As World War II closed and the cold war
unfolded, it was largely the United States that first
focused on Southeast Asia as an arena for global conflict
within Southeast Asia.

THE UNITED STATES

Long before World War II, the United States was
clearly on record in support of independence for colonial
areas. Although specific dates were not proposed, it was
generally expected that transition procedures not unlike
those established by the United States for the Philippines
would, in most cases, be appropriate. Yet, the United
States had made its commitment to the Philippines soon
after the defeat of the Spanish in 1898 and had still not
actively encouraged similar policies among other colonial
powers by the 1930s, despite Woodrow Wilson's enunciation
of an official program of Philippines independence in 1912.

This apparent ambivalence continued after World War II
when the United States was caught between its desire to
support the nationalist movements in Southeast Asia and
the need to support the rebuilding of Europe,[1] even at
the cost of a return to the colonial past. The United
States tried to support both its European allies and
Southeast Asia, and its policies shifted from one side to
the other over time. The dilemmas of trying to
rationalize a regional foreign policy position (support
for independence of former colonies) and a global policy
position (containing Communism) became particularly acute
after the 1949 Communist takeover of China. For example,
the United States had pressured the Dutch to reach an
accord with the Indonesian nationalists in the period from
1945 to 1949 and continued to do so until West Irian was
turned over to Indonesia. In Vietnam, however, once it
became clear that the Communist Lao Dong party would
control an independent Vietnam, the French were encouraged
to remain in Indochina, eventually financed by the United
States, and finally replaced by the U.S. military there.
In the end, and perhaps in necessary deference to its
global perspective, the United States seemed unable to
resolve either the contradictions in its policies of
support for new independent states versus the European
colonial powers or the contradictions between global and
regional perspectives in its foreign policy.

Two underlying perspectives governed much of U.S.
foreign policy after World War II. First, even though the

United States ended World War II as the only major military force in Asia, its policies were governed by a strong Atlantic-European bias. Second, the vision of communism as a global ideology came to obscure regional and national differences in the political evolution of many developing states. The global perspective became even stronger following the fall of China in 1949 and the invasion of Korea in 1950. These two events were critical in the development of the U.S. policy of "containment" of communism, and they signaled the end of any hope of U.S. decisions predicated upon purely regional issues. Containment was a global issue, and all actors in the global system would be required, in U.S. eyes, to participate.

The U.S. containment policy took form in the global alliances of which the North Atlantic Treaty Organization (NATO) was the anchor, but the policy stretched through Southeast Asia and around the world, virtually surrounding the Eurasian heartland then dominated by the two "monolithic" Communist giants--the Soviet Union and Communist China. This policy was bulwarked by a long-standing international relations theory of control of the heartlands and rimlands of Asia.[2] Added to these regional alliances were the United States' bilateral treaties with Japan, South Korea, and Taiwan, as well as the ANZUS pact with Australia and New Zealand. Each of three regional alliances--NATO in Europe, the Central Treaty Organization (CENTO) in the Middle East and South Asia, and the Southeast Asian Treaty Organization (SEATO)--was linked to the others through a swing member: Turkey was a member of both NATO and CENTO, whereas Pakistan was a member of both CENTO and SEATO. From the global perspective and in terms of conventional military action, the U.S. alliance system appeared nearly impregnable. An attack at any point in the system would bring a chain reaction to deter "open armed aggression . . . by making it abundantly clear that an attack on the Treaty area would occasion a reaction so united, so strong, and so well placed that the aggressor would lose more than it could hope to gain."[3] This treaty system, parts of which still function, was the foundation of U.S. cold war policies.[4] During the 1950s and 1960s, the U.S. expected that other states should actively support the side of freedom in this global confrontation of communism.

Southeast Asia was one of the regions in which communism seemed likely to break through the U.S. alliance network.[5] The newly independent states there usually seemed to be on the brink of chaos. As early as the late 1940s, there were Communist rebellions in Indonesia, Burma, Malaysia, and the Philippines. Although each of these outbreaks was controlled by the incumbent government, there was a pervasive fear that these regimes could not survive. The Vietnamese Communists continued to gain strength. The U.S. view was summarized in the "domino theory," which symbolized the sequential fall of all of the states of the region to communism should any one fall. Although the domino theory was not publicized as a policy justification until years later, its antecedents are found in documents prepared as early as 1949, following statements made by then Secretary of Defense Louis Johnson.[6] The policy implications of the domino theory were two fold: (1) The United States and its allies should confront Communist forces militarily wherever they appeared; and (2) the states of the region should aid the United States in that fight by joining the SEATO alliance. However, the U.S. commitment to SEATO was limited--signatories were not automatically enjoined to use force. This limited commitment represented the U.S. administration's view that Southeast Asia was a major area of interest to the United States but not a vital one.[7]

The U.S. containment policy in Southeast Asia became a classic example of the difficulties inherent in regionalizing a global foreign policy strategy.[8] In the first instance, only two regional states, Thailand the Philippines, joined SEATO, whereas South Vietnam, Cambodia, and Laos were included under the treaty as protocol states.[9] Most of the states of the region, including Cambodia and Laos, opposed SEATO as an unnecessary export of the cold war to Southeast Asia.[10] They, too, were concerned about communism, but they were not so worried about the direct Soviet or Chinese military assault that SEATO was designed to counter. Rather, the worry of these states was local Communist insurgency stimulated by political and economic instability.

The success of the U.S. containment policy in either global or regional terms is a subject of enormous debate.[11] In Southeast Asia, SEATO was effective as a regional force to counter Communist expansion only so long as the United States remained willing to maintain a direct military commitment to the containment policy. Other interpretations of U.S. policy suggest that U.S. action in Vietnam (through SEATO or bilaterally) was a holding operation designed to give other states of the region enough time to stabilize their political and economic systems and to resist communism on their own.

Whatever the validity of these interpretations of U.S. foreign policy, the period from the mid-1950s through the 1960s has been called the Pax Americana.[12] It was not necessarily a period of peace, but it was a time in which the United States, despite symbolic setbacks, held sway throughout the globe. Soviet influence and power were growing and U.S. policies were defeated in some regional contests, but, overall, the United States was the only state possessing clearly global capacities.

An evaluation of U.S. policy in Southeast Asia, however, detects greater deficiencies when the global context is set aside. U.S. policies, from their earliest versions after World War II, showed a lack of knowledge and understanding of Southeast Asia. There had been historical periods in which U.S. economic interest in the region was great, but as the economies of the Southeast Asian colonies become more tightly linked with Europe during the nineteenth and twentieth centuries, U.S. concern for the region increasingly focused on the Philippines. By the outbreak of World War II, U.S. policies of support for independence for other regional colonies had receded considerably. The isolationist policy of the interwar years was not one to encourage active policies toward Southeast Asia.

In any case, the global political specter of communism prevented any careful consideration of policy alternatives following World War II. Carefully structured policies of economic development to broaden the national political base of support for Southeast Asian regimes held little sway against the moralist military drive to fight communism. It is quite likely that during the 1950s and 1960s the American public, conservative in world view and lacking any real knowledge of Southeast Asia, would not have backed a strong policy of economic support for these countries. Perhaps more damaging for U.S. foreign policy, however, was the propensity to define any anti-Communist regime as "freedom-loving" and, therefore, deserving of U.S. support. There may have been value in numbers in the global confrontation, but the United States' willingness to accept and support boldly repressive regimes throughout the cold war era cost precious time during which reform-minded governments in these countries might have been able to move socioeconomic development to the point that Communist or other insurgencies would have withered for lack of constituencies.

The U.S. commitment to South Vietnam was a direct outcome of the containment policy. The United States entered the conflict at the French defeat in order to demonstrate to its Communist adversaries (the Soviet Union, China, and their surrogates in Vietnam) that they could not expect to expand the Communist world through the use of force and, conversely, that the United States was willing to use its power to protect the free peoples of the world. The polemics on both sides appear more obvious now, but from the perspectives of policymakers at the time acting with limited information, the judgment that communism must be stopped seemed clear. That Vietnamese nationalism or historical ethnic and cultural patterns were issues to be considered in Vietnam or Indochina did not reverse the global policymaking context.[13]

The U.S. policy of containment began to unravel by the end of the 1960s, although it was never clearly abandoned as a policy; indeed, elements of the idea of stopping Communist expansion, if not containing it in the Eurasian heartland, are still evident. However, the policies of Nixon and Kissinger in moving toward detente with the Soviet Union and establishing relations with the People's Republic of China undermined the arguments for containment. The confusion of the American public over the evident contradiction between detente, on the one hand, and the war in Vietnam, on the other, was important in sustaining domestic opposition to U.S. policy there. The majority of Americans could not distinguish between global and regional issues because U.S. policy makers did not develop such a distinction.[14] The policy that brought the United States into Vietnam--cold war containment--and the policy that challenged U.S. credibility there--detente--were global policies applied, rightly or wrongly, to a regional context in which the "fit" could not be sustained. Whether different policies would have been "more correct" or would have had a different outcome cannot be determined. But the point can be made that the rationale for specific policies in Southeast Asia (or elsewhere) cannot automatically rely on global justifications. This experience also suggests that before the United States embarks on active policy in a region such as Southeast Asia, a major educational campaign must be undertaken with the American public.

Further limitations on the U.S. policy of containment came from the Soviet Union, which, by the late 1960s, had significantly increased its global capabilities. In 1969, Soviet Premier Leonid Brezhnev proposed a "collective security" system for Asia. Although his proposal received scant support in Asia, it became the cornerstone of Soviet policy in Southeast Asia and a sign of the USSR's increasing interests in the region.

There were other factors, primarily economic ones, that eroded the U.S. stature globally and in Southeast Asia. The growing economic strength of West Germany and Japan rivaled that of the United States; thus ending in the early 1970s the dominant position of the U.S. dollar as the single global reserve currency and forcing the United States to drop its fixed-price policy for gold. Another challenge to the United States of economic and also psychological significance was the success of the Organization of Petroleum Exporting Countries (OPEC) in raising oil costs after 1973. Although the United States (and other industrial economies) made the transition from low-cost energy to high-cost energy more smoothly and more rapidly than anticipated, at the time the effect on the global image of the United States in both the political and the economic spheres was unmistakable.

As early as 1969, Nixon sought to establish a new basis for U.S. foreign policy. What has become known as the Nixon Doctrine (or for Southeast Asia, the Guam Doctrine) recognized this changing status for the United States. The principal points were these:

1. Maintenance of its treaty commitments;

2. Extension of the nuclear shield to any national whose survival is vital to U.S. security, if threatened by a nuclear power;

3. Provision of such military or economic support as required by treaty or requested by a government to meet aggression, but with the expectation that each nation will assume primary responsibility for its own defense.

There can be no doubt that this doctrine represented a major change in U.S. policy vis-a-vis Southeast Asia. Some leaders in the Association of Southeast Asian Nations (ASEAN) saw the doctrine as a "device to cover an American abandonment of responsibility in the region."[15] The domestic travails that later engulfed the Nixon administration as well as the insecure U.S. leadership that followed confirmed this view for many regional leaders. The emphasis of the Carter administration on human rights issues as a primary consideration for full American support heightened the belief that U.S. leadership neither understood the problems of Southeast Asia nor maintained a sufficient commitment to Southeast Asia to act as a positive force. Even in the creation of SEATO, the United States had assessed Southeast Asia to be a major rather than a vital area, but that perspective, too, was lost during the height of the Vietnam war.

The shock of the U.S. military withdrawal had a positive side in the sense that the United States realized it could no longer police Southeast Asia and shore up fading domestic elites. The converse of abandonment is a recognition, implicit in the third point of the Nixon Doctrine, that regional actors themselves must play the primary role in determining their own future. To the extent that this recognition has been linked to better understanding of regional problems as the basis for U.S. decisionmaking (rather than global issues), the United States has improved the likelihood of successful policies in the region.

At the same time, the core of U.S. interests in the region was redefined. This core is the geopolitical position of Southeast Asia on the sea lanes between the Pacific and Indian Oceans--that is, between East Asia and the Middle East. Not only does this fact have important military and strategic importance for the United States, but it also recognizes that Japan depends on these sea lanes for oil from the Middle East. What is more, the United States has increasingly acknowledged the economic potential of Southeast Asia as an important interest to the United States. The potential of the region as a market has been realized since colonial times, but with real economic growth in the region exceeding six percent over a recent five-year period, that market potential has become even greater.[16]

U.S. policy interests are now focused on ASEAN. This regional organization, in contrast to the U.S.-sponsored SEATO, was founded by five regional states and has added a sixth member. Although leftist critics have sometimes labeled it a pawn of U.S. policy in the region, ASEAN has provided the non-Communist regional states with a united forum through which to deal with extraregional powers. This organizational structure alone increased the capacities of the regional state to bargain with extra-regional powers, and, as the member states familiarized themselves with the routines of regional

communication and cooperation, this capacity has increased
further. There are issues on which the United States and
ASEAN disagree. For example, the use of the Strait of
Malacca for military vessels, especially those carrying
nuclear weapons, is a concern. So, too, is the general
principle of nationalization of these waterways. But to
the extent that the United States recognizes and deals
with the regional as well as the global aspects of these
issues, the prospects for functional and long-lasting
solutions are increased.

This is not to say that the United States can abandon
its perspective on global politics with respect to
Southeast Asia. On the contrary, the dramatically
expanded Soviet presence in the region, through its
support of Vietnam, has again concentrated global
attention on the region. Moreover, the bipolar division
of the region into ASEAN states supported by the United
States and Vietnam-dominated Indochina supported by the
Soviet Union has the potential of producing a major global
conflict in the region. However, U.S. policy toward this
polarized region has been dictated in large measure by
U.S. interests in improving relations with China,[17] as
global policy goals, once again, obscure regional issues
and needs.

It is critical that the United States continue to
formulate its policies based on a full and clear
understanding of the regional variables influencing any
situation, even where global variables may ultimately
determine the policy.[18] However, before global policy
goals are (or should be) transferred directly to the
regional level, their relationship to "basic cultural and
philosophical values and experience and contemporary
trends and developments"[19] must be understood and
accounted for in policy prescriptions.

THE SOVIET UNION

Soviet policymakers have traditionally directed their
focus--inherited from czarist times and reinforced by the
experiences of two world wars--toward Europe, although a
historical sense of eastward expansion has also drawn
Russian and Soviet adventurers and state leaders toward
Asia for centuries.[20] Moreover, the ideological
homestead of Marxism was the industrial West, not the
agrarian peasant culture of Asia--although in simple
terms, Marxist concepts have easily transferred to Asia.

Many of the young intellectuals of Southeast Asia, trained
in Europe during the colonial period, were quick to
identify with these broadly conceived Marxist notions as a
rationale for opposing colonialists as well as the
traditional aristocratic elite who still had some vestiges
of respect and authority. Nevertheless, "whatever role
the Soviet Union plays in Asia and whatever aims and
interests she may have are those of a European and a
global power in Asia, not those of an Asian power."[21]

The first impetus for Soviet policy in Southeast Asia
was support for nascent Communist parties and their
opposition to colonial regimes. Soviet policies were
ambiguous and confusing on such issues as whether
Communist elements in places like Southeast Asia should
cooperate with bourgeois nationalists against colonial
authority. However, only Ho Chi Minh among Southeast
Asian Communists remained active in the Comintern during
the 1930s, by which time this issue had been resolved in
favor of confrontation with the nationalist leadership.[22]

Following World War II, the Soviet Union had sought to
counter U.S. influence and success in Western Europe by
establishing itself as the champion of the newly emerging
countries in Asia and Africa. Although the late 1940s may
have held possibilities for cooperative strategies between
the United States and the USSR as envisioned in the
concept of the United Nations, the confrontation between
them was beyond reversal by the time the United States
announced the Marshall Plan for European reconstruction.
Turning away from Europe, the Soviet Union stimulated a
number of Communist rebellions in Southeast Asia, such as
the 1941 uprising along the Sittang River in Burma,
following strong Communist agitation at the Southeast
Asian youth conference held in Calcutta in 1948.[23] In
addition, soon after the Communist leader, Musso, returned
from Moscow to Indonesia, a coup was attempted in
Sumatra.[24]

Yet in the years immediately after World War II,
Soviet policy in regions as remote as Southeast Asia could
be little more than reactive with respect to U.S.
initiatives. The USSR was mainly a passive rider on the
roller-coaster movements of national Communist parties in
the region. Foreign assistance projects were largely
symbolic. In Indonesia, for example, Soviet assistance
with the Chiligon Steel Project and the Senayan sports
complex was largely political in nature, designated, as it
was, to enhance Sukarno's stature as a leader of the
nonaligned states and strengthen Soviet influence in

Indonesia. Despite such support, Soviet policy never achieved the level of influence it sought: "The more Moscow gave Sukarno materially and verbally, the more he seemed to feel he could disregard Soviet policy recommendations and do as he pleased, including pursuing many policies, such as closer relations with China, inimical to the interests of the U.S.S.R."[25]

The policy benefits of supporting the national Communist parties in Southeast Asia were dubious. Over time, these parties have usually proven too headstrong and nationalistic to follow consistently Comintern or Soviet direction. The number of ill-fated Communist military rebellions throughout the region is indicative of the problem: Years of leadership training, cell building, development of auxiliary mass organizations, and nurturing of political respectability have again and again been wasted because of badly timed and poorly planned military action against the incumbent regime. Moreover, although the Soviet Union is viewed by some regional Communist groups as "safe" because of its distance from the region (as compared with the Chinese Communists), this same distance has undercut the relevance of Soviet ideological thinking for the region's Communists, who have found Maoist theories of peoples' wars of liberation more meaningful than Soviet Marxist-Leninism. The Maoist emphasis on communal interests with precedence over those of the individual found ready-made cultural support throughout Asia. The concept of class struggle, when adapted (as in China) to landlords and other forms of agrarian class discrimination, met a very receptive clientele in Asia. Moreover, as the first generation of Asian Communist leaders, educated in Europe and intellectual and elitist in outlook, gave way to younger leaders, the revolutionary Maoist ideas gained further support.

Under Khrushchev, the Soviet Union began to attack the U.S. containment policy by proposing several "zones of peace," including Southeast Asia, to gain friendships among Communist and non-Communist states. Approaches to the latter group required the dilution of Soviet ideological fervor and, in some cases, even the sacrifice of local Communist parties for better relations with bourgeois governments--a strategy that was successful in the global system vis-a-vis the United States but costly in the Communist system vis-a-vis China.[26]

The Soviets have more recently (since the late 1960s) found themselves in strong competition with the Chinese, particularly as the Chinese pressed their revolutionary ideological differences throughout the region.[27] During the war against the United States, Vietnam was careful to balance its relations with the Soviets and the Chinese while maximizing its own independent positions. Sihanouk in Cambodia was also able to manipulate Soviet interests to balance the Chinese, and Sukarno used the Soviet connection until it became too conservative after 1963, then vaulted to a close relationship with China. The Burmese, though in many respects close to the Soviets structurally and ideologically, have allowed them only a limited economic role and even less of an ideological role.[28] This transition in Sino-Soviet competition took place when the Chinese moved away from supporting insurgency movements and more toward state relations even with non-Communist states.[29]

In 1975, with the fall of South Vietnam and the U.S. withdrawal from Southeast Asia, the regional context for Soviet policy changed abruptly. Not only did its major adversary leave the region, but the USSR soon gained an ally in Vietnam, with whom it signed a treaty of friendship in 1978. This alliance was turned to Soviet advantage as the Vietnamese agreed to Soviet use of port facilities and airfields, giving the USSR a new strategic flank position in its competition with the People's Republic of China (PRC). In this sense, the Soviet Union seems to have developed its own version of a containment policy for China. The Vietnamese hesitated to allow the Soviets full use of vacated U.S. military facilities at Cam Rahn Bay and elsewhere, but their dependence on Soviet support (given the sapping of Vietnamese energies in Cambodia and the surprisingly universal isolation of Vietnam) made continued refusal impossible.

For the most part, this new Soviet position in Southeast Asia was not gained through diplomatic or political skill. Rather, it was a function of the collapse of the U.S. containment policy, the subsequent unwillingness of the United States to try to wean Vietnam away from the Communist orbit with reconstruction and development assistance, and the previously underestimated animosity of the Vietnamese toward the Chinese. Maintenance costs for the Soviet position in Vietnam are relatively low, at an estimated U.S. $3 to 5 million per day, although additionally the cost has included the alienation of other regional states, particularly the ASEAN states. However, the Soviet link to Vietnam is key to Moscow's "two foremost global objectives--containing

China and competing with the United States for worldwide influence and power."[30]

Access to these military facilities has given a tremendous boost to Soviet strategic policy in the global system. In the regional context, or perhaps in the international context of the Third World in general, the Soviet Union may have lost some status through its support to Vietnam. However, the strategic value of the military facilities in Vietnam far exceeds these costs when the USSR's global position is considered. The superior access of the United States to both major oceans, as compared with Soviet access, is obvious. But the USSR's naval facilities in Vietnam significantly increase the Soviet ability to counter U.S. operations in Southeast Asia, South Asia, and the Middle East. When the second strategic gain—that of flanking China—is considered as well, the full value of Soviet support to Vietnam becomes evident. Soviet redeployment of military force to Asia began as early as 1963 and included increased military support to North Vietnam;[31] moreover, although the Soviets have shown some willingness to discuss Cambodian issues,[32] there is no reason to expect that they would readily relinquish this strategic position. On the other hand, the Soviet Union does not appear to be interested in expending substantial resources for conflict in Southeast Asia; instead it seems to be urging restraint on Vietnam so as to minimize the possibilities of a Thai-Vietnamese direct conflict.[33]

THE PEOPLE'S REPUBLIC OF CHINA

The foreign policy of the People's Republic in Southeast Asia continues to be influenced by traditional Chinese views of the world: "One could not be Chinese without having a dedicated conviction of the innate worth and superiority of Chinese culture. . . . In short, Peking's intractable mood comes out of China's history, not just from Lenin's book."[34] China has promoted Southeast Asia as a traditional sphere of influence that should be "militarily quiescent" and "politically accessible."[35] The PRC has at different times followed each of the traditional Chinese strategies—leading by example or by force. However, China's foreign policy initiatives, particularly in the early years after World War II, were often limited to rhetoric because its resources were devoted to domestic needs. More recently,

China has undergone a major shift in its foreign policy strategies in conjunction with the leadership change from Mao Tse-tung to Deng Xiaoping.

China followed the Soviet lead in developing the global strategy of peaceful coexistence in the early 1950s, compromising in Korea and participating in the 1954 Geneva talks on Vietnam. It also played a prominent role at the Bandung conference of nonaligned states in 1955, presenting an image of support for nationalist and anti-imperialist forces.[36] Moreover, China led by Chou En-lai replaced Nehru (and India) as the "central figure of the Afro-Asian assemblage."[37]

After Geneva, China began separating itself from the Soviet Union and peaceful coexistence and capitalized instead on its image as the revolutionary model for the Third World--particularly in Asia, where the similarities in traditional agricultural bases are obvious.[38] Because Southeast Asia traditionally fit within the nearer circles of the Chinese world, China has expected to maintain a special relationship there and, since independence, has sought the "development of a safe belt, if not a sphere of influence, through the establishment and strengthening of friendly or neutralist regimes in such peripheral areas as Southeast Asia."[39]

However, revolutionary China had major difficulties in dealing with the essentially conservative nationalist governments in Southeast Asia. Relationships have, of course, been complicated by PRC support for the Communist parties there, some of which have been outlawed or are maintaining a state of rebellion, but even in Vietnam relations have not been stable. China has sometimes balanced diplomatic relations against revolutionary policy by lessening its support to insurgents when government-to-government relations were good and raising its support of the revolutionaries when formal relations were poorer.[40] Another problem in such relations is the presence throughout Southeast Asia of large numbers of ethnic Chinese who control significant portions of the economy wherever they reside but who have usually spurned assimilation into the culture of their adopted countries or have sometimes been involved with Communist insurrections in the region.

The U.S. policy of containment struck directly at China's own self-interested Southeast Asian strategy to limit the power of other global actors in the region. This policy probably mitigated China's growing conflict with the Soviet Union for some years, whereas Chinese support for communist insurgents probably prolonged the American presence in the region. The PRC's commitment to these groups has not encouraged incumbent regimes in the region to accept the Chinese, but its primary goal was to curtail the U.S. influence. Already feeling that the Soviet Union had given up its revolutionary zeal in the Geneva meetings of 1954, China then used the Bandung forum in 1955 to "challenge" the United States with conciliatory comments that had enormous propaganda value among the states attending the conference.[41]

The decline in fraternal Communist relations with the Soviet Union was hidden by the united front against U.S. involvement in Vietnam. What began in the 1950s as China's attempt to revolutionize its own agrarian society led to a rejection of the Soviet model of urban industrial development. The Chinese hardened their revolutionary line to contradict the Soviet position of peaceful coexistence.[42] Because of the remnants of China's traditional world view, such a split might have been inevitable in any case, with the Chinese finding it impossible to accept second place to the Soviet Union in the global Communist hierarchy. As early as 1964, China reportedly offered the Vietnamese an assistance package in excess of US$1,000 million per year, if the Vietnamese would refuse further Soviet aid.[43] The doctrine of "wars of national liberation" announced in September 1965 was an indirect criticism of Vietnam's increasing reliance on the Soviets and their more sophisticated military program.[44] When the Soviet Union replaced the United States in Vietnam, the division between the PRC and the USSR deepened.

Finally, as a counter to Soviet influence in Southeast Asia after its alliance with Vietnam, China came full circle and began to focus on state-to-state relations, even with non-Communist governments and even those states that maintained an American presence.[45] It reversed the radical revolutionary line that it had initially developed to oppose the Soviet Union, in order to seek a new regional balance of power. China improved its links to the non-Communist ASEAN states, particularly Thailand, which had become the frontline state against Vietnamese expansion through Cambodia.[46] That this support for the Thai monarchical regime came at the expense of the Communist party of Thailand shows clearly that traditional balance of power politics carries more weight in Chinese policy formulation than ideology. Burma has received a great deal of attention, as Peking tries to counter Soviet influence on the southern flank.[47] Prime Minister Tun Abdul Razak, explaining Malaysia's lessening fear of Chinese supported insurgents, observed that China wants "Southeast Asian goodwill and would prefer 'bourgeois' governments that were not hostile to it rather than radicals who could come under the influence of its arch-enemy, the Soviet Union."[48]

Vietnam has for centuries been a buffer state within the Chinese sphere of influence, protecting the southern flank;[49] moreover, the 1979 Chinese military incursion into Vietnam, a challenge to the Vietnamese invasion of Cambodia, can be interpreted not only as a gesture of support for its allies in Cambodia but also as an expression of Chinese frustration with Soviet influence in Indochina. Historically, the Chinese have taken military action to bring ungrateful vassals into line. In this case, the Vietnamese not only rejected China's ideological leadership but also had refused to acknowledge Chinese revolutionary support since the 1940s. In addition, the 1979 border skirmishes aimed to reestablish China's premise that extraregional powers do not belong in Southeast Asia. Little changed: The Soviet Union was not dislodged from Vietnam nor the Vietnamese from Cambodia, and China's military move into Vietnam demonstrated the weakness of its military threat to Vietnam, although it has placed pressure on Vietnam's northern border. At the same time, the Soviet Union offered little protection to its ally, Vietnam, and the perceived value of Soviet protection declined in the aftermath of China's invasion of Vietnam. Vietnamese domination of Cambodia is not acceptable to China, and while it is not clear how China can end this situation, its present policies have added significantly to Hanoi's problems at very little cost to China.[50]

China has faced more than three decades of frustration in Southeast Asia. The region has provided opportunities for its global adversaries, first the United States and now the Soviet Union, to maintain positions on China's southern flank and to operate a strategic containment of China itself. On the regional level, China has seen very few successes among other Communist groups while experiencing several spectacular failures, most notably the destruction of the Indonesian Communist party (PKI) in 1965 and the ouster of the Khmer Rouge from Cambodia in January 1979. China has sometimes added to this frustration by supporting insurgency movements and taking an ambivalent or inconsistent approach to the ethnic

Chinese living in Southeast Asia, but its newer policy of developing state-to-state contacts has stabilized its relations with most of the regional states, lessened their fears and propensities to rely on extraregional support, and isolated the Soviet Union and Vietnam.[51]

JAPAN

Japanese foreign policy since its defeat and occupation by the United States after World War II has been dominated by that relationship. The U.S. constitutional prescription for Japan--that it not redevelop a military capacity--has meant that Japan has played no role in power politics. Yet under U.S. protection, and despite the presence of hostile neighbors in China and the Soviet Union, Japan is the only state in modern history to develop as a global actor without a military capacity. Japan's future as a military power is now a critical foreign policy issue, but the fact remains that for thirty years Japan has survived and prospered in the global economic system with no direct military capacity.

Japan entered the twentieth century as the single Asian model for modernization. Its rising industrial capacities and its defeat of the Imperial Russian naval fleet in 1905 demonstrated to all of Asia that European powers were not invincible.[52] Yet their language, their own cultural introversion, and their lack of access to the growing core of Southeast Asian intellectuals prevented the Japanese from achieving leadership in the growth of anticolonialism and nationalism in the region. As Japanese militarism grew in the 1930s, the Japanese challenged non-Asian privileges in China, and when they entered Southeast Asia after the outbreak of World War II in the Pacific, they were received as liberators by many people in the region. Although disillusionment followed as the harsh realities of war and Japanese exploitation were felt, the Japanese also took steps to strengthen independence movements, to provide basic military training to many of the local population, and (as defeat neared) to establish independent governments against the return of European colonial power. But, overall, the legacy of these experiences has not left the Japanese in a strong position in Southeast Asia.

After the war and throughout the 1950s, when the Japanese as well as the new states of Southeast Asia were rebuilding their domestic economies, Japan took little cohesive action in Southeast Asia. There were war reparations paid to some states and Japan began to "build her position in Southeast Asia on the basis of economic diplomacy,"[53] but aggressive economic investment by Japanese corporations did not begin until early in the 1960s.

Japan's primary foreign policy goals are intimately linked with its commercial policies and especially the search for trade in raw materials and hard currency.[54] In effect, Japan has "hidden behind" the U.S. alliance while "enlarging overseas contacts for the purpose of maximizing economic well-being."[55] This trade orientation gave Japanese policy a dual focus: The industrial states of the West were the market zone, whereas Asia and particularly Southeast Asia became the raw materials zone and, more recently, the manufacturing zone. When Japan began to push this strategy, the results were dramatic. For example, after the Thai government approved a policy of active inducement of foreign capital in 1963, the Japanese share of the auto market there rose from approximately ten percent to more than eighty percent in less than ten years.[56] This pattern was repeated throughout the region. By the late 1960s, nearly two-thirds of Japanese private investments in Asia and three-quarters of Japan's foreign aid for Asia were directed to Southeast Asian countries.[57] Southeast Asia has been less important to Japan than the Western countries, the oil-producing countries, or China, Taiwan, and Korea. Nevertheless, Japanese investments in Southeast Asia have been heavy. Southeast Asia is also geographically important to Japan; it lies on China's southern flank and straddles the sea-lanes that provide Japan with Middle Eastern oil.

The growing economic imbalances between Japan and Southeast Asia have had important political consequences both for the region and for the future of Japan's relations and investments there,[58] but Japanese investment policies and practices have done little to establish a positive image. Although shrewd economic decisions became the hallmark of Japanese corporations, the Japanese seem to lack a sense of interpersonal/intercultural relations, have demonstrated a limited appreciation of the still-growing nationalist feelings in Southeast Asia, and have exhibited an overall unwillingness to accept local responsibility for personal or corporate development. These traits and behaviors have often alienated Southeast Asians. For example, Japanese businessmen in Southeast Asia have sought the best local business expertise, but these people came invariably from the Chinese community, a group already resented by the local population. Japanese corporate policies for introducing local management have remained very limited; they have retained rigid fiscal control so that "spill-over" to the local economy was minimal; and their rigid demeanor and strict business practices alienated the more ebullient Southeast Asians, thereby leaving an image, rightly or wrongly, of exploitation.

The frustration of this real and imagined exploitation has from time to time erupted in anti-Japanese activities. The most widespread of these took place in 1974, when Japanese Prime Minister Kakuei Tanaka toured Southeast Asia. He was greeted by student riots first in Thailand and then in Indonesia.[59] These outbreaks of violence, although they had local as well as anti-Japanese overtones, stimulated debate in Japan about its role in Southeast Asia and its seeming inability to relate to other Asians.[60]

The outcome of this debate was a series of policies aimed at countering the negative image. In 1977, Japanese Prime Minister Takeo Fukuda attended the second ASEAN summit meeting in Kuala Lumpur, where he stressed the need for Japan to develop a closer personal and cultural understanding and to support ASEAN's economic security plans.[61] This was followed by an announcement that has become known as the Fukuda Doctrine for Southeast Asia. It restated the Kuala Lumpur aims of (1) establishing relationships of mutual trust and confidence, (2) guaranteeing Japan's policy of nonmilitarism, and (3) offering Japan's "good offices" in stabilizing Indochina and ASEAN relationships. The doctrine also included nearly US$3 billion in assistance and loans for ASEAN industrial and development projects.

The Fukuda Doctrine represented the high point of Japan's approach to Southeast Asia. Although the fault does not lie primarily with the Japanese, few of the ASEAN development projects have been successful. Indeed, there has been little change in Japan's relations with Southeast Asian states. The ASEAN States, for example, were suspicious of Japan's overtures to Vietnam, fearing that increased activities there would draw Japanese resources away from them and strengthen Vietnamese military capacities.[62] Moreover, Japan itself has become more engulfed in global problems, especially economic relations

with China and the United States. As a policy, the
broader Pacific Basin cooperation has also drawn Japan's
attention away from the narrower focus of Southeast
Asia.[63] And pressures from the United States for Japan
to increase its military capabilities have not been well
received in Southeast Asia.

The fact of Japanese economic domination in Southeast
Asia will remain, whether or not it is made more or less
palatable with development assistance or with changes in
Japanese personal or official behavior. The states of
Southeast Asia may be better able to deal with Japan
collectively in the future, as ASEAN has begun to
demonstrate, but for now they must recognize that they are
vulnerable to economic as well as political penetration.
In short, there is a single state--Japan--in a position to
accomplish economically what no other state has the will
to accomplish politically.

NOTES

1. Evelyn Colbert, Southeast Asia in International
Politics, 1941-1956 (Ithaca: Cornell University Press,
1977), pp. 86-96.

2. H. J. Mackinder, in Democratic Ideals and
Reality: A Study in the Politics of Reconstruction (New
York: Henry Holt and Co., 1919), contended that control
of the global heartland--Central Europe through Russia--by
a single power would inevitably lead to that power's
dominance of the world, whereas Nicholas J. Spykman, in
America's Strategy in World Politics (New York: Harcourt
Brace and Co., 1942) and The Geography of Peace (New
York: Harcourt Brace and Co., 1944), argued that unitary
control of the rimlands--Western Europe, Asia, and
Africa--surrounding Mackinder's global heartland would be
a sufficient power counterbalance. See also Bruce M.
Russett, The Asia Rimland as a "Region" for Containing
China (New York: Asia Foundation, SEADAG Papers, 1966).

3. John Foster Dulles, "Manila Conference Address,"
U.S. Department of State, Bulletin 31 (1954), p. 432.

4. Lloyd C. Gardner, Arthur Schlesinger, Jr., and
Hanson J. Morgenthau, The Origins of the Cold War
(Waltham, Mass.: Ginn and Co., 1970).

5. Edwin O. Reischauer, Beyond Vietnam: The United
States and Asia (New York: Vintage Books, 1967), p. 59.

6. N. Chomsky and H. Zinn, eds., The Pentagon
Papers: The Defense Department History of United States

184

Decisionmaking on Vietnam (Senator Mike Gravel edition), vol. 1 (Boston: Beacon Press, 1971), p. 32.

7. Donald E. Nuechterlein, "Southeast Asia in International Politics: A 1975 Perspective," *Asian Survey* 15 (July 1975), p. 575.

8. Donald G. McCloud, "United States Policies Toward Regional Organizations in Southeast Asia," *World Affairs* 133 (September 1970), pp. 133-145.

9. Russell H. Fifield, *The Diplomacy of Southeast Asia* (New York: Praeger Publishers, 1958), p. 317.

10. Leszek Buszynski, *SEATO: The Failure of an Alliance Strategy* (Singapore: Singapore University Press, 1983).

11. There is a substantial body of literature critical of the standard interpretations of U.S. foreign policy. See, for example, Arthur M. Schlesinger, Jr., *The Bitter Heritage: Vietnam and American Democracy, 1941-1966* (Greenwich, Conn.: Fawcett Publications, 1967); and William Appleman Williams, *The Tragedy of American Diplomacy* (New York: Dell Publishing Co., 1962).

12. This phrase was popularized by a study highly critical of U.S. post-World War II foreign policy. See Ronald Steel, *Pax Americana* (New York: Viking Press, 1967); see also Amaury de Riencourt, *The American Empire* (New York: Dell Publishing Co., 1968).

13. For a detailed analysis of the evolution of U.S. involvement in Vietnam see George McT. Kahin and John N. Lewis, *The United States in Vietnam* (New York: Delta Books, 1967), especially Chapter 7 ("Americanization of the War") and Chapter 8 ("Escalation").

14. Paul M. Kattenburg, *The Vietnam Trauma in American Foreign Policy, 1945-1975* (New Brunswick, N.J.: Transaction Books, 1980), p. 315.

15. Donald E. Weatherbee, "The United States in Southeast Asia: Continuity and Discontinuity" (paper presented at the International Studies Association meeting, March 1982), p. 4.

16. The *Asia 1984 Yearbook*, pp. 8-9, lists the following percentages as average real growth in GNP for the years 1978-1982: Burma, 7.1; Indonesia, 6.8; Malaysia, 7.52; the Philippines, 4.6; Singapore, 8.86; and Thailand, 6.5. For Vietnam, the International Monetary Fund reports growth in GDP as 3.7 for 1980, 5.1 for 1981, 8.2 for 1982, and an estimated 5.9 for 1983. Figures are not available for Laos or Cambodia, however.

17. Leszek Buszynski, "The United States and Southeast Asia: A Case of Strategic Surrender," *Journal*

of Southeast Asian Studies 14 (September 1983), p. 243.

18. Donald E. Weatherbee, "U.S. Policy and the Two Southeast Asias," Asian Survey 18 (April 1978), pp. 408-421.

19. Norman D. Palmer, "The United States and the Security of Asia," in Changing Patterns of Security and Stability in Asia, edited by Sudershan Chawla and D. R. Sardesai (New York: Praeger Publishers, 1980), p. 139.

20. George Alexander Lensen, ed., Russia's Eastward Expansion (Englewood Cliffs, N.J.: Prentice-Hall, 1964).

21. Malcolm Mackintosh, "Soviet Interests and Policies in the Asia-Pacific Region," Orbis 19 (Fall 1975), p. 764.

22. Colbert, Southeast Asia in International Politics, pp. 116-117.

23. John F. Cady, The United States and Burma (Cambridge, Mass.: Harvard University Press, 1976), pp. 196-197.

24. Colbert, Southeast Asia in International Politics, p. 83.

25. Robert C. Horn, "Soviet Influence in Southeast Asia: Opportunities and Obstacles," Asian Survey 15 (August 1975), p. 660.

26. Vernon V. Aspaturian, "The Foreign Policy of China," in World Politics, edited by James N. Rosenau, Kenneth W. Thompson, and Gavin Boyd (New York: Free Press, 1976), p. 85.

27. William E. Griffin, in The Sino-Soviet Rift (Cambridge, Mass.: MIT Press, 1964), pp. 20-30, provides an overview of the ideological differences between the two Communist powers.

28. Horn, "Soviet Influence in Southeast Asia," pp. 662-663, 667.

29. Melvin Gurtov, China and Southeast Asia--The Politics of Survival (Lexington, Mass.: Heath Lexington Books, 1971), p. 176.

30. Donald S. Zagoria and Sheldon W. Simon, "Soviet Policy in Southeast Asia," in Soviet Policy in East Asia, edited by Donald S. Zagoria (New Haven, Conn.: Yale University Press, 1982), p. 153.

31. Mackintosh, "Soviet Interests and Policies in the Asia-Pacific Region," pp. 767-768.

32. Far Eastern Economic Review, February 10, 1983, and March 10, 1983.

33. Zagoria and Simon, "Soviet Policy in Southeast Asia," in Zagoria, Soviet Policy in East Asia, p. 168.

34. See John K. Fairbank, The People's Middle Kingdom and the U.S.A. (Cambridge, Mass.: Belknap Press of Harvard University Press, 1967), pp. 37, 46. See also Udo Weiss, "Imperial China's Tributary Trade and the Foreign Trade Policy of the People's Republic of China: A Comparison of Attitudes," Asian Quarterly 1 (Bruxelles, 1976).

35. Gurtov, China and Southeast Asia, p. 167.

36. Donald F. Lach and Edmund S. Wehrle, International Politics in East Asia Since World War II (New York: Praeger Publishers, 1975), pp. 165-166.

37. Colbert, Southeast Asia in International Politics, p. 321.

38. Robert C. North, The Foreign Relations of China (Belmont, Calif.: Dickenson Publishing Co., 1969), p. 122.

39. Shao-chuan Leng, "Chinese Strategy Toward the Asian Pacific," Orbis 19 (Fall 1975), p. 776. In a subsequent footnote, the author cautions against overemphasis of traditional values and perspectives in Chinese foreign policy.

40. Gurtov, China and Southeast Asia, p. 163.

41. Lach and Wehrle, International Politics in East Asia, pp. 171-172.

42. Ibid., p. 182.

43. Roland-Pierre Paringaux, "The Indochinese Power Seesaw," The Guardian (October 29, 1978), cited in Chan Heng Chee, "The Interests and Role of ASEAN in the Indochina Conflict," in Indochina and the Problems of Security and Stability in Southeast Asia, edited by Khien Theerauit and MacAlister Brown (Bangkok: Chulalongkorn University Press, 1981), p. 188.

44. D. R. Sardesai, "Vietnam's Quest for Security," in Chawla and Sardesai, Changing Patterns of Security and Stability in Asia, p. 225.

45. Shao-chuan Leng, "Chinese Strategy Toward the Asian Pacific," pp. 779, 787-88.

46. Thailand had previously been China's principal "target for revolution" because of its location on the Southeast Asian mainland, its links to the United States, and its reactionary government. See Peter Van Ness, Revolution and Chinese Foreign Policy (Berkeley: University of California Press, 1970), pp. 181-184.

47. Edwin W. Martin, "Burma in 1975: New Dimensions to Non-Alignment," Asian Survey 16 (February 1976), p. 173.

48. Asia 1974 Yearbook, p. 211.

49. North, The Foreign Relations of China, p. 81.

50. John F. Copper, "China and Southeast Asia," in Southeast Asia Divided: The ASEAN-Indochina Crisis, edited by Donald E. Weatherbee (Boulder, Colo.: Westview Press, 1985), p. 61.

51. Shao-chuan Leng has shown graphically what China's policy of support for state-to-state relations has meant: In 1970 the New China News Agency released 374 endorsements of six revolutionary movements in Southeast Asia, whereas in 1973 the number dropped to 32 in support of five insurgency movements. Malaysia and Thailand have been the primary beneficiaries of this change, falling from 131 and 188 endorsements in 1970 to 11 and 15, respectively, in 1973. See Shao-chuan Leng, "Chinese Strategy Toward the Asian Pacific," p. 790. See also William Hetan, "China and Southeast Asian Communist Movements: The Decline of Dual Track Diplomacy," Asian Survey 22 (August 1982), pp. 779-800.

52. John Bastin, The Emergence of Modern Southeast Asia: 1511-1957 (Englewood Cliffs, N.J.: Prentice-Hall, 1967), p. 145.

53. Fifield, The Diplomacy of Southeast Asia, p. 83.

54. Hans H. Baerwald, "Japan," in Asia and the International System, edited by Wayne Wilcox, Leo O. Rose, and Gavin Boyd (Cambridge, Mass.: Winthrop Publishers, 1972), p. 52.

55. Donald C. Hellmann, Japan and East Asia: The New International Order (New York: Praeger Publishers, 1972), p. 61.

56. Reijiro Toba, "Japan's Southeast Asia Policy in the Last Decade," Asia Pacific Community 19 (Winter 1982).

57. Simon, "East Asia," in Rosenau et al., World Politics, pp. 534-535.

58. Masataka Kosaka, "Japan's Major Interests and Policies in Asia and the Pacific," Orbis 19 (Fall 1975), pp. 801-802. See also Hideo Matsuzaka, "The Future of Japan-ASEAN Relations," Asia Pacific Community 21 (Summer 1983), pp. 11-22.

59. "Tanaka Blows Up a Storm," and "Students: An Asian Barometer," Far Eastern Economic Review (January 21, 1974), pp. 13-14, 20-26.

60. Susumu Awanohara, "Japan Looks for a Friendly Image," Far Eastern Economic Review (January 28, 1974), pp. 12-14.

61. William W. Haddad, "Japan, the Fukuda Doctrine, and ASEAN," Contemporary Southeast Asia 2 (June 1980).

62. Guy Sacerdoti, "A Doctrine of Suspicion," Far Eastern Economic Review (September 11, 1981), p. 36.

63. The Pacific Community concept, following Japanese and U.S. interests, takes in all of the littoral states of the Pacific as an economic unit. Five key countries--the United States, Japan, Canada, Australia, and New Zealand--are expected to develop special relationships with other countries in the region. A major problem with the concept is the lack of Chinese or Soviet participation. See Zakaria Haji Ahmad, "The Pacific Basin and ASEAN: Problems and Prospects," Contemporary Southeast Asia 2 (March 1981), pp. 332-340. See also Sean Randolph, "Pacific Overtures," Foreign Policy 57 (Winter 1984-1985), pp. 128-142; and Jusuf Wanandi, "ASEAN and Pacific Basin Economic Cooperation," Indonesian Quarterly 13 (January 1985), pp. 74-82.

CHAPTER 9

Foreign Policy Responses to the Bipolar World

At the end of World War II, the states of Southeast Asia, newly independent except for Thailand, were led by elites with little international experience or training in diplomacy and were given few defined national interests to guide them. The tenets of the European international system, first introduced to Southeast Asia through conquest and colonial domination, had been accepted as the elements of a global political system. The Chinese imperial system had collapsed early in the twentieth century under pressure from Europeans and Americans much as the Southeast Asian system had disintegrated two centuries earlier. The new multistate system envisioned (in theory) that member states would be sovereign in their territory and equal among themselves internationally. This concept was significantly different from that pertaining to traditional Southeast Asia.

State leaders in Southeast Asia adapted to the confusing, protocol-controlled diplomatic system with little difficulty. At first, they drew much of their policy directly from their experience in shaping statehood. As expected in any subordinate system, the states of Southeast Asia found it necessary to mold foreign policies in response to demands and pressures from the global system; then, as the world became more and more polarized from the early 1950s through the 1970s, the Southeast Asian states found their foreign policy options increasingly limited.

FOREIGN POLICY IN THE NEW ERA OF
INDEPENDENCE, 1945-1957

Especially for those states in which independence was
strongly contested by the former colonial power, by
competing elites within the nationalist movement, or by
ethnic groups seeking separate statehood, foreign policy
was initially an extension of the "domestic" revolution:
The new states sought international recognition and
diplomatic and material support. The simplicity of this
goal made their task easier and gave them a moralist
outlook on international politics. Freedom, independence,
and democracy were the watchwords of twentieth-century
political rhetoric in the West, and the Allied victory in
World War II seemed to confirm the moral certitude of
these positions. Yet support from the global system for
independence for former colonies was scant at best; most
major world powers were hostile or ambivalent, and moral
indignation among the Southeast Asian elite grew strong.

The first postindependence foreign policies of these
states were conditioned by the acts of the returning
colonial power. This fact was most obvious in Burma,
Indonesia, and Vietnam, where varying degrees of conflict
with Europe prompted a rejection of the political
alignments of the former colonial power once independence
had been achieved. Burma, although not forced (as
Indonesia had been) to fight a war of independence, was
nevertheless frustrated in its relations with the British
during and after the war. Burma rejected membership in
the British Commonwealth and developed a foreign policy of
"active neutrality."[1] Indonesia, because of its
revolutionary struggle with the Dutch, was even more
vigorous in repudiating policies that might have been seen
as signs of alignment with the Netherlands or even the
Western bloc. Vietnam was the most extreme case,
rejecting the West entirely and ultimately allying
ideologically with the Communist world.

It is not difficult to see why, in the immediate years
after independence, these new states of Southeast Asia
were reluctant to commit themselves to wholehearted
support of one or the other of the major power blocs.
Indeed, the fresh experience of colonial domination left
them well aware of their vulnerability.

The Philippines, Malaysia, and eventually Singapore,
having acquired independence in a friendlier atmosphere,
were quicker to cooperate and even ally themselves with
the former colonial powers. The Philippines welcomed the
return of U.S. forces after World War II and remained

firmly aligned with the United States later. It provided sites for two major military bases and joined SEATO at the time of its organization. After independence in 1957, the Federation of Malaya (known as the Federation of Malaysia after 1963)[2] implemented a foreign policy closely linked to that of the British, and Singapore followed the same strategy after its independence in 1965. Defense agreements were maintained with the British by both states. Thailand had a continuous record in foreign policy because it had avoided colonization, but it moved closer to the United States as the conflict in Indochina expanded and became the second regional member of SEATO in 1954. Cambodia and Laos maintained foreign policies of neutrality established by International agreement--namely, the Geneva agreements of 1954 and the Zurich agreements of 1961, respectively.

Foreign policies among Southeast Asian states at the outset of independence did not reflect high degrees of regional cooperation or even frequent communication among geographic neighbors because their varying colonial experiences linked them to disparate European metropoles and because the foreign policy behavior in the traditional Southeast Asian system did not provide examples of regional cooperation. Even though good relations with immediate neighbors was one of Indonesia's first publicly outlined foreign policy goals,[3] there was little precedent on which to build such relations.

In foreign policy and international relations, the traditional centrist view of the state formed the basis on which leaders dealt with other states in the early years of independence. The states of Southeast Asia were still economic and at times ideological competitors. Their competitive stance often served to strengthen links to states and movements outside the region. Domestic power in the centrist system, as in the traditional state, extended from the center--literally, the capital--and reached only so far as military force could be sustained. This factor had a significant effect on elite precepts and the implementation of foreign policy.[4]

Economic competition among the states of Southeast Asia has traditionally involved exports of kapok, pepper and spices, quinine, copra, palm oil, tin, and rubber. (Rice, as the dietary staple of the region, has been in sufficient demand in some states to take up most of the surplus produced in others.) In recent years, these states have also competed in the search for foreign capital as well, while oil has become a surplus commodity for some and a deficit for others.

At the outset of independence, Vietnam (first North Vietnam) was the only regional state to establish a Communist government. Indonesia, by contrast, moved through three periods of different ideological perceptions but has always maintained a concept of its own leadership role in the archipelago if not the entire region. Burma and Cambodia, as well as Indonesia, played prominent parts in the nonaligned movement of the 1950s and 1960s, but their mutual interest in nonalignment had little impact on policies within the region. U Nu, Sihanouk, and Sukarno were instead preoccupied with the global stage.

The foreign policies of the time were largely the prerogative of the governmental elite and, in fact, were dominated by such strong charismatic, leaders as Sukarno in Indonesia and Sihanouk in Cambodia, who kept competing elements of the elite group off balance in order to broaden their own latitude in foreign policy making.[5] Thus, foreign policy became nearly the personal domain of premiers, presidents, dictators, and other leaders, while such figures as Sukarno in Indonesia, U Nu in Burma, and Sihanouk in Cambodia shaped foreign policy to fit the needs of their continuing domestic revolution, as they saw it.[6] This was less the case in Thailand, where the foreign ministry had a longer tradition and greater expertise. Few interest groups were strong enough to influence policy, except perhaps negatively in the form of suspicion of subversive activities among Chinese or other ethnic minorities and fear of Communist insurgents. In general, however, public opinion had a very limited role in foreign policy, although mass demonstrations orchestrated by or against the government occasionally were successful in shaping foreign policy.

RESPONSES TO THE COLD WAR
AND GLOBAL BIPOLARITY, 1950-1970

The states of Southeast Asia looked out at an increasingly hostile world as they sought to develop their first foreign policy positions in the 1950s. The last hope for continued cooperation among the wartime allies collapsed with the Soviet rejection of the Marshall Plan for Europe (1947) and the disputes over Poland, Greece, and Turkey. The victory of the Communist forces in China (1949) and the outbreak of war in Korea (1950) brought the cold war directly to Asia,[7] so that "from 1945 to the early 1960s, most decisions and actions of the major Asian statesmen were responses to the cold war conflict between Washington and Moscow."[8]

As the world became increasingly polarized, the options of Southeast Asian leaders became narrower. The choice of aligning with either the Eastern or Western bloc meant the end of meaningful relations with the other. The United States applied incentives in the form of foreign assistance to attract support, whereas the Soviet Union stimulated rebellions to try to replace conservative governments with Communist regimes. Those states braving nonaligned policies found some latitude between the two blocs as well as a degree of issue-by-issue flexibility, whereas each superpower contributed some foreign assistance in the hope of "winning" the allegiance of that state. It should not be surprising that Southeast Asians chose widely divergent paths in their initial foreign policy formulations. Variations in their pre-independence experiences ensured this divergence.

The Philippines, 1946-1970. The Philippines found it easy to choose a foreign policy position closely aligned with that of the United States. Its former colonial status and its disagreements on economic relations as well as postwar compensatory payments did, indeed, impart a negative tone to the Philippines' bilateral relations with the United States, but, at the global and regional levels, Philippine support for U.S. global leadership was strong. Manila's frustration over relations with the United States focused primarily on the U.S. Congress, where the war compensation claims were delayed for years and various trade quotas and other economic restrictions were initiated.

Despite the U.S. failure to protect the Philippines against the Japanese, the Filipinos moved quickly back under the wing of the United States after the war. The Philippines not only joined SEATO as a founding member and provided military facilities for U.S. naval and air forces; it also contributed men to the U.S. effort in Vietnam and for years supported the United States on the question of UN membership for Taiwan (as opposed to PRC membership). Until April 1949, the Philippines had established formal relations only with the Republic of China in Asia.[9] Philippine foreign policy has been governed by a staunch anti-Communist view, as when the Philippines advocated SEATO action in Laos in 1961.[10] Filipino anti-communism has also been strengthened by an important element of "Sino-phobia."[11] Through most of the 1950s and 1960s Philippine foreign policy was "a mirror image of American policy," best interpreted as "American policy with a lag-time of five to ten years."[12]

The closeness of the Philippine-U.S. relationship has also set the tone for Philippine foreign policy in Southeast Asia. In attempts to shun its image as the client of a non-Asian state, the Philippines embarked from the early 1950s on a policy of cultivating closer ties to Asians.[13] It was some time before these policies gained momentum, but by 1963, "for the first time since independence, the Philippines' relations with Asia . . . became more important than her relations with the West."[14] The Philippines did take some policy initiatives quite contradictory to U.S. positions. Always outspoken against colonialism, the Philippines gave strong support to Indonesia's struggle to claim Irian Jaya.

The Philippines also wanted a closer relationship with Indonesia as a way of confirming its "Asian-ness." The regional organization MAPHILINDO (a confederation comprising Malaysia, the Philippines, and Indonesia) was one such attempt to link the Philippines directly to Indonesia and Malaysia, the other two states in the Malay world.[15] In addition, the Filipino strategy for MAPHILINDO also was designed to put Malaysia in a diplomatic and political "box" vis-a-vis Philippine designs on Sabah, part of Malaysian territory in North Borneo. Manila based this position on its role as successor to the old Sultanate of Sulu and demanded that the claim be settled by the World Court. The motives behind the Philippine claims to Sulu seem to have originated with claims of the heirs of the last Sultan of Sulu. These claims had long interested Diosdado Macapagal; when he became president of the Philippines, the Sulu claim appeared to have some domestic political value. As a foreign policy issue, the Sulu claim was apparently one of many Philippine efforts to separate itself from the United States. Although the Sulu claim challenged another tenet of Filipino foreign policy--that pertaining to the development of closer ties to its Southeast Asian neighbors--this negative impact in the region may have been balanced by the increased awareness of Filipinos gained from the Sulu publicity that they were part of the Malay world.[16] This claim was put forth with varying intensity from 1961 until 1968, and it severely inhibited the Filipino transition toward an Asian foreign policy.[17] The concern among Filipinos for an Asian identity is strong and stems from the successive and very intensive Spanish and U.S. colonial experiences that obliterated much of their indigenous cultural identity.

Hence, throughout the 1950s and especially in the 1960s, there was a dualism in Philippine foreign policy. The Philippines felt the need to establish stronger economic ties within Southeast Asia while simultaneously recognizing that the United States remained its principal source of economic support and security. This extraregional link was often disdained by other Asian states; moreover, on several occasions it brought with it certain policies, such as Philippine support for Indonesia's confrontation with Malaysia, that did little to serve long-range Philippine interests.[18]

Malayasia, 1957-1970. Malaysia found an easy relationship in sustaining its links to the British. It chose to participate in the British Commonwealth, and its principal security concern, stemming from a twelve-year Communist insurgency, was met through a mutual defense and assistance treaty signed with the British in 1957. Economic links to Britain remained strong, but Malaysia became anxious over possible British entry into the European Economic Community (EEC) and the potential negative impacts on Malaysian exports of palm oil, rubber, and tin.[19]

However, Malaysia has also tried to maintain some measure of an "independent" foreign policy by limiting the ability of the British to use forces stationed in Malaya in support of such organizations as SEATO,[20] even though its strong anti-Communist views had placed Malaysia among the first to provide technical support to South Vietnam after the fall of the French.[21] Under the leadership of Tunku Abdul Rahman, Malaysia took other independent stances: It strongly criticized South Africa's policies of apartheid, supported the claim of Communist China for UN membership, and opposed such military interventions as the Soviet move into Hungary and the Chinese takeover of Tibet.[22] Despite this mix of policies, Malaysia's firm links to the British and its strong anti-communism made it difficult to sustain its position in the nonaligned movement, as when in 1965 it feared it would not be seated at the Algiers conference of nonaligned powers.[23]

The configuration of Malaysia itself became a major foreign policy issue. Indonesia challenged the addition of North Borneo and Sarawak to form the Federation of Malaysia, describing the new state as a British neocolonial creation. At the same time, the Philippines pushed its claim to North Borneo. These three states had briefly created the Malay-oriented regional organization, MAPHILINDO, but in 1963 Malaysia severed diplomatic relations with both Jakarta and Manila. Within two years of Malaysia's formation, a new foreign policy issue arose when Singapore was separated from Malaysia. Except for the dispute with the Philippines over North Borneo, these conflicts were resolved by 1967 when Malaysia and its neighbors formed ASEAN.

After the confrontation with Indonesia ended and ASEAN was formed in the late 1960s, Malaysia began to move away from its close and cordial relations with the British.[24] At the same time, relations with the Soviet Union expanded after 1967, when several trade missions were exchanged, and diplomatic relations were established in 1968. It appears that, having brought its domestic insurgency under control and having settled its differences with its neighbors, Malaysia was, by 1970, prepared to step into the global arena without the protective blanket of the British military.

Singapore, 1965-1970. Singapore's foreign policy has been linked closely to that of Malaysia. It obtained self-government in 1959, but foreign affairs and defense remained under British control, and Singapore was the primary British base for support of the Britain-Malaya defense agreement. After two years as part of the Federation of Malaysia (1963-1965),[25] Singapore found itself alone—a reincarnation of the Malaccan entrepot center of the traditional Southeast Asian system but without the coercive power to control its own economic and political future in the region. Moreover, its largely Chinese population located in the midst of the largely ethnic Malay archipelago area of Southeast Asia left it isolated and held in considerable suspicion by its neigbors, Indonesia and Malaysia.

Singapore sought to break this isolation in 1966-1967 with a foreign policy that gave strong support to nonalignment and Third World states in general, in addition to substantial criticism of Western and particularly U.S. imperialism. However, domestic economic realities intervened, and Singapore soon turned back to the West in search of trade, aid, and investment.[26] It maintained its global, investment-oriented policies until late in the 1960s.

Although Singapore was strong in its anti-Communist position and supported the U.S. action in Vietnam, it also

avoided any temptation to replace its old commitment to
the withdrawing British with a similar commitment to the
United States, reportedly feeling that the latter was not
dependable in the longer term.[27] China has also posed
problems for Singapore, which does not have official
relations with the PRC, even though their common heritage
draws them together and their economic links are strong at
the private level. In short, Singapore has felt
particularly vulnerable to China's policies of
infiltration and subversion because of the close cultural
bond between China and the Chinese in Singapore. As the
leading center of capitalist development in Southeast
Asia, Singapore has approached the PRC with cautious
policies.

Thailand, 1945-1970. Thailand, the only Southeast Asian
state to avoid colonization, has developed an image as a
state capable of bending to necessity, and in Southeast
Asia it holds a reputation for skilled and knowledgeable
diplomacy. It has been noted of Thai foreign policy that
the "glory of the tradition has perhaps been overstated
and the role of luck understated," while at the same time
"Thai statecraft has been much more principled, much less
like the bamboo" than has generally been recognized.[28]
Perhaps equally important, through most of the twentieth
century and especially in the 1950s and 1960s, has been
the Thai propensity to lean away from China and to
cultivate relations with any states that opposed
China.[29] In 1949, following the Communist victory in
China, Thailand also developed a strong anti-Communist
position that led it to closer technical, military, and
economic relations with the United States. As the
conflict in Vietnam and Indochina heightened, Thailand
moved yet closer to the United States, and by 1954 it was
sufficiently committed in support of U.S. foreign policy
to enter the SEATO alliance system. However, Thailand
also attended the Bandung conference, where cordial
conversations with Chou En-lai left the Thais wondering
whether or not they had overcommitted themselves in SEATO
to the cold war.[30] They overcame these misgivings, but
when the United States approved neutrality for Laos in
1962, the Thais first felt the "weakening of American
determination to hold the line on the Southeast Asian
mainland."[31] Nevertheless, Thai-U.S. relations remained
strong, with increasing economic and military support
through the 1960s[32] until the announcement of the Guam
Doctrine in 1969.

Thailand has long supported regional cooperation as a means of ensuring the independence of Southeast Asia's small states; furthermore, Bangkok became the headquarters for SEATO. However, when it became evident that SEATO could not provide effective security in the Laos crisis of 1960-1962, Thailand began to search for regional alternatives and was a leader in the founding of both the Association of Southeast Asia (ASA) and, later, the Association of Southeast Asian Nations (ASEAN).[33]

Despite its emphasis on regional cooperation, Thailand's relations with its immediate neighbors--Burma to the west and Laos and Cambodia to the north and east--have not been good. These borders constitute some of the least stable areas in Southeast Asia. The Thai-Burmese border has never been secure, and the Burmese frequently have suspected the Thais of encouraging instability there. Border problems also had serious implications for Thai-Cambodian relations, particularly as each state interpreted older Thai-French border treaties to its own advantage.[34] Thailand found Cambodian Prince Sihanouk's neutralist policies and his continued assertions of the inevitable Communist triumph in Southeast Asia particularly grating. After Sihanouk accepted North Vietnam's use of Cambodian territory, relations with Thailand worsened further.

Vietnam, 1954-1970. Foreign policies in Vietnam have of course been dominated by the long war fought there. The conflict with the French began in 1946. In 1950 the French resurrected the former emperor Bao Dai in an effort to provide a governmental alternative to Ho Chi Minh and the Communists, and to set the stage for the 1954 Geneva agreements that divided Vietnam along the 17th parallel.

The partition of Vietnam brought severe economic and social disruptions in both the North and South and greatly expanded influence for the major benefactors of each side--the United States for the South and the Soviet Union and China for the North. The South, particularly, was not able to overcome its image as a client, even though the Diem government sometimes ignored American advice and refused directives. This image largely determined the scope of its relations with other states. Its immediate neighbors, Laos and Cambodia, maintained official neutrality toward both Vietnams but held little optimism that the South would emerge victorious. Most of the nonaligned states, including Burma and Indonesia in Southeast Asia, avoided direct relations with South

Vietnam; Sukarno actively supported the North. Other Asian states such as Malaysia and Singapore as well as Japan gave verbal support to non-Communist South Vietnam but were careful not to be drawn into outright alignment with the United States and South Vietnam. Only a few Asian allies such as South Korea, Taiwan, the Philippines, and Thailand were left to provide varying amounts of men, material, and other support in South Vietnam's war against the North.

Meanwhile, the Sino-Soviet rift brought difficulties to North Vietnam as it tried to balance its two increasingly provocative mentors. Hanoi was determined to "go its own way" in matters of ideology and felt that the Sino-Soviet dispute prevented the two Communist powers from working together to provide Vietnam with maximum support for its revolution.[35] Practical considerations of continuing material support, ideological implications, and traditional power and cultural positions all figured in North Vietnam's calculations, as did domestic power coalitions and competing ideological groups within the Lao Dong party politburo.[36] Although there was evidence of Sino-Vietnamese differences even as early as the 1954 Geneva talks,[37] North Vietnam did not have sufficient strength to consider seriously a strongly pro-Soviet policy in the face of Chinese opposition. Yet from 1957 to about 1960, the Vietnamese were drawn closer to Moscow, whereas after 1963, as the war intensified, they came again to rely on the Chinese.[38] The Soviet Union downplayed the importance of the Vietnamese revolution, hoping to contain the conflict as a regional struggle and minimize U.S. involvement.[39]

North Vietnam also played an active part in stimulating subversion in Laos and Cambodia, although Hanoi accepted Sihanouk's neutrality and his opposition to Thailand and South Vietnam. In Laos, particularly, the North Vietnamese practiced the time-honored regional policy of extending their own power into territory where a power vacuum existed. They soon controlled much of southeastern Laos for supply routes to the South. Elsewhere in Southeast Asia, North Vietnam sought support among the nonaligned states, especially Burma and Indonesia, and as Jakarta under Sukarno moved to the Left in the early 1960s, the North Vietnamese found their first solid support within the region.

Beyond the region, North Vietnam's primary relations were all within the communist world. A few nonaligned states had relations with North Vietnam, but only Sweden among the countries of Western Europe maintained full diplomatic relations with Hanoi in the early 1960s.[40]

Cambodia and Laos, 1953-1970. Cambodia and Laos entered the contemporary era in the most precarious positions of any of the Southeast Asian states. French colonial rule had probably saved Cambodia from the relentless pressure of the Thais from the west and the Vietnamese from the east.[41] Cambodia's decline from the heights of the Khmer kingdom at Angkor in the thirteenth century had been nearly continuous until it was interrupted with the establishment of the French protectorate in the 1860s. Laos, by contrast, had only the barest historical framework in the state of Lan Chang, which appeared in the 1350s, but in its present form "only by cartographic and diplomatic convention can Laos seriously be considered as a single state."[42]

The foreign policies of Cambodia and Laos were governed largely by their proximity to the conflict in Vietnam. For Laos, where neutrality was "guaranteed" by an international agreement signed in Zurich in 1961 by all the major powers and all the relevant regional actors, foreign policy was largely a search for ways to implement that neutrality in the face of continuing overwhelming pressure from North Vietnam. More than this, foreign policy was the guarantee for Cambodia's existence--in the global system against Communist confrontation and in the regional system against the irredentist claims of its neighbors, especially Thailand.[43] Like South Vietnam, the Laotian government of Prince Souvanna Phouma received much support from the United States, while the opposing Pathet Lao were supported by North Vietnam, China, and the Soviet Union. The presence of the Americans on the one hand and the North Vietnamese on the other effectively divided Laos territorially, rendering neutrality ineffective and probably ensuring that Laos could not continue as a truly independent state.[44]

Cambodia, in the period until the fall of Prince Norodom Sihanouk (1970), maintained a more aggressive and independent foreign policy position. Like that of Laos, Cambodian neutrality was "guaranteed." Surrounded by hostile or potentially hostile neighbors in Vietnam, Thailand, and China, Cambodia could not risk antagonizing any of these states.[45] Sihanouk also recognized, however, that a vulnerable Cambodia might need external assistance and acknowledged this legally when the Cambodian National Assembly in 1957 passed a neutrality act that included a clause allowing for foreign assistance against military invasion.[46] Sihanouk accepted both U.S. and Soviet technical and economic aid as well as U.S. military assistance, and he strongly encouraged the United States to provide support to Laos in the early 1960s.[47]

Cambodia's relations with Thailand and South Vietnam were poor, at best, because Cambodian neutrality was seen in Bangkok and Saigon as tacit support for Communist North Vietnam. This became even more critical after 1965, when Cambodia acquiesced to North Vietnam's use of Cambodian territory for logistical and supply purposes. Relations with the United States deteriorated and were broken in 1965, not to be restored until 1969.

As pressures from Thailand, South Vietnam, and North Vietnam increased in the late 1960s, Cambodia sought to "tighten" its neutral position; however, both the Right and the Left by this time had insurgent armies--the Khmer Serai backed by Thailand and the Khmer Rouge backed by China.

Burma, 1948-1970. Of the Southeast Asian states with a foreign policy of neutrality, Burma has been the most constant. The Burmese chose "positive" neutrality, which translated into an issue-by-issue choice of involvement or noninvolvement, alignment or nonalignment, or an independent position. Perhaps because Burma had so long been governed as a subunit of British India, there was very little domestic support for postindependence linkages in the British Commonwealth. This became generalized as a foreign policy strategy of avoiding most forms of special relationships.[48] Burma's foreign policy has been governed by two principles: (1) small, weak, and underdeveloped states should stay out of global blocs; and (2) geographic proximity to China and the obvious inequality of the two countries means that Burma must be circumspect in all of its foreign policy decisions so that China will have no provocation.

Burma, from the early 1950s, also set a course of friendly relations with Thailand. The historic antagonisms and contemporary border and ethnic problems between the two made this course a difficult one, and Thai alignment with the United States through SEATO further separated the two neighbors.[49] Burma, contrary to the strategies of many other regional states, has not sought to expand its borders; because of the extremely tenuous relations to the various ethnic minorities residing near its border, however, it sought early to secure formal border agreements with all of its neighbors.[50] Thailand and Burma did sign a common border agreement in 1963, but continued movement of Karen and Shan dissidents across the border, as well as smuggling of consumer goods into Burma, have continued to cause difficulties in relations.

The Burmese have accepted foreign assistance from a number of sources including the United States, Russia, Japan, China, Britain, and Israel. On the whole, however, they have been extremely sensitive to "strings" on foreign assistance, and assistance programs have been terminated on several occasions because of suspected anti-Burmese activities on the part of the donor. The United States has felt the brunt of Burmese sensitivities, having been invited to end its foreign assistance programs in 1953 and again in 1966. On the other hand, Chinese support to Rangoon increased steadily through most of the 1960s.[51] Israeli assistance was particularly appreciated because Israel did not represent a leading member of one or another of the power blocs.[52]

Within the region, Burma has maintained good relations with all states, and it is active in the nonaligned movement and in the United Nations. However, it has rejected invitations to participate in regional organizations such as ASEAN, although it has occasionally sent observers to regional meetings. The patterns of isolation became evident as the Burmese espoused self-sufficiency even when it brought economic or other deprivation.[53]

Indonesia, 1945-1970. Indonesia, the largest and most populous state in the region, has had greater fluctuations in its foreign policy than any other state of Southeast Asia. It is not surprising that these foreign policy changes have been closely linked to shifts in domestic politics. However, although veering at times more to the Left or to the Right, Indonesia has retained consistently a concept of an "independent and active" foreign policy in which some distance or aloofness has been maintained at all times, even toward its apparent major global benefactors of the moment. The underlying caution in this policy strategy may derive from the bitter experience of the revolution[54] and the development of an underlying elite perception of the world as a hostile place[55]--a perspective that, in all probability, also developed through the revolutionary experience. Indonesia first developed a pro-Western neutralism--a commitment to nonalignment that envisioned the establishment of

exclusive relations with Western countries.[56] Indonesia
hosted the Asian-African Conference at Bandung in 1955,
and, along with Burma and Cambodia, it increasingly voiced
its concern and resentment over the impositions of both
the Western and Eastern power blocs. By the mid-1950s,
Indonesia had developed an "independent foreign policy" to
protect itself from the "duplicitous" Dutch and their
Western allies.

Through the 1950s, Indonesia was more or less balanced
in its criticism of both East and West. However, as
President Sukarno became more convinced of his mission in
the world, Indonesian foreign policy took a tone decidedly
more critical of the "old established forces" of the West
and more tolerant of the "new emerging forces" of the East
and the Third World. Sukarno carried these concepts into
the regional context in Indonesia's confrontation with
Malaysia, a state he labeled as a neocolonial creation.
Whether Sukarno seriously intended to "crush" Malaysia or
whether the anti-Malaysia policy was really designed for
Indonesian domestic purposes, it was an economic disaster
for Indonesia as most sources of Western capital
disappeared.[57]

As Sukarno's claims of encirclement by the old
establishment forces became more frequent, Indonesia's
relations with the United States slowly deteriorated
through the early 1960s. There were increasingly frequent
examples of conflict in these relations, as, for example,
when U.S. covert aid to the rebellion in the Eastern
islands was publicized, or when Indonesia's claim to West
Irian was defeated at the UN. These conflicts further
shifted Indonesia's foreign policy to the Left but did not
preclude development of another U.S.-sponsored assistance
package following Indonesia's takeover in West Irian.

By 1964, Indonesia's relations with the West had
declined badly and a "Jakarta-Hanoi-Peking Axis" appeared
on the horizon.[58] Also by this time, Indonesia'
confrontation with the established world order had reached
its peak, taking the form of withdrawal from the United
Nations. Indonesia's conservative military leaders were
sufficiently concerned to send peace feelers to Malaysia,
apparently without Sukarno's knowledge.[59] Nevertheless,
Indonesia's leftward movement in foreign policy continued
until Sukarno was removed from power after October 1965.

The Suharto government that emerged in 1966 and 1967
dramatically reversed Indonesian foreign policy. Within
two years, Indonesia's confrontation with Malaysia was
ended, and both states became members of a new regional

association. Relations with Communist China were frozen
in 1967, and the activities of the Soviet Union were
sharply reduced. Negotiations with the Soviet Union for
the rescheduling of debt payments were very slow, and
Indonesia did not respond positively to the Soviet
proposal for a Southeast Asian collective security
pact.60

Indonesia again embarked on a pro-Western foreign
policy, although it continued to search for opportunities
to exercise its "independent and active" foreign policy.
Most of the political attention of Suharto's New Order
government was given to economic stabilization. Major
Western donors formed the Inter-Governmental Group on
Indonesia (IGGI) both to guarantee steady financial
support and to provide a framework for making difficult
economic decisions, but Indonesia' relations with the IGGI
inhibited Jakarta's flexibility in foreign policy
formulation. Ultimately, regional relations under the New
Order government became a higher priority. Although
careful to avoid being criticized for trying to dominate
the region, Indonesia began to develop its leadership
potential within the ASEAN framework.

FOREIGN POLICY RESPONSES

The foreign policies of all of the states of Southeast
Asia were limited by their respective lack of resources,
organization, and experience in international diplomacy.
Early foreign policy initiatives tended to be short-term
responses to contemporary issues and were formulated
within the context of the immediate past experiences:
Revolutionary states tended to reject former colonial
authority, whereas those states experiencing a
non-revolutionary transition to independence tended to
stay close to the former metropole. Relations within the
region were slow to develop as the regional states
remained dependent upon former colonial metropoles or
became dependent on one or the other leaders of the global
power blocs. However, as these states gained experience,
new foreign policy forms and strategies--combining a more
balanced core of historical and cultural experience with
the newly defined goals of the independent state--began to
emerge.

NOTES

1. See George P. Jan, "Neutralism in Asia," in International Politics of Asia, edited by George P. Jan (Belmont, Calif.: Wadsworth Publishing, Co., 1969), pp. 133-159. This chapter includes articles by P. J. Eldridge and Mohammed Ayoob on nonalignment and neutralism.

2. The addition of the territories of Sabah, Sarawak, and Singapore made up the expanded state, although Singapore was subsequently expelled in 1965.

3. Mohammed Hatta, "Indonesia's Foreign Policy," Foreign Affairs 31 (April 1953), p. 352, included this objective as one of Indonesia's six major foreign policy goals.

4. Franklin B. Weinstein, Indonesian Foreign Policy and the Dilemma of Dependence (Ithaca: Cornell University Press, 1976). Weinstein argues convincingly that the Indonesian elite sees Indonesia as a helpless maiden in international politics, likely to be taken advantage of at any moment. This insecurity is less apparent within the Thai elite, who can draw strength from an unbroken diplomatic tradition.

5. Arnfinn Jorgensen-Dahl, Regional Organization and Order in South-East Asia (London: Macmillan Publishers, 1982), p. 159.

6. Werner Levi, The Challenge of World Politics in South and Southeast Asia (Englewood Cliffs, N.J.: Prentice Hall, 1968).

7. Paul M. Kattenburg, The Vietnam Trauma in American Foreign Policy, 1945-1975 (New Brunswick, N.J.: Transaction Books, 1980), pp. 12-13.

8. H. Wriggins, "The Asian State System in the 1970s," in Asia and the International System, edited by Wayne Wilcox, Leo E. Rose, and Gavin Boyd (Cambridge, Mass.: Winthrop Publishers, 1972), p. 346.

9. Evelyn Colbert, Southeast Asia in International Politics, 1941-1956 (Ithaca: Cornell University Press, 1977), p. 104.

10. David Wurfel, "The Philippines," in Governments and Politics of Southeast Asia, edited by George McT. Kahin (Ithaca: Cornell University Press, 1964), p. 758.

11. Peter Lyon, War and Peace in South-East Asia (London: Oxford University Press, 1969), p. 44.

12. Robert O. Tilman, "The Foreign Policies of the Smaller Asian States: Malaysia, Singapore and the Philippines," in Wilcox et al., Asia and the International System, p. 218.

13. Russell H. Fifield, Diplomacy of Southeast Asia (New York: Praeger Publishers, 1958), p. 84.

14. David Wurfel, "A Changing Philippines," Asian Survey 4 (February 1964), p. 706.

15. Filipino historians have also sought links in the past to Indonesia during the Srivijayan period. See, for example, Juan R. Francisco, "Srivijaya Art in the Philippines," in The Art of Srivijaya, edited by M. C. Subhadradis Diskul (Paris and Kuala Lumpur: UNESCO and Oxford University Press, 1980), pp. 50-51. See also Malcolm Churchill, "Indian Penetration of Pre-Spanish Philippines," Asian Studies 15 (1977), pp. 21-45.

16. Jorgensen-Dahl, Regional Organization and Order in South-East Asia, pp. 191-194.

17. Lela Garner Noble, In Pursuit of the National Heritage: The Philippine Claim to Sabah (Tucson: University of Arizona Press, Association for Asian Studies Monograph Series, 1977).

18. Russell H. Fifield, National and Regional Interests in ASEAN: Competition and Cooperation in International Politics (Singapore: Institute of Southeast Asian Studies, Occasional Paper no. 57, 1979), pp. 41-42.

19. R. S. Milne, "Malaysia: A New Federation in the Making," Asian Survey 3 (February 1963), p. 82.

20. J. Norman Parmer, "Malaysia," in Kahin Governments and Politics, p. 361.

21. Asia 1976 Yearbook (Hong Kong: Far Eastern Economic Review, 1976), p. 216.

22. Parmer, "Malaysia," in Kahin Governments and Politics, p. 362.

23. J. Norman Parmer, "Malaysia 1965: Challenging the Terms of 1957," Asian Survey 6 (February 1966), p. 117.

24. Lyon, War and Peace in South-East Asia, p. 95.

25. Nancy McHenry Fletcher, The Separation of Singapore from Malaysia (Ithaca: Southeast Asia Program, Data Paper no. 73, 1969).

26. Fifield, National and Regional Interests, p. 38.

27. Robert O. Tilman, "Foreign Policies of the Smaller Asian States: Singapore," in Wilcox et al., Asia and the International System, pp. 215-216, especially fn. 27.

28. James E. McCarthy, "National Image and Diplomacy: The Case of Thailand," Southeast Asia, An International Quarterly 2 (Fall 1972), p. 428.

29. Wilson, "Thailand," in Kahin, Governments and Politics, p. 66.

30. Donald E. Nuechterlein, Thailand and the Struggle for Southeast Asia (Ithaca: Cornell University Press, 1965), pp. 122-131.

31. David A. Wilson, "Thailand: Old Leaders and New Directions," Asian Survey 8 (February 1968), pp. 120-121.

32. Frank C. Darling, "Thailand: Stability and Escalation," Asian Survey 8 (February 1968), pp. 120-121.

33. Wilson, "Thailand: Old Leaders and New Directions," p. 88.

34. Ganganath Jha, The Foreign Policy of Thailand (New Delhi: Radiant Publishers, 1979), pp. 113-121.

35. William J. Duiker, The Communist Road to Power in Vietnam (Boulder, Colo.: Westview Press, 1981), p. 256.

36. Lyon, War and Peace in South-East Asia, p. 72.

37. Donald F. Lach and Edmund S. Wehrle, International Politics in East Asia Since World War II (New York: Praeger Publishers, 1975), p. 166.

38. Donald S. Zagoria, Vietnam Triangle: Moscow, Peking, Hanoi (New York: Pegasus Books, 1967), pp. 102-109.

39. Duiker, The Communist Road to Power, p. 224.

40. Robert A. Scalapino, "The Foreign Policies of the Smaller Asian States: Vietnam," in Wilcox et al., Asia and the International System, p. 178.

41. Lyon, War and Peace in South-East Asia, p. 79.

42. Ibid., pp. 85-86.

43. Bernard K. Gordon, "Cambodia: Where Foreign Policy Counts," Asian Survey 5 (September 1965), pp. 433-448.

44. Langer and Zasloff have pointed out that "from its inception the Lao Communist movement was made up of individuals closely associated with the North Vietnamese." See Paul F. Langer and Joseph J. Zasloff, North Vietnam and the Pathet Lao, Partners in the Struggle for Laos (Cambridge, Mass.: Harvard University Press, 1970), p. 171.

45. Roger M. Smith, "Cambodia," in Kahin, Governments and Politics, pp. 662-663.

46. Ibid., p. 663.

47. Ibid., p. 664.

48. Colbert, Southeast Asia in International Politics, pp. 105-108.

49. Josef Silverstein, "Burma," in Kahin, Governments and Politics, p. 166.

50. Lyons, War and Peace in South-East Asia, pp. 53 and 54.

208

51. Frank N. Trager, "Burma: 1967--A Better Ending than Beginning," Asian Survey 8 (February 1968), pp. 112-113.

52. Silverstein, "Burma," in Kahin, Governments and Politics, p. 168.

53. John F. Cady, The United States and Burma (Cambridge, Mass.: Harvard University Press, 1976), pp. 256-257.

54. Michael Leifer, Indonesia's Foreign Policy (London: Allen & Unwin, for the Royal Institute of International Affairs, 1983), p. 26 and passim.

55. Weinstein, Indonesian Foreign Policy and the Dilemma of Dependence.

56. Franklin B. Weinstein, "The Foreign Policies of the Larger Asian States: Indonesia," in Wilcox et al., Asia and the International System, p. 128.

57. Guy J. Pauker, "Indonesia in 1963: The Year of Wasted Opportunities," Asian Survey 4 (February 1964), pp. 692-693.

58. Justus M. van der Kroef, "The Sino-Indonesian Partnership," Orbis 8 (Summer 1964), pp. 332-356.

59. Weinstein, "Indonesia," in Wilcox et al., Asia and the International System, p. 139.

60. John M. Allison, "Indonesia: The End of the Beginning?" Asian Survey 10 (February 1970), pp. 144-145.

CHAPTER 10

Foreign Policy Responses in a Multipolar World

FOREIGN POLICY AFTER 1970

When the bipolar system began to crumble in the late 1960s, the Southeast Asian states found greater ambiguity in the global system. However, in the meantime they had also gained confidence and experience in international affairs and were prepared to assert their own interpretations of interstate relations. The end of the U.S. containment policy and strategic domination with the fall of South Vietnam was one of a series of events that fragmented the bipolar global system, at least so far as Southeast Asia was concerned. Two other events that had long-term implications for Southeast Asia were the Sino-Soviet rift, which had its beginnings in 1959 and peaked in the Ussuri River conflict in 1970, and the Sino-American rapprochement beginning in 1971.

In the first two decades after World War II, the Southeast Asian states (except North Vietnam) recognized that Soviet interests in the region lay primarily in countering U.S. involvement, but that interest could command only very limited Soviet economic or military assistance. By the early 1970s, however, Soviet capabilities, particularly naval strength, extended the USSR's power into Southeast Asia and raised for the first time the possibility of direct superpower confrontation in a "spectator" region.[1] The Soviet bid for a more prominent regional role came in the form of a proposed collective security system for Southeast Asia. Southeast Asian leaders, including those in North Vietnam, also recognized that China's assertion of greater independence made Southeast Asia a critical strategic zone. Although Japan was not a strategic threat, its growing economic

209

domination in Southeast Asia left many regional leaders feeling that Japan's old World War II slogan of a "Co-Prosperity Sphere" for Asia had come to fruition through peaceful means. The withdrawal of the British from Malaysia and Singapore left the states of the archipelago in a weakened defensive posture, despite a new defense agreement with the British and the presence of Australian and New Zealand forces. The vivid displays in the United States of public unwillingness to sustain the global anti-Communist containment policy in Vietnam and, finally, the less than satisfactory result of the U.S. military operation in Vietnam, meant that external military force was no longer available to prop up incumbent elites. Whether such support had been welcomed in the region (publicly it usually had not been), the fact remained that when U.S. military force became unavailable, elites in Southeast Asia found themselves rethinking many long-standing foreign policy positions. As a result, the Asian international system became "more autonomous, generating its own dynamic pattern of relationships independent of the Moscow-Washington conflict."[2]

The Philippines After 1970. The earlier dualism in Philippine foreign policy intensified in the last years of the 1960s as relations with the United States weakened and the presence of U.S. military bases became a more sensitive issue. In addition, domestic "disappointments and the expectations for a better life" forced Philippine leaders to look for new, more pragmatic policy options.[3] Relations within Southeast Asia, despite ASEAN membership, remained uncertain, in part because of the still-festering Sabah conflict between Malaysia and the Philippines. By 1968, however, Filipino foreign policy began to change. President Marcos made state visits to Indonesia, Malaysia, and Thailand, and Japanese economic activity continued to grow, especially in joint ventures for natural resource exploitation,[4] as the Philippines sought to build deeper relationships in Asia.

Another important foreign policy change for the Philippines was "the lifting of its hardline policy against trading and diplomatic relations with communist states."[5] President Marcos announced a "reorientation" in Filipino foreign policy at the beginning of 1971, stressing his desire to broaden contacts around the globe.[6] The new configuration of Filipino foreign policy became more evident throughout 1971--for example, when the Philippines shifted its support and voted in favor of UN membership for the People's Republic of China. Unofficial trade contacts also were opened between the two countries.

The Philippines soon broadened this new strategy through unofficial contacts with the Soviet Union and a number of Eastern European countries. Official relations were established with seven Eastern European countries in 1972.[7] In 1975, relations were established between Manila and Peking, and in 1976 with Moscow and Hanoi. The Filipino strategy in improving relations with Communist states was an effort to pressure the United States and to mitigate the perceived weakening of U.S. security guarantees for Manila. However, particularly with respect to China and Vietnam, the competing claims to the Spratley Islands of all three states as well as Taiwan meant that stable diplomatic relations among them might lessen the potential for regional conflict.[8]

Philippine foreign policy also drew away from its position of near-total dependence on the United States by developing better relations with neighboring states. The former quixotic search for "Asian-ness" through cultural ties with Indonesia, as well as the claim to the Sabah territory in Malaysia, was gradually replaced with policies more realistically in tune with regional cooperation, especially those established through ASEAN. The Philippines became the earliest advocate of an ASEAN summit, and the Marcos administration, as early as 1971, raised the issue of an ASEAN free-trade zone.[9] In terms of economic cooperation within ASEAN, however, the Philippines has been frustrated by lack of movement toward freer intra-ASEAN trade and, in particular, has viewed Indonesia's proposals for limited adjustments as unsatisfactory.[10] On the other hand, Manila has not given strong support to the ASEAN proposal for regional neutralization, "accepting the intellectual arguments of neutralization," but labeling it as a long-range program.[11] By the mid-1970s, nevertheless, Filipino relations within ASEAN were aimed at forging "closer and stronger" bilateral ties to build a "true multilateral alliance that would benefit all member nations through economic cooperation rather than through military entanglements."[12]

Constituting another thread of the newly diversified Philippine foreign policy were the contacts with the nonaligned states. In the early 1970s, the Philippines minimized the use of force against Muslim insurgents to "avert worsening relations with Arab states."[13]

Reaching further toward the nonaligned Muslim states, the Philippines sponsored a national Muslim conference and attended the Islamic Foreign Ministers' Conference in Malaysia.[14] In February 1976, the Philippines hosted the Group of 77. Formulated at that conference was the Manila Declaration, which called for the indexing of raw materials prices, debt rescheduling, increased aid on more concessionary terms, tariff preferences for imports to developed countries, and unrestricted technology transfers.[15] Manila also unsuccessfully sought observer status in the nonaligned meetings in August of 1976, but the delegation was limited to guest status.[16] The UNCTAD meetings were successfully hosted in Manila in May 1979.[17]

Yet, despite this broader base for Filipino foreign policy, the United States remains strong in the international perspective of the Philippines. The Philippines threatened in the mid-1970s to close the U.S. bases, but they continue to operate. The mercurial issue of these U.S. military bases, sometimes used by the government as leverage against the United States and sometimes by the opposition to challenge Marcos, has been dealt with through increased compensation to Manila and reduction of the extraterritorial rights of the United States. Many of the broader inequities in economic relations between the two countries have been resolved through bilateral agreements, but the fact remains that, although the U.S.-Filipino security agreements offer Manila substantial protection from external threat, the U.S. military bases there also ensure that the Philippines will become an automatic target for any opponent of the United States in a general war.[18]

In response to the demise of the cold war and the breakdown of global bipolarity, the Philippines has taken advantage of the wider range of options available to it and oriented its policies "toward independence, pragmatism, and development."[19] Issues such as the Sabah dispute with Malaysia have receded, and concern over U.S. withdrawal from the region has lessened. Expanding Filipino relations with neighbors in Asia have "led to more realistic policies" in both the regional and global systems.[20] Although recently disrupted by domestic political problems, especially after the assassination of Benigno Aquino, the Philippines has nonetheless built over the past two decades a foreign policy framework that, while continuing its links to the United States, sustains a greater balance in the regional and global systems, reduces its dependence on extraregional powers, and provides greater expression of Filipino interests in foreign policy.

Malaysia After 1970. Malaysia's early foreign policy was strongly anti-Communist and closely linked to the British through the Commonwealth and through bilateral defense agreements. By the late 1960s, the British had clarified their intent to withdraw from Southeast Asia, but Malaysia remained under the defense umbrella of the new Five Power Defense Pact, which included Britain, Australia, New Zealand, Malaysia, and Singapore. Malaysia opposed British withdrawal and also saw Britain's decision to join the European Economic Community (EEC) as another sign of declining interest in Asia. Nevertheless, Britain remained Malaysia's key contact in Europe and Malaysia continued to rely on British advice and service, until British protectionism and such acts as the great fee increases for foreign students studying in the U.K. forced the Malaysians to broaden their international contacts.

In 1970, Malaysia formally shifted toward a nonaligned foreign policy, the antecedents of which harked back to the late 1960s when Malaysia opened closer relations with nonaligned, particularly Muslim, countries. Introduced as early as 1968 was "a political entrepreneurship role in Malaysian foreign policy."[21] Under this new policy, links with Communist countries, especially the Soviet Union and China, were expanded, despite Malaysia's experience with Communist insurgents and strong anti-Communist stance. Trade with the Soviet Union became more important when the Soviets increased their purchases of Malaysian rubber. Trade missions and cultural exchanges with China began in 1970 as a result of the widening Sino-Soviet rift; China sought to improve relations with Southeast Asian states in order to balance the growing Soviet influence in the region, thereby giving Malaysia an opportunity to trade with China. Malaysia's new policies brought diplomatic recognition to East Germany and most other Communist states in Eastern Europe by 1973. After more than a year of negotiations, Malaysia led the way for other ASEAN states in opening diplomatic relations with the People's Republic of China in 1974.

Malaysia's new nonaligned stance also included advocating an end to the U.S. presence in Vietnam. Hence, in 1970, Malaysia called for U.S. troop withdrawals and proposed the neutralization of Southeast Asia with superpower guarantees.[22] In 1982, Malaysia embarked on a "Look East" policy focusing on Japan and Korea. The policy called for Malaysia to emulate the economic development practices of these two Asian states, but in implementation the policy has led to confusion, criticism, and divisiveness at home.[23]

The dramatic increase in Malaysia's participation in various Islamic organizations has brought Malaysian opposition to U.S. support for Israel. In addition, pan-Islamic issues have become entangled in Malaysia's bilateral relations with the Philippines, where repression of Moro Muslims has driven refugees into Malaysian territory. Malaysia hosted the Fifth Islamic Conference in Kuala Lumpur during 1976, but trade with and investment from Islamic countries have grown but slowly since.[24]

Finally, Malaysia's new foreign policies have included regional perspectives. Within Southeast Asia, the growth of ASEAN gave Malaysia a stronger self-identity and a willingness to articulate regional policy positions, such as the Southeast Asian neutrality proposal. Despite the nagging dispute with the Philippines over Sabah, relationships within ASEAN prospered. Although the observation that Malaysia practiced "self-induced subordination to Indonesia on foreign policy matters"[25] is an overstatement, relations with Indonesia became quite close during the 1970s.[26]

The high point of Malaysia's new nonaligned foreign policy may have been ASEAN's adoption of the Malaysian proposal for neutralizing Southeast Asia. Recognizing that Western, particularly British and American, protection was no longer dependable against China, the Malaysians formulated their neutralization proposal based on the perception that "apart from its own internal and subregional problems, the biggest single 'external' problem of Southeast Asia is the uncertainty surrounding China's future intensions."[27] Whether practicable or not, the neutralization policy brought a global character to Malaysian foreign policy and endowed it with greater legitimacy among nonaligned states.

Malaysia's foreign policy denotes clearly the transition from an insecure and inexperienced state in the regional and global systems to an effective and pragmatic actor in those systems. Jettisoning its outmoded dependence on the British, Malaysia has built solid relationships with its nearest neighbors, expanded its global support base to include Islamic and nonaligned states, and come to terms, to the extent possible, with its greatest external threat--China. Malaysia has ranked its foreign policy priorities as ASEAN, the Muslim countries, the nonaligned movement, and the Commonwealth countries, in that order.[28] In this process, it has resurrected the traditional foreign policy foci of states on the Malay peninsula: the Strait of Malacca, in relations with Indonesia; competing entrepot centers, in relations with Singapore; and concern for extraregional powers, in relations with China.

Singapore After 1970. Not fully independent until 1965, Singapore took an initially strong stance toward nonalignment and a somewhat confrontational position within the region.[29] This "go-it-alone" strategy peaked in the crisis with Indonesia over Singapore's decision in October 1968 to hang two Indonesian marines still held captive from the old Indonesian confrontation, despite appeals from Indonesia's President Suharto and Malaysia's Prime Minister Tunku Abdul Rahman.[30] Also in 1968, Singapore and the Soviet Union exchanged ambassadors and established diplomatic relations.

In subsequent years, Singapore developed a policy of "positive neutrality" and a clear recognition of its own position, size, and long-term economic needs. For example, it began to stress regional cooperation, especially in economic areas, while maintaining a publicly self-effacing position with regard to Malaysia and Indonesia to lessen its conspicuously Chinese character. At the same time, as a latter-day incarnation of the traditional Southeast Asian entrepot city-state, Singapore adopted a policy of accepting and encouraging a balanced presence of global powers in the region--a position strikingly different from Malaysia's advocacy of regional neutrality. Singapore's foreign minister, S. Rajaratnam, said that "Singapore was 'puzzled and alarmed' that China had never developed an Asia policy . . . [and that Singapore] welcomed the increased interest shown by Japan and the Soviet Union in Southeast Asia but at the same time stressed the need for a continuing U.S. presence in the post-Vietnam era."[31] Although it did not invite the Americans to occupy the facilities of the departing British, Singapore has consistently argued for a continued U.S. "economic and strategic presence" in the region.[32]

Despite the British disengagement policies, Singapore hosted the Commonwealth Heads of State Conference in 1971 and continued to rely on the British for security support. Singapore also strengthened economic ties with the EEC. Although it expected continued British interest and particularly economic support, Singapore realized that capital and investment would be needed from Japan, Western Europe, the United States, and Eastern bloc countries. More recently, Singapore, with the largest oil refining capacity in the region, has prudently strengthened relations with Middle Eastern states.

Relations with Japan were built slowly in the 1970s. Investment in Singapore as well as political relations were strengthened by Japanese Prime Minister Kakuei Tanaka's visit in 1974. Singapore, favoring an active regional role for all global powers, has been more supportive of Japan's increasing military capabilities than have other Southeast Asian states.

Singapore has also developed a unique foreign policy position toward China. Recognizing both Indonesian and Malaysian suspicions of China, Singapore has repeatedly stated that it will not open formal relations with China until all other ASEAN states have done so; yet Singapore's informal relations with China have been very active and correct. There is brisk trade between the two, mostly directed from China to Singapore, even though Singapore also has extensive unofficial contacts with Taiwan and has sent military officers there for training.[33]

Regional relations, especially those pertaining to the archipelago, are critical to Singapore. Since the 1974 visit of Indonesian President Suharto, when several basic economic agreements were signed, a triangular relationship has grown. There have been many disagreements, such as water problems between Malaysia and Singapore and competing freight rates between Indonesia and Singapore, but these have not proven insurmountable. However, the imbalanced economic strength among the three will continue to cause friction until both Malaysia and Indonesia "catch up" with Singapore. Nonetheless, Singapore has led ASEAN initiatives against protectionist policies in Japan, the United States, the EEC, and Australia.[34] Singapore also maintains sympathetic views toward Thailand as a result of the joint fears of Communist expansion and Thailand's vulnerable strategic position on the mainland of Southeast Asia.

Singapore's nonalignment has always had a certain capitalist tilt given the nature of its economy, but it refused to join the Asia and South Pacific Area Council (ASPAC) because of the council's anti-Communist profile. Singapore does retain relations with Eastern Europe as well as the West, and it maintained relations with both North and South Vietnam in the past. Singapore's official position on nonalignment in the early 1970s was summarized by President D. B. Sheares: "Singapore is neutral and non-aligned insofar as we are asked to take sides between competing power blocs. . . . But where our survival is concerned, we cannot afford to be neutral. We will not stand non-aligned if we are threatened by superior force."[35]

It is within Southeast Asia itself that Singapore, originally pessimistic about the prospects for cooperation, has found a rewarding foreign policy forum. With a somewhat self-effacing posture, Singapore has used ASEAN to rationalize its position among the regional states. Singapore's economic policies follow this theme: "to be complementary within ASEAN, to be competitive worldwide."[36] The ASEAN theme of greater economic cooperation, although progress has been slow, has stimulated changes in regional economic policies advantageous to Singapore.[37] Maritime relations between Indonesia and Singapore have been stabilized and joint military exercises held. Since the early 1970s, Singapore has maintained a position as a regional entrepot and transshipment center, despite the efforts of other regional states to develop better port facilities.[38]

The developments of the 1980s in Indochina have prompted closer ASEAN coordination and cooperation. Singapore was the advocate of the Cambodian opposition coalition, led the ASEAN campaign to seat the coalition in Cambodia's vacant spot at the New Delhi nonaligned meetings, and was also instrumental in pressuring Japan to withhold economic aid to Vietnam.[39] At the same time, however, Singapore's strong verbal opposition to Vietnam has been mitigated by extensive trade that exceeded US$200 million by 1983.[40] Meanwhile, the Soviet Union's growing role in Indochina has prompted Singaporean leaders to restate their view that the United States must continue or expand its security role in the region.[41]

Singapore's foreign policy reflects the tenets of the traditional Southeast Asian entrepot states. As a modern regional commercial center, however, Singapore has had to emphasize tourism and regional finance instead of commodity flows.[42] First, it has sought to stabilize relations throughout the region. In this strategy it has had to ignore the traditional propensity to employ military and especially naval force to maintain its position but, instead, has used the tactic of establishing regional cooperation--through ASEAN--as the cornerstone of its foreign policy.[43] Second, it has actively sought the involvement of extraregional powers both to enhance its own economic position and to increase its own security. In short, Singapore has recognized that it is dependent on the world economy for survival. At the regional level, Singapore must patiently rely on economic growth within ASEAN to provide it with widening local markets for its financial and technical services. At the global level, Singapore must deal with the prospect of "graduating" to developed status.[44]

Thailand After 1970. Because of its proximity to the military conflicts and long-standing ethnic and historical animosities in the region, Thailand has always been watchful of the revolution in Vietnam and the spread of Vietnamese power throughout Indochina. With its strongly anti-Communist policies, Thailand soon found itself intimately linked to the U.S. sponsorship of South Vietnam and U.S. global containment policies. This linkage was particularly intense during the period in which Thailand was under military control and its foreign ministry was kept in the background in the development of Thai foreign policy.[45] The U.S. departure from Vietnam proved a very difficult time of transition for successive Thai governments, as the Thais extricated their troops from direct combat, reduced the U.S. presence on Thai soil, and tried to improve relations with a range of states with which they had had virtually no previous contact.

Early in 1969, Thailand began publicly to signal a changing policy when Foreign Minister Thanat Khoman informed the Thai parliament that "there should be less reliance on non-Asian countries to enable countries in the region to fill the vacuum of a U.S. withdrawal from the area."[46] At the same time, talks aimed at a planned withdrawal from Vietnam began, although President Richard Nixon visited Thailand in July of 1969 and reiterated U.S. support for SEATO. Thailand also was criticized in the United States by anti-war groups, the media, and congressional opponents of the war. The pace of the Thai-U.S. separation quickened in the early 1970s as the Thai government, under civilian control from late 1973 through 1976, underwent a period if intense introspection focusing on domestic institutions as well as foreign relations.[47] As part of this reformulation, the government sought control over U.S. activities in Thailand by regulating contracts more strictly, limiting the numbers of U.S. personnel at certain sensitive bases, and restricting or terminating some intelligence posts focused on areas other than Indochina.

Thailand moved quickly to support the anti-Communist Lon Nol government in Cambodia, although it declined to send troops there to assist them against the Vietnamese and Cambodian Communists.[48] With the fall of Saigon and, later, of the Lon Nol government in Cambodia, Thailand's separation from the U.S. moved to conclusion. A subsidiary problem arose when U.S. forces from Thai bases were used to rescue the freighter Mayaguez from the Cambodians. The Thais subsequently notified the United States that all U.S. military personnel remaining on Thai soil would be subject to new and more restrictive regulations, and when the United States rejected these limitations, the remaining troops left within a few months.

The emerging Thai foreign policy sought to balance more evenly Thailand's relations with extraregional powers.[49] As Thailand reduced its links to the United States, it initiated other policies designed to improve relations with old enemies, particularly China but also the Soviet Union and Eastern European countries. The Thais had long had formal relations with the Soviet Union, but in 1968 and 1969 they began encouraging trade mission activities and other exchanges as well. Moreover, there were reports of secret Thai missions to China early in 1970.[50]

Thailand dropped its opposition to UN seating for the People's Republic in 1971, although it did support Taiwan's continuing membership. Communications, sports delegations, and unofficial visits to China followed for several years before formal relations were established in 1975. Relations and contacts with other Communist states, including a trade delegation to North Korea in 1974, were also expanded, but the most important of these were with the Vietnamese. The Thais had made intermittent overtures to Hanoi beginning in 1972, but with little success.[51] Shortly after the North Vietnamese captured Saigon, they asked the Thais to release South Vietnamese aircraft and other equipment left on Thai soil; much of the equipment was eventually turned over to the Vietnamese, and diplomatic relations were established. Communications between the two remained limited because of their different ideologies and, more important, their competing interests in Indochina.

The long border between Thailand and Laos and Cambodia, as well as the historical ethnic problems and territorial irregularities among these states, has meant that Thai relations with the two other states have been difficult at best.[52] The strong anti-Communist position of the Thais led them to provide military forces to fight against the Pathet Lao.[53] However, more important to the Thais was the fact that, as long as Laos and Cambodia were free of Vietnamese control, Thailand was able to maintain working relationships with them. Thailand, for example, was the first non-Communist country to recognize the Khmer Rouge regime in Cambodia,[54] and maintained relations with Laos even after the last neutral coalition became a Communist government. By the mid-1980s, Thai-Laotian relations were strained by border disputes, a conflict many felt had been prompted by Vietnam.[55] The preponderant influence of the Vietnamese in Indochina also helped to rejuvenate Thai-U.S. relations.

The consolidation of Vietnam's control over both Laos and Cambodia has placed a great strain on Thailand. These territories had served as a buffer between Vietnamese and Thai kingdoms even before the arrival of the French. The consolidation under Vietnam's control was a direct threat to Thailand: From the Thai foreign policy perspective, Cambodia is no longer independent; the Vietnamese army has moved to (and over) the Thai border; there are now thousands of refugees in Thailand; and Thailand has had to substantially increase its military expenditures.[56] All these factors threaten twenty years of Thai foreign policy. Despite Thailand's efforts to establish relations with Vietnam following the unification of that country, the two states remain opponents in almost every respect.

Thailand has meanwhile tried to strengthen relations with friendly states in Southeast Asia, particularly the ASEAN group. Continuing problems on the Thai-Malaysian border have not inhibited the overall development of good relations between the two states. The Thai foreign ministry, which established an ASEAN bureau in 1975, initially looked to the ASEAN states for diplomatic support as the situation in Indochina became more threatening.

Thailand's security and foreign policy perspectives have undergone basic revision since Vietnam established control over the traditional buffer states between them, because the Cambodian takeover established Thailand as the "frontline" state against the Vietnamese controlled and Communist Indochina. The Thais have moved much closer--perhaps too close--to China, as a function of their common short-term goal of dislodging the Vietnamese from Cambodia.[57] Although this close relationship with

China has strained Thai relations with its ASEAN partners, particularly on the question of the best strategy for approaching Vietnam, it has also served to bring Thailand and the United States into closer alignment again. However, until the Indochina situation is normalized and the threat to Thailand of military invasion or subversion reduced, Thai foreign policy will continue to exhibit elements of vacillation as it deals with an imminent internal as well as external threat.[58] Much like traditional kingdoms of the past, Thailand is experiencing countervailing pressure at its borders, and, with the Cambodian buffer removed, competing Thai and Vietnamese power will clash until a new equilibrium is established.

Vietnam After 1970. As the United States wavered in its military support in the late 1960s, South Vietnam had to seek alternatives. By 1968, negotiations between Washington and Hanoi had become a reality that Saigon could not ignore. Faced with the possibility of being abandoned through an agreement that did not include them, the South Vietnamese delegation arrived in Paris late in December. South Vietnam tried to sustain relations with its military allies--Australia, New Zealand, South Korea, Taiwan, Thailand, and the Philippines--but as these states reevaluated their cold war policies, South Vietnam became more and more isolated. In 1969, both the Philippines and Thailand stated that their troops would withdraw from South Vietnam. Eventually all of South Vietnam's allies indicated that their support would end with the U.S. withdrawal.[59]

Diplomatically, too, South Vietnam found itself increasingly alone as previously neutral or nonaligned states, having already accorded formal recognition to North Vietnam, began to accept the Provisional Revolutionary Government (PRG) in the South. The PRG was recognized at the 1973 nonaligned conference in Algiers. By that time, more than a dozen states reportedly had sent representatives to the PRG-controlled zones in the South.[60] South Vietnam countered with a diplomatic strategy encouraging states to recognize both the Democratic Republic of Vietnam in Hanoi and the Republic of Vietnam in Saigon, but not the provisional government in the South.

For North Vietnam, the closing years of U.S. involvement in Indochina also brought complications: Counter policies had to be developed to South Vietnam's initiatives seeking expanded support and recognition; and pressure had to be maintained on the war-weary United States, without appearing too intransigent to the latter's friends and allies. North Vietnam had to accomplish these objectives while skirting the growing rift between the Soviets and the Chinese, knowing that their policies were changing unpredictably because of the new global politics of detente. Moreover, the continued resurgence of "parochial interests" among Communist states in general meant that support for North Vietnam may no longer have been an important priority.[61] And, of course, it was necessary to sustain the war effort in the South.

The Soviet Union and China advocated different positions for Hanoi in negotiating with the United States. China held a relatively harder line than Moscow and urged the Vietnamese to persevere in their war, even after the U.S. offer to begin negotiations in 1968.[62] China also stressed military tactics requiring less advanced military equipment (presumably available only from the Soviet Union). For its part, North Vietnam, balancing the appearances of friendship with China and the USSR to avoid the political gulf between them and hoping to receive as much aid as each might be willing to give, expanded its relationship with the Soviet Union to counter China's traditionally dominant position in Southeast Asia.

As the likelihood of a North Vietnamese victory rose, more states began to accord recognition to Hanoi and its revolutionary arm in the South. Sweden, which opened diplomatic relations with North Vietnam early in 1969, was the first Western state to do so, but in the next several years many other states followed. North Vietnam, however, rejected several ASEAN invitations but opened more active relations with India, a state whose independent foreign policy had leanings more suitable to its views.

With the collapse of Saigon, the unified Vietnam found itself suddenly free of global bipolar constraints. At the same time, the fall of the U.S.-supported Lon Nol government in Cambodia removed from Indochina the last vestige of Western colonial and imperial power, although it was not long before extraregional power returned in the form of the Chinese, who provided support to the Khmer Rouge against the threats from Vietnam.

Meanwhile, Hanoi embarked with exhilaration on a new foreign policy that, it felt, would enhance the global solidarity of the proletarian international and recognize the special relationship of the fraternal peoples of Vietnam, Laos, and Cambodia in the regional system.[63] Specifically, five foreign policy goals have been identified as fundamental to Vietnam: (1) protecting political independence from all non-Vietnamese challenges; (2) stabilizing independence free from external economic, military, or material aid; (3) guaranteeing ethnic and territorial unity and integrity; (4) ensuring Vietnamese defense against any military threat; and (5) establishing Vietnam as the dominant influence in Indochina and as a major influence throughout Southeast Asia.[64]

No longer needing to straddle the Sino-Soviet rift, Hanoi moved quickly to improve its ties with the Soviet Union. In Peking in 1975, Le Duan, general secretary of the Vietnamese Communist party, refused to renounce Soviet "hegemonism" in Asia, thus formally rejecting China's view in favor of the Soviets.[65] New technical aid agreements were signed in early 1975, and Moscow financed the building of a Ho Chi Minh mausoleum in Hanoi.[66] Relations with China cooled dramatically.

Vietnam began a global diplomatic initiative that raised the number of states recognizing it to ninety-seven and brought membership in twenty-two international organizations.[67] It also worked to stabilize its relations with the regional ASEAN states, exchanging its criticism of them as "stooges and henchmen for the United States" for diplomatic recognition and the beginnings of dialogue. Relations with Thailand remained strained but were somewhat improved over those of earlier years.

Vietnam's global foreign policy strategy may have been a bid to establish a credible position as a nonaligned state; indeed, much of the official rhetoric from Hanoi in the late 1970s supports this interpretation. However, having tipped the Sino-Soviet scale in favor of Moscow, Vietnam needed another counterweight--the United States--if it was to sustain a nonaligned position. Vietnam clearly expected aid from the United States, as was indicated in the Paris Agreement and in other statements and documents. Hanoi tried to open the door to the United States by returning the remains of some U.S. servicemen killed in action and stating publicly its desire to normalize relations with the United States. Through 1978, Vietnam continued a broader diplomatic program in Southeast Asia to ease U.S. and ASEAN fears, enunciating a four-point policy of (1) noninterference in the domestic affairs of others, (2) exclusion of foreign bases from the region, (3) regional economic cooperation and peaceful settlement of disputes, and (4) support for a modified version of ASEAN's proposed ZOPFAN.[68] The opportunity for conciliation, if there was one, was not taken up by the United States, which rejected requests for aid and blocked Vietnam's admission to the United Nations. Hanoi and Moscow signed a Treaty of Friendship in 1978; then, once this commitment was made, Hanoi turned to confrontation, insisting that Moscow support elimination of China's ally in Cambodia.[69]

Vietnam's Indochina policies were probably strengthened by the treaty with the Soviet Union, allaying Vietnamese fears of Chinese rivalry and domination in Southeast Asia with the counterpoise of Soviet protection to ward off this domination.[70] Relations between Vietnam and China worsened rapidly after the end of Vietnam's war with the United States, although Vietnam had recognized "no later than 1972, that China was not favoring the unification of Vietnam."[71] Significantly complicating these relations was the growing friendship between the new Cambodian regime of the Khmer Rouge and China after 1975.

Vietnam's perspectives must recognize the long history of conflict in Indochina dating back to the seventeenth-century Vietnamese expansion into Kampuchea Krom (Cochinchina).[72] The historical roots for the conflict may predate the organization of any Communist party in Indochina, but the immediate causes related to Khmer Rouge paranoia toward the Vietnamese and the concomitant breakdown in communications between Phnom Penh and Hanoi as well as Phnom Penh's growing relations with China. As violence in Cambodia increased, the numbers of refugees moving into Vietnam grew also, thereby providing the nucleus for a Cambodian resistance group. From the Vietnamese perspective, continued Khmer Rouge military activities in Vietnamese border areas threatened stability in several "new economic zones," and, from a strategic standpoint, Vietnam may have feared that a prolonged border war with Cambodia would be transformed into a two-front war with China.[73] The invasion took place with Soviet approval, but the Chinese retaliated violently, sending their own troops across the border into Vietnam.

Other things being equal, the Vietnamese should have welcomed the victory of the Khmer Rouge in Cambodia, as it brought another Communist government to power and eliminated a right-wing military government with close ties to the United States. The conflict with the Khmer Rouge initially focused on the border with Vietnam in areas that had been under Vietnamese control for nearly a decade. However, the roots of the conflict were deep in

Vietnamese-Cambodian relations and in differing interpretations of such concepts as the "Indochina Federation" or Vietnam's desire to a "special relationship" in Indochina, which the Khmer Rouge interpreted to mean Vietnamese domination.[74] Moreover, there were differences in their respective interpretations of socialism and the global situation of communism, based on the "contrasting socioeconomic and political settings" that faced them in their revolutions.[75] Precipitated over a border dispute, the Vietnamese-Cambodian conflict gave scope to these deep differences until it escalated into a Vietnamese campaign to destroy the Khmer Rouge.

Vietnam appears to believe that neutralism in Laos and Cambodia cannot work--that the probabilities of external intervention from states like the United States or China make neutralism impossible. Vietnam's actions since 1979 confirm its intent to ensure that governments in Laos and Cambodia must be reliable and supportive of Hanoi. In addition to the obvious military presence that Vietnam maintains in both Laos and Cambodia, a series of conferences on joint economic planning and integration have been held.[76]

The regional power balance shifted in three ways as the result of the Vietnamese conquest of Cambodia. First, Indochina was consolidated under the leadership of Communist Vietnam, although Vietnam may have been so drained by war that it cannot fulfill its leadership role. Second and linked to the first, Vietnam has reestablished the traditional interstate pattern of conquering neighboring states but maintaining them in suzerainty rather than destroying or annexing them. Third, the Soviet Union gained a strategic military access to former U.S. facilities in Vietnam. There is little doubt that Vietnam will retain its dominant position in Cambodia and Laos. It seems unlikely that sufficient political pressure will be applied to force withdrawal, although the Vietnamese have become nervous as the Soviet and Chinese have opened negotiations and, perhaps, will reach a rapprochement.

Hanoi at first seemed confident that the Cambodian issue would be settled quickly, but, as resistance groups have made stabilization impossible, so Vietnam's global isolation increased in the early 1980s.[77] China, the United States, and the ASEAN states were successful in sustaining global opposition to Vietnam's occupation of Cambodia.[78] More recently, trade with non-Communist countries has begun to increase; Australia moved to improve relations after the change to a Labor government; and there are some signs that linkages between Jakarta and Hanoi may be warming, although recent UN votes in opposition to seating Vietnam's client Cambodian regime have been even stronger than in years past.[79] Vietnam would like to "localize" the conflict--move it out of the United Nations, persuade other Southeast Asian states to accept the status quo, and undermine the Chinese ability to influence any negotiations.[80]

Despite their apparent success, the primary opposition forces--China, the United States, and the ASEAN states--have not been fully united in their challenges to Vietnam in Cambodia. China, unable to force any decisions, appears satisfied to maintain pressure on Vietnam through Cambodia and along the China-Vietnam border.[81] The United States, perhaps still psychologically vulnerable from the Vietnam conflict, seems only too willing to follow China's lead without seriously examining its own regional interests.[82] Meanwhile, the ASEAN states cannot agree whether China or Vietnam is the greater enemy of regional stability.[83] Thus, Vietnam's "special relationship" and its imposition of traditional suzerainty over Laos and Cambodia are likely to continue, with some detailed adjustments possible in order to allow the world to more or less gracefully accept them.

Cambodia and Laos After 1970. These two countries, caught in the middle of the cold war confrontation, also found themselves hopelessly intertwined in ethnic competition and regional changes that made the preservation of independence a near impossibility. Both had followed foreign policies of neutrality as the only potential refuge from these larger conflicts. Other nations' policies "came to them" in the sense that the strategies of global and regional politics were played out within their borders. They were the pawns and their foreign policies became desperate but ultimately futile struggles to survive as independent states. As the war in Vietnam escalated, U.S. pressures on both Laos and Cambodia intensified, in part as a response to the growing presence of the Vietnamese within the border regions of both countries.

Cambodia had some success in sustaining neutralist policies until 1965, when the North Vietnamese began using its territory, and it became more and more enmeshed in the regional aspects of the war. After Sihanouk's tacit acceptance of Vietnemese troops on Cambodian soil, the political Right began to coalesce; then, after 1969, when Lon Nol became prime minister, Cambodia moved away from neutralism, although the transition was not immediate. During 1969 and 1970, relations with Communist states remained positive. Sihanouk was the only head of state to attend the funeral of Ho Chi Minh, and Prime Minister Lon Nol visited Peking. At the same time relations with the United States were formally resumed in 1969 after a four-year break. In 1969, Cambodia also joined the International Monetary Fund as well as the Asian Development Bank, both of which were supported by the West.

Until then, Sihanouk had been able to sustain a neutralist position cultivating relations with China and the Soviet Union while also receiving in state visits conservative leaders such as President Suharto of Indonesia and Emperor Haile Selassie of Ethiopia. Conversely, as late as 1968, Sihanouk reiterated Cambodia's rejection of membership in or protection from SEATO.[84]

Recognizing Cambodia's vulnerability, Sihanouk made a great effort to secure Cambodia's borders, despite the presence of the North Vietnamese army. Cambodia sought and received formal bilateral confirmations of its borders from states as diverse as Britain, Japan, Pakistan, Guinea, and Ceylon. Sihanouk also continually sought border guarantees from the North Vietnamese and the National Liberation Front, as well as from the South Vietnamese and the Thais. Border problems were acute on the Mekong, and as relations with Thailand deteriorated, the Thai-sponsored Khmer Serai took advantage of sanctuaries on the Thai side of the border. Encroachment on Cambodian territory embodied one of the traditional patterns of interstate behavior in the region; from independence on, Cambodia was threatened with territorial loss to both the Thais on the west and the Vietnamese on the east (although the latter threat was the more serious).

In effect, these conflicts were contemporary versions of the traditional interethnic conflicts that had been interrupted by the French. From its zenith in the twelfth century during the Angkor period, Cambodia experienced continuing pressures from Champa, Annam, and the Vietnamese dynasties on the east and Ayudhya on the west. Vietnamese pressure represented the political expansion of a rising ethnic or cultural group at the territorial and political expense of the declining Cambodian politico-cultural entity. Thai concerns, however, were generally more conservative, focusing less on territorial expansion than on the neutralization of any competing political entity in the Mekong basin. Colonial domination also exacerbated the conflicts by establishing artificial boundaries between states. Shifts and changes that began in the mid-1960s and continued in the 1980s reflected both the region's readjustment to its own internal power dynamics and the rise or decline of particular ethnic groups at the expense of others.

Cambodia's neutrality ended in 1970, and U.S. military forces entered Cambodia from South Vietnam for the first time. Cambodia was briefly dependent on the United States and its two nearest allies, Thailand and South Vietnam, for protection and support. Sihanouk, meanwhile, went into exile in Peking as China's policy of seeking a Cambodian counterbalance to an increasingly aggressive and independent Vietnam began to take shape. However, Cambodia under Lon Nol was not able to join effectively with the Thais or the South Vietnamese to deal militarily with either the North Vietnamese army or the local Communist insurgents. In the end, Cambodia's pro-Western regime was a local victim in the breakdown at the global system level, when the United States retired from the direct military part of its containment policy.

Even before the close of the United States' involvement in Indochina, Cambodia had begun to slide into another global conflict. China, seeking to flank the growing power of Vietnam, gave its support to the Royal Government of Cambodia in exile in Peking and, later, to opposition forces inside Cambodia, while the Soviet Union maintained relations with the rightist Lon Nol government until forced to close its embassy when embarrassed by public criticism of its lack of support for Third World countries.[85]

Following the collapse of the U.S. supported regimes in Indochina, the new government in Phnom Penh entered a secretive period during which it focused largely on reformulating domestic society. Most of its brief foreign policy expressions were announcements of its intention to follow a Maoist line, but in actuality its foreign policy was ultranationalist and often xenophobic. Its links to the radical Left in China were very close, dating back to before the Cultural Revolution, and political maneuvering among the Khmer Rouge factions followed the fortunes of political groups in the PRC: When "Teng's rightists staged their comeback against Chiang's radicals, Pol Pot intensified his purges," and the Stalinist faction tightened its control and increased the level of internal and external violence in Cambodia.[86]

The new Cambodian government was in continual conflict along the Vietnamese border, but it managed to reach border agreements with Thailand and even to establish normal diplomatic relations with Bangkok. Cambodia also took a more conciliatory posture toward ASEAN than did Vietnam or Laos, ignoring the organization for the most part but also avoiding such labels as "imperialist tool" for ASEAN.

As the Cambodia's drift toward Peking became clearer in the late 1970s, Cambodian-Vietnamese relations deteriorated. Border clashes became more frequent and rhetoric more heated. Concomitantly, as relations between Vietnam and China worsened, Cambodia once again became vulnerable in a conflict over which it exercised little or no control. The resolution of this conflict began in December 1978 with the Vietnam invasion of Cambodia and the subsequent installation of a pro-Vietnamese government under Heng Samrin.

This new stage of Vietnamese control in Cambodia completed a process begun in the 1700s that was only temporarily inhibited by French colonial intervention. Even the French had unwittingly enhanced the Vietnamese position in Indochina, and especially in Cambodia, by relying heavily on Vietnamese bureaucrats in colonial administration throughout the area. Although current reports of Vietnamese colonization in Cambodia are disputed,[87] it is evident that Vietnamese control of Cambodia will not be ended through diplomatic means. There is no countervailing force in the region to challenge Vietnam's control and no global power with the will to intervene. China's brief intrusion across the northern border of Vietnam was intended to pressure Vietnam into withdrawal from Cambodia, but it also demonstrated that China, like other global powers, does not want to enter an armed Indochina conflict.

Laos was less able to sustain neutrality. Neutralist coalition governments were established there in 1957, 1962, and 1975, but none was able to withstand the pressures from one side or another for long. By 1970, the estimated total of U.S. assistance to Laos had reached US$500 million,[88] with many clandestine military operations and groups getting military support. Direct military action by the North Vietnamese army in Laos was increasing at the same time, as was North Vietnamese support of the Laotian Patriotic Front (Pathet Lao) forces.[89]

Laos tried to demonstrate its neutralist complexion by maintaining diplomatic relations with the Soviet Union, China, and both North and South Vietnam, but when the movement of South Vietnamese troops into Laos early in 1971 provoked only mild Laotian protests and relations with the Thai military continued to expand, the neutral image was lost. In late 1971, the United States announced that it would no longer comply with the 1962 Geneva Agreements guaranteeing Laotian neutrality.

However, in 1972 a new coalition government was formed in Laos. Prince Souvanna Phouma engineered a compromise with rightists, who may already have realized that U.S support was waning. The last neutralist government did not have time to stabilize: With the fall of Phnom Penh and Saigon in 1975, the remaining rightist leadership fled Laos. The coalition government was abolished, the king abdicated, and the Lao People's Revolutionary party replaced the Patriotic Front. Laos had again passed from neutrality to alignment, this time in conjunction with the Communist bloc.

Abandoning neutrality for the third time in 1975, Laos found itself caught in the global struggle between the Soviet Union and China as well as in the regional struggle between Thailand and Vietnam. At the global level, Laos through the late 1970s sought a balance between the USSR and the PRC, but at the regional level it turned wholly to Vietnam and reduced relations with Thailand to a minimum. This imbalance in regional positions further reduced Laotian flexibility in foreign policy. Following Vietnam's intervention in Cambodia, the Vietnamese position in Indochina became preponderant and Laos had little room for independent foreign policy.[90]

In the early 1980s, there were signs that Laos was seeking more latitude in relations with non-Communist states. The prospect of new initiatives from the United States providing aid in exchange for information on American MIAs was rumored, but nothing substantive followed. Relations with Thailand also improved somewhat. With an estimated five Vietnamese army divisions stationed in Laos,[91] nothing extraordinary could be expected. Then, in the mid-1980s, Laotian relations with Thailand turned to disputes over border disagreements, which appeared to have been prompted by Vietnam's desire both to ease pressure on the Thai-Cambodian border by increasing it along the Thai-Lao border and to generally ensure that Thai-Laotian relations did not become too cordial.[92]

It would appear that the "cornerstones of the three Indochinese states' foreign policy are their 'special relationship' between themselves and their several collective treaties with the USSR and COMECON."[93] As Cambodian opposition to this relationship is fatally fragmented, and Laotian opposition is nearly non-existent,[94] these two states appear destined to fill roles as traditional vassal states in Vietnam's extended Indochina system. For the present there is no other power center either among regional states or among interested extraregional states that has the combination of will and capacity to alter this situation.

Burma After 1970. Nonalignment, neutrality, and even isolation are policies that Burma has maintained more consistently since independence than any other state in the region. In foreign and domestic politics, Burma has evolved a peculiarly "Burmese way to socialism" at home and a Burmese way toward independence in foreign policy. For instance, it has steadfastly maintained stable relations with its neighbors, especially India, China, and Thailand. Recognizing the dominant position of China in the area, the Burmese have consistently made foreign policy decisions within the context of their perceptions of China's likely reactions to each decision, according China a de facto veto power over Burma's foreign policy. China, on the other hand, has used its financial, material, and moral resources to extend or withdraw support from the Burmese Communist insurgents as a reward mechanism for "correct" Burmese policy decisions. One outcome of this Chinese influence has been a very carefully managed and limited relationship between Burma and the Soviet Union. Yet relations with China have not always been harmonious. They turned sour in 1967 but improved again after 1970, although concerns remain about the treatment of Chinese living in Burma. The treatment of Indians in Burma has also been a source of difficulty, and border problems with Thailand have never been satisfactorily resolved. Thai-Burmese relations were particularly threatened when Thailand granted political asylum to former Burmese Prime Minister U Nu.

Other aspects of Burma's foreign policy have been designed to sustain its nonaligned posture. For example, Burma was among the few states maintaining relations with both North and South Vietnam and North and South Korea, although its relations with the North were severely strained when North Korean assassins attempted to murder South Korea's President Chun Doo Hwan during his state visit to Burma in 1983. Burma also has good relations with the Soviet Union and the United States, although Burma carefully restricts the aid from and involvement with both. Burma has received technical assistance from Japan and the United Nations through the United Nations Development Program (UNDP). Its relations with the British have been correct but not warm; and its relations with West Germany and Finland are friendly. Indeed, Burma has found in the latter a sympathy for its neutralist positions and its proximity to a global power.

Within Southeast Asia, Burma has maintained policies of friendly but limited and always bilateral cooperation. It welcomed the changes in Indochina that ended the U.S. involvement but withheld recognition of the Heng Samrin regime in Cambodia after the Vietnamese expansion in Indochina, arguing that the Khmer Rouge, however inhumane its policies, was the only legitimate government there.[95] Burma has shown some interest in ASEAN. It attends meetings occasionally as an observer but has declined membership, despite rumors to the contrary. Continuing to respect Chinese wariness of ASEAN and its capitalist-oriented members, Burma has indicated that it would join a regional organization only if all Southeast Asian states were members.

Border issues have occupied the major part of Burma's foreign policy toward its immediate neighbors. As among the traditional states, Burma has experienced severe problems with ethnic minority groups occupying the border regions of the state and effectively rejecting the authority of the state. Its first concern was the border with China, and an agreement was reached in 1960 demarcating the border and transferring disputed territory. In 1967, Burma reached separate border agreements with both India and Pakistan, and settled disputes over the islands in the Naaf River. Border pacts were reached with Thailand in 1963 and again in 1968, but the Thai-Burmese border remains a virtual sieve as people and goods travel to take advantage of or escape the economic distortions in Burma. China's reductions in support of Burmese Communist insurgents have forced the Communists into alliances with non-Communist ethnic minorities and drug-smuggling groups along the Thai-Burmese border.

Burma is the only Southeast Asian state that has sustained a more or less constant foreign policy course, despite the pressures and changes in global and regional systems. Perhaps its geographic position has aided the situation. It was beyond the fringes of the cold war confrontation in Indochina and lies between two underdeveloped giants--India and China. Its attraction to neutralism has meant not an inactive foreign policy but rather a policy of selectively deciding each issue on its own merit. In addition, Burma has been very active in what has been called "conference diplomacy.[96] Finally, the willingness of the Burmese to impose strict developmental goals on themselves--rejecting assistance moneys if the terms were not suitable--has given them a measure of insulation against overcommitment to any one donor state. The U.S. Agency for International Development, for example, has twice been invited to close its program and leave Burma.

Beginning in 1968, Burma began to change its foreign policy perspectives following a six-year term of nearly reclusive policy. In that year, Ne Win made several trips to other states in Southeast Asia and by 1973 had visited all of the ASEAN countries. He also visited India, Pakistan, and China. In 1969, travel restrictions were relaxed somewhat to encourage tourism, and Burma chartered a plane from an American airline to shuttle tourists between Hong Kong and Rangoon.[97] Burma accepted assistance for offshore oil exploration from Gulf Oil Corporation in 1972, the first time it had taken aid from a private, nongovernmental organization.[98] And in the early 1970s, Japanese investment and assistance began to expand, also focusing on petroleum exploration.[99] By the mid-1970s, Burma was again accepting assistance from the World Bank and the Asian Development Bank, both of which it had previously rejected. Early in the 1980s, it received a new US$30 million agricultural assistance grant. However, Burma maintained its aloof perspective on both global and regional politics, desite persistent speculation that ASEAN membership was planned.[100]

Burma's success in maintaining consistently nonaligned policies may have been aided by its geographic isolation from the Indochina conflict. Burmese neutrality and links to both the ASEAN states and to Vietnam have led to suggestions that Rangoon might play a major role in negotiations for a settlement of the Cambodian conflict.[101] Moreover, with the transfer of the Sino-Soviet split to Southeast Asia, Burma's policy options between the two Communist giants had to be very carefully managed. Characteristically, the Burmese have resurrected relations with Western states such as the United States, which became a more legitimate partner for the Burmese with the end of its military involvement in Vietnam. U.S.-Burmese cooperation remains modest, but joint efforts in narcotics control, for example, have been accomplished.[102]

Burmese foreign policy continues to be governed both by its proximity to China and by a not always healthy suspicion of foreigners and of Western modernization. As long ago as the mid-1960s, the closure of World Bank operations in Rangoon was prompted by "an antipathy to having foreigners observe closely the Burmese economy."[103] Its development policies remain based on an obscure perception that Burma must follow its own model for development. (For example, tractor power for agricultural production has recently been rejected in favor of the water buffalo because of continued shortages of parts and gasoline in the domestic market.)[104] Thus, despite Burmese desires for goods and technology from the West, Burma has held fast to its generally aloof and nonaligned policies.[105]

Indonesia After 1970. Although not subject to direct military confrontation in Indochina, Indonesia has been the target of considerable competition among global powers--a fact that has had an impact on its foreign policy. Size, resources, and strategic regional position have combined to make Indonesia attractive to both East and West.

In 1965, Indonesia turned toward the West. The government that evolved following the October coup embarked on a foreign policy course designed to stabilize Indonesia's domestic inflation problems and to establish a development program keyed to financial assistance from major Western donors. Gone was the flamboyant Sukarno rhetoric of newly emerging forces in global confrontation with the established world order. "Reality," said one writer, "was gaining control over romance."[106]

Foreign policy suddenly became one of the least interesting topics in Jakarta. The Suharto government met with international creditors to reschedule debt payments and review austere development plans. Indonesia also redressed its foreign policy in Southeast Asia by ending its confrontation with Malaysia and expanding relations with Singapore, Thailand, the Philippines, and Burma.

Indonesia's traditional description of an "independent and active" foreign policy was retained, but it came to stand for a pragmatic mixture of policies that acknowledged the position of its Western creditors while allowing enough breadth of action within non-Western circles to defend an essentially nonaligned policy.[107] The recognition of its creditors included strong commercial and assistance-oriented relations with the United States and Japan, although distrust and fear of economic domination has at times inhibited relations, particularly with Japan. Also included in this policy was a reconstituted role for the Dutch. Links to the Inter-Governmental Group for Indonesia (IGGI) became a target of domestic criticism because of perceived Indonesian dependence on the donors, who, it was claimed, were concerned with protecting their investments at the expense of Indonesia's development.[108] This criticism also addressed issues of domestic corruption and arbitrary governmental decisionmaking, but in large measure it reflected the deep-seated concern, present since independence, that Indonesia not be drawn too close to either the East or the West in global politics.[109] Worries about economic dependence continued to grow, focusing increasingly on Japan and culminating in the January 1974 riots, which broke out when Japanese Prime Minister Kakuei Tanaka arrived in Jakarta.

Limits on Indonesia's Western "tilt" remain. Nevertheless, Indonesia's international stance has been more pro-Western under the New Order government than at any time since independence. It has been argued that this shift away from nonalignment was possible because there is no longer an effective domestic opposition to restrain the government: "The New Order's freedom to carry out a foreign policy of development . . . reflects the latitude afforded by the absence of serious political competition."[110] On the other hand, when the New Order came to power the country was near bankruptcy, and "Indonesia's long-standing allegiance . . . to non-alignment in foreign policy has been overshadowed by its critical need for enormous economic assistance . . . [which] can only come from the developed countries of the West and Japan."[111]

Indonesia has retained or expanded its position in several non-Western organizations. By 1969, it was ready to support a summit meeting of nonaligned states, and Indonesian foreign minister Adam Malik attended the summit in Algiers in 1973. Indonesia has also participated in

Islamic organizations, although it has not taken strong positions in the Middle East conflicts. An oil-exporting nation, Indonesia also became a member of OPEC. In each of these organizations, Indonesia has kept a low profile.

In bilateral relations, Indonesia has sought to retain its image of independence. In 1968, it began a policy of dual recognition for divided states when it established contacts with South Korea and informal relations with South Vietnam while retaining relations with North Korea and North Vietnam. This policy was followed again in 1972, when Indonesia established relations with East Germany. Relations with the Soviet Union were maintained, although arduous negotiations were required before the Soviet Union accepted the debt rescheduling called for by Indonesia's Western creditors. The Indonesians remained very cool toward the USSR because Moscow had refused to supply military spare parts after the coup of 1965. Nevertheless, the Soviet Union maintains one of its largest embassies in Jakarta.[112]

Since 1965, the Chinese have been a major foreign policy enigma for Indonesia. Because of suspected complicity in the 1965 coup, Indonesia "froze" its relations with China. The exact terms of the freeze are not clear: although the entire diplomatic staffs of each country departed from their posts under duress, relations are not considered to be formally broken. Informal contacts have been maintained, and some trade continued, largely through Singapore or Hong Kong. Although rumors of improved relations have frequently been aired, and although various Indonesian government officials have at times declared that relations would be restored "soon," it was not until 1985 that Indonesia's first trade mission since 1967 visited Peking and trade relations were formalized through an exchange of memoranda.[113]

China represented a double threat to the New order government in Indonesia. Because of China's alleged collusion with the Indonesian Communist Party (PKI), the Indonesian military was particularly fearful of Chinese support for internal subversion. These fears were only exacerbated by the position of the ethnic Chinese living in Indonesia, who for generations have rejected assimilation and are often seen as the very agents for subversion. The normalization of Indonesia's relations with the then new Malaysia was made easier by the fact that the Chinese population of Singapore had already been separated from Malaysia,[114] although Indonesia's relations with the independent Singapore have been shown to be more extensive and intensive than generally understood.[115]

Long fearing problems in an independent Timor,[116] the Indonesian government in 1976 took decisive action in Portuguese Timor, despite the expected furor of world opinion. Jakarta obviously feared the possibility of a Communist client state in the archipelago and, holding little hope that Timor could ever sustain independent economic or political status, acted to annex the territory to Indonesia. It has since become clear that the annexation of Timor is permanent, although the Indonesians "are realistic about the speed with which measures of integration will effect change" in Timor.[117]

In regional politics, Indonesian foreign policy has matured since the mid-1960s. By the early 1970s, relations with Malaysia were growing very strong, enhanced by such changes as the new unified spelling system and an agreement on reciprocal recognition of university degrees.[118] With the fall of Indochina in 1975, Indonesia assumed an even more active role in regional politics. It has gained a significant leadership role within ASEAN, and now holds the permanent secretariat in Jakarta for which Indonesia pressed very hard against an alternative bid from Manila.[119] The Indonesian concept of "national resilience" has been transformed into "regional resilience" to connote the greater unity and confidence of the Southeast Asian states. Indonesia has also expanded its regional role by strengthening its relations with non-ASEAN states, particularly Burma. And it had an active part in the Indochina settlements under the International Commission of Control and Supervision following the U.S. withdrawal from Vietnam. The specific policies have changed from time to time, but Indonesia has consistently sought regional leadership "based on an exclusive pattern of relations among the resident states," although it does not yet have the power to shape the pattern.[120]

Indonesia's foreign policy has become more dynamic, compared with the early years of the New Order, although there has been no return to the flamboyant policies and practices of the Sukarno days. Moving with increased confidence, the New Order government has tried to reestablish Indonesia's "rightful" position as regional leader, especially with respect to ASEAN.[121] Tangible evidence of this new active foreign policy is found in Indonesia's opening of bilateral contacts with the Vietnamese in an effort to find a solution to the

Cambodian conflict.[122] Further evidence is seen in Indonesia's new initiatives and dialogue with the Soviet Union.[123] That Indonesia seeks a significant regional leadership role, at least in the archipelago, comparable to that of the great historical kingdoms of Srivijaya, Majapahit, and Mataram seems beyond doubt. Whether Indonesia can accept this leadership role and successfully meet the challenge posed by Vietnam in the consolidated Indochina is less clear.

Brunei. The Sultanate of Brunei gained full independence as late as January 1, 1984,[124] and developed a foreign policy plan that will bring it directly and positively into regional politics. As early as 1981, Brunei began to seek association with ASEAN and its members.[125] Malaysia has had its differences with Brunei and with the British handling of the independence process, and there were suspicions of Indonesian plans for annexation, but these problems have not inhibited Brunei's ASEAN membership, which was strongly supported by Indonesia.

Brunei's major concern as Southeast Asia's second ministate is the maintenance of its oil production, which approaches 200,000 barrels per day.[126] Even as the terms of independence were being developed, security was a major concern. Brunei wanted to retain a battalion of British Army Gurkhas under the sultan's command. However, the British balked at this prospect, feeling that any national security threat would likely "originate from sources within the country . . . yet the philosophy behind the deployment of the Gurkhas stems from the perception of an external threat."[127]

Brunei has also developed close relations with Islamic states and oil-producing states. Since independence, Brunei increasingly "looks to international bodies to amplify its voice." It has become an active participant in ASEAN, the British Commonwealth, the Islamic Conference Organization, and the United Nations.[128] Brunei has also developed close bilateral relations with Japan as its major trading partner for oil, natural gas, and beef.

FOREIGN POLICY RESPONSES

The states of Southeast Asia have gained considerable strength and experience in responding to the challenges of international politics. In the course of managing domestic politics in the years since independence, they have also shed many of the foreign trappings of government and politics inherited from the colonial period or adopted erroneously in the immediate postindependence period. Although they all remain weak in terms of foreign policy capabilities, as a region, the states have defined a common ground for regional diplomacy where none existed previously and, at the same time, have placed some limits on the ability of extraregional powers to act in the region. Regional interaction and cooperation have grown significantly and the client-state status of these states has diminished. Although many of the more dramatic goals of revolution and independence remain unfulfilled, the regional states have adopted more low-keyed approaches to domestic growth and development as well as international relations. As in domestic politics so it is in foreign policy: Patterns of regional interaction, diplomacy, and leadership have taken on more autochthonous meanings.

NOTES

1. Donald C. Daniel, "The Soviet Navy in the Pacific," Asia Pacific Community 4 (Spring/Early Summer 1979), pp. 66-84.
2. H. Wriggins, "The Asian State System in the 1970s," in Asia and the International System, edited by Wayne Wilcox, Leo E. Rose, and Gavin Boyd (Cambridge, Mass.: Winthrop Publishers, 1972), p. 349.
3. Estrella D. Solidum, "Philippine Perceptions of Crucial Issues Affecting Southeast Asia," Asian Survey 22 (June 1982), p. 536.
4. John H. Adkins, "Philippines 1972: We'll Wait and See," Asian Survey 13 (February 1973), p. 146.
5. Asia 1969 Yearbook (Hong Kong: Far Eastern Economic Review, 1969), p. 262.
6. Dick Wilson, The Neutralization of Southeast Asia (New York: Praeger Publishers, 1975), p. 68.
7. Asia 1975 Yearbook, p. 262.
8. M. Rajendran, ASEAN's Foreign Relations: The Shift to Collective Action (Kuala Lumpur: Arenabuku, 1985), p. 85.
9. Asia 1972 Yearbook, p. 270.
10. Guy J. Pauker, "Hegemonial Aspirants in Southeast Asia," in Diversity and Development in Southeast Asia: The Coming Decade, edited by Guy J. Pauker, Frank H. Golay, and Cynthia H. Enloe (New York: McGraw-Hill, 1977), p. 55.

240

11. Wilson, The Neutralization of Southeast Asia, pp. 69-70.

12. Asia 1975 Yearbook, p. 263.

13. Rolando V. del Carmen, "Philippines 1974: A Holding Pattern--Power Consolidation or Prelude to Decline?" Asian Survey 15 (February 1975), p. 136.

14. Bernard Wideman, "An Approach to the Muslim Rebels," Far Eastern Economic Review (November 22, 1974), p. 12.

15. Guy J. Pauker, "The North-South Conflict," in Pauker et al., Diversity and Development in Southeast Asia, p. 83.

16. Lela G. Noble, "The Philippines," Asian Survey 17 (February 1977), p. 139.

17. Asia 1979 Yearbook, p. 270.

18. Carlos F. Nivera, "National Threat Perceptions in the Philippines," in Threats to Security in East Asia-Pacific, edited by Charles E. Morrison (Lexington, Mass.: D. C. Heath and Co., 1983), pp. 129-130.

19. Solidum, "Philippine Perceptions of Crucial Issues Affecting Southeast Asia," p. 546.

20. Lela Garner Noble, "The National Interest and the National Image: Philippine Policy in Asia," Asia Survey 13 (June 1973), p. 575.

21. Stephen Chee, "Malaysia's Changing Foreign Policy," in Trends in Malaysia II (Singapore: Institute of Southeast Asian Studies, 1974), p. 47, cited in Wilson, The Neutralization of Southeast Asia, p. 65.

22. Marvin Rogers, "Malaysia/Singapore: Problems and Challenges of the Seventies," Asian Survey 11 (February 1971), p. 127.

23. Asia 1984 Yearbook, p. 194.

24. Ibid.

25. Stephen Chee, "Malaysia and Singapore: Separate Identities, Different Priorities," Asian Survey 13 (February 1973), p. 157.

26. Donald G. McCloud, "Indonesian Foreign Policy in Southeast Asia: A Study of the Patterns of Behavior" (Ph.D. dissertation, University of South Carolina, 1974), pp. 120-124, 136-142.

27. Wilson, The Neutralization of Southeast Asia, p. 67.

28. Lee Poh Ping, "The Indochinese Situation and the Big Powers in Southeast Asia: The Malaysia View," Asian Survey 22 (June 1982), p. 516.

29. R. S. Milne, "Singapore's Exit from Malaysia: The Consequences of Ambiguity," Asian Survey 6 (March 1966), pp. 175-184.

30. McCloud, in "Indonesian Foreign Policy in Southeast Asia," provides a quantitative measure of the depth to which Indonesia-Singapore relations plunged following this incident. Although relations were not severed, for all intents and purposes communications and all other official transactions stopped for a period of months following the hanging of the marines.

31. Asia 1970 Yearbook, p. 250.

32. Chee, "Malaysia and Singapore: Separate Identities, Different Priorities," p. 161.

33. Asia 1976 Yearbook, p. 273.

34. Shee Poon-Kim, "Singapore in 1977: Stability and Growth," Asian Survey 17 (February 1978), p. 198.

35. Asian 1974 Yearbook, p. 272.

36. Prime Minister Lee Kuan Yew, "National Day Speech" (August 17, 1980), cited in Lim Joo-Jock, "Singapore in 1980--Management of Foreign Relations and Industrial Progress," in Southeast Asian Affairs, 1981, edited by Leo Suradinata (Singapore: Institute of Southeast Asian Studies, 1981), p. 276.

37. Robert L. Rau, "The Role of Singapore in ASEAN," Contemporary Southeast Asia 3 (September 1981).

38. Frank H. Golay, "The Potential for Regionalism," in Pauker et al., Diversity and Development in Southeast Asia, p. 115. See also Chia Siow Yue, "ASEAN Economic Cooperation: Singapore's Dilemma," Contemporary Southeast Asia 2 (September 1980).

39. Asia 1983 Yearbook, p. 241.

40. Far Eastern Economic Review (April 5, 1984).

41. Lau Teik Soon, "National Threat Perceptions of Singapore," in Morrison, Threats to Security in East Asia-Pacific, p. 123.

42. Lee Boon Hiok, "Constraints on Singapore's Foreign Policy," Asian Survey 22 (March 1982), p. 526.

43. Jon S. T. Quah, "Singapore in 1984--Leadership Transition in an Election Year," Asian Survey 25 (February 1985), p. 230.

44. Lee Boon Hiok, "Constraints on Singapore's Foreign Policy," pp. 532-533.

45. McCarthy, "National Image and Diplomacy," Southeast Asia: An International Quarterly 2 (Fall 1972), p. 448.

46. Asia 1970 Yearbook, p. 290.

242

47. Somsakdi Xuto, "Thai Security Perceptions in Historical Perspective," in Morrison, Threats to Security in East Asia-Pacific, pp. 158-159.

48. Clark D. Neher, "Thailand: Toward Fundamental Change," Asian Survey 11 (February 1971), p. 136.

49. Leszak Buszynski, "Thailand: The Erosion of a Balanced Foreign Policy," Asian Survey 22 (November 1982), pp. 1037-1055.

50. David Morell, "Thailand: Military Checkmate," Asian Survey 12 (February 1972), p. 165.

51. Asia 1975 Yearbook, p. 308.

52. Khien Theeravit, "Thai-Kampuchean Relations: Problems and Prospects," Asian Survey 22 (June 1982), pp. 561-567.

53. Ganganath Jha, Foreign Policy of Thailand (New Delhi: Radiant Publishers, 1979), pp. 106-113.

54. Asia 1977 Yearbook, p. 318.

55. Juree Vichit-Vadakan, "Thailand in 1984: Year of Administering Rumors," Asian Survey 25 (February 1985), p. 234.

56. Theeravit, "Thai-Kampuchean Relations," pp. 569-571.

57. Buszynski, "Thailand: Erosion of a Balanced Foreign Policy," p. 1052.

58. Xuto, "Thai Security Perceptions in Historical Perspective," in Morrison, Threats to Security in East Asia-Pacific, p. 159. See also Sarasin Viraphol, "The Soviet Threat: Development of the Thai Perception," Asian Affairs: An American Review 11 (Winter 1985), pp. 61-70.

59. Asia 1972 Yearbook, p. 301.

60. Asia 1974 Yearbook, p. 289.

61. Allan Goodman, "Is It Too Late to End the Vietnam War?" Southeast Asia: An International Quarterly 1 (Fall 1971), p. 367.

62. Asia 1969 Yearbook, p. 244.

63. Joseph J. Zasloff and MacAlister Brown, Communist Indochina and U.S. Foreign Policy: Postwar Realities (Boulder, Colo.: Westview Press, 1978), p. 60.

64. Lee E. Dutter and Raymond S. Kania, "Explaining Recent Vietnamese Behavior," Asian Survey 20 (September 1980), pp. 931-942. See also Carlyle A. Thayer, "Vietnamese Perspectives on International Security: Three Revolutionary Currents," in Asian Perspectives on International Security, edited by Donald Hugh McMillen (London: Macmillan Publishers, 1984), pp. 57-76.

65. D. R. Sardesai, "Vietnam's Quest for Security," in Changing Patterns of Security and Stability in Asia,

edited by Sudershan Chawla and D. R. Sardesai (New York: Praeger Publishers, 1980), p. 239.

66. Asia 1976 Yearbook, p. 318.

67. Asia 1977 Yearbook, p. 329.

68. Sheldon Simon, "Vietnam: Regional Dominance Arising from the Failure of Great-Power Balances," in The Great-Power Triangle and Asian Security, edited by Raju G. C. Thomas (Lexington, Mass.: D. C. Heath, 1983), p. 85.

69. Ibid., pp. 85-86.

70. William J. Duiker, The Communist Road to Power in Vietnam (Boulder, Colo.: Westview Press, 1981), p. 339.

71. Philippe Devillers, "An Analysis of the Vietnamese Objectives in Indochina," in Indochina and Problems of Security and Stability in Southeast Asia, edited by Khien Theeravit and MacAlister Brown (Bangkok: Chulalongkorn University Press, 1981), p. 92.

72. Werner Draguhn, "The Indochina Conflict and the Positions of the Countries Involved," Contemporary Southeast Asia 5 (June 1983), pp. 95-99.

73. Craig Etcheson, The Rise and Demise of Democratic Kampuchea (Boulder, Colo., and London: Westview Press and Frances Pinter, 1984), pp. 192-194.

74. Stephen P. Heder, "The Kampuchean-Vietnamese Conflict," in The Third Indochina Conflict, edited by David W. P. Elliot (Boulder, Colo.: Westview Press, 1981), p. 35.

75. Ibid.

76. William J. Duiker, "Vietnam in 1984--Between Ideology and Pragmatism," Asian Survey 25 (January 1985), p. 103.

77. Douglas Pike, "Vietnam in 1981: Biting the Bullet," Asian Survey 22 (January 1982), p. 73.

78. Paul M. Kattenburg, "Living with Hanoi," Foreign Policy 53 (Winter 1983-1984), pp. 131-149.

79. Michael Eiland, "Kampuchea in 1984: Yet Further from Peace," Asian Survey 25 (January 1985), p. 110.

80. Pao-min Chang, "Beijing Versus Hanoi--The Diplomacy over Kampuchea," Asian Survey 23 (May 1983), p. 607.

81. John F. Copper, "China in Southeast Asia," in Southeast Asia Divided: The ASEAN Indochina Crisis, edited by Donald E. Weatherbee (Boulder, Colo.: Westview Press, 1985), p. 61.

82. Kattenburg, "Living with Hanoi," p. 149.

83. Donald E. Weatherbee, "Indonesia in 1984--Pancasila, Politics, and Power," Asian Survey 25 (February 1985), pp. 194-195; and Donald E. Weatherbee,

"The View from ASEAN's Southern Flank," Strategic Review 11 (Spring 1983), pp. 54-61.

84. Asia 1969 Yearbook, p. 121.

85. Asia 1974 Yearbook, p. 113.

86. Etcheson, The Rise and Demise of Democratic Kampuchea, pp. 162-180.

87. "The Long Road Back," Far Eastern Economic Review (November 29, 1984), p. 30. For a critical view of Vietnamese colonization in Cambodia, see Edmund F. McWilliams, Jr., "Hanoi's Course in Southeast Asia," Asian Survey 24 (August 1984), pp. 879-880.

88. Asia 1971 Yearbook, p. 215.

89. Paul F. Langer and Joseph J. Zasloff, North Vietnam and the Pathet Lao: Partners in the Struggle for Laos (Cambridge, Mass.: Harvard University Press, 1970), pp. 151-163.

90. Geoffrey C. Gunn, "Foreign Relations of the Lao People's Democratic Republic: The Ideological Imperative," Asian Survey 20 (October 1980), pp. 990-1007.

91. Asia 1984 Yearbook, p. 206.

92. Arthur J. Dommen, "Laos in 1984--The Year of the Thai Border," Asian Survey 25 (January 1985), pp. 119-120.

93. Dennis Duncanson, "Ideology, Tradition and Strategy in Indochina's Foreign Policy," Asian Affairs: Journal of the Royal Society for Asian Affairs 15 (February 1984), p. 44.

94. Draguhn, "The Indochina Conflict," p. 102.

95. Aung Kin, "Burma in 1980--Pouring Balm on the Sore Spots," in Suradinata, Southeast Asian Affairs, 1981, p. 121.

96. Josef Silverstein, Burma: Military Rule and the Politics of Stagnation (Ithaca: Cornell University Press, 1977), pp. 167-196.

97. Josef Silverstein, "Political Dialogue in Burma: A New Turn on the Road to Socialism," Asian Survey 10 (February 1970), p. 139.

98. Jon A. Wiant, "Burma: Loosening Up on the Tiger's Tail," Asian Survey 13 (February 1973), p. 186.

99. Ibid., p. 177.

100. Hugh MacDougall and Jon A. Wiant, "Burma in 1984: Political Stasis or Political Renewal," Asian Survey 25 (February 1985), p. 243.

101. Aung Kin, "Burma in 1980--Pouring Balm on the Sore Spots," in Suryadinata, Southeast Asian Affairs, 1981, p. 122.

102. Edwin W. Martin, "Burma in 1975: New Dimensions to Non-Alignment," Asian Survey 16 (February 1976), pp. 175-176.

103. David J. Steinberg, Burma: A Socialist Nation of Southeast Asia (Boulder, Colo.: Westview Press, 1982), p. 123.

104. Far Eastern Economic Review (August 15, 1985), pp. 64-66.

105. MacDougall and Wiant, "Political Stasis or Political Renewal," p. 243.

106. Werner Levi, The Challenge of World Politics in South and Southeast Asia (Englewood Cliffs, N.J.: Prentice-Hall, 1968), pp. 14, 22.

107. Lalta P. Singh, "Indonesian Foreign Policy: The Linkage Between Domestic Power Balance and Foreign Policy Behavior," Southeast Asia: An International Quarterly 1 (Fall 1971), pp. 379-394.

108. Allan A. Samson, "Indonesia 1973: A Climate of Concern," Asian Survey 14 (February 1974), p. 163.

109. Franklin B. Weinstein, Indonesian Foreign Policy and the Dilemma of Dependence (Ithaca: Cornell University Press, 1976).

110. Weinstein, "Indonesia," in Wilcox et al., Asia and the International System, p. 142. For an excellent detailed development of this thesis, see Weinstein's Indonesian Foreign Policy and the Dilemma of Dependence.

111. Robert C. Horn, "Soviet Influence in Southeast Asia: Opportunities and Obstacles," Asian Survey 15 (August 1975), p. 661.

112. Asia 1975 Yearbook, p. 191.

113. The Indonesia Times (August 5, 1985), p. 6.

114. Michael Leifer, Indonesia's Foreign Policy (London: Allen & Unwin, for the Royal Institute of International Affairs, 1983), p. 175.

115. McCloud, "Indonesian Foreign Policy in Southeast Asia," pp. 180-195.

116. Donald E. Weatherbee, "Portuguese Timor: An Indonesian Dilemma," Asian Survey 6 (December 1966), pp. 683-695.

117. Donald E. Weatherbee, "The Indonesianization of East Timor," Contemporary Southeast Asia 3 (June 1981), p. 17.

118. Allan A. Samson, "Indonesia 1972: The Solidification of Military Control," Asian Survey 13 (February 1973), p. 136.

119. Arnfinn Jorgensen-Dahl, _Regional Organization and Order in South-East Asia_ (London: Macmillan Press, 1982), p. 185.

120. Leifer, _Indonesia's Foreign Policy_, pp. 180-181.

121. Peter H. Lyon, "Indonesia: Reconciling Variable Roles, Regional Leadership, and "Great Power Intrusions," in Thomas, _Great-Power Triangle and Asian Security_, pp. 97-101.

122. Juwono Sudarsono, "Indonesia in Regional Affairs" (paper prepared for the Fletcher School/CSIS/Asia Society Conference on Indonesia, October 6-8, 1983), pp. 16-19. See also Weatherbee, "The View from ASEAN's Southern Flank," pp. 56-57.

123. Weatherbee, "Pancasila, Politics, and Power," p. 195.

124. S. J. Fulton, "Brunei: Past and Present," _Asian Affairs: Journal of the Royal Society for Asian Affairs_ 15 (February 1984), pp. 5-14.

125. Donald E. Weatherbee, "Brunei: The ASEAN Connection," _Asian Survey_ 23 (June 1983), p. 723.

126. Ibid., p. 725.

127. Hamzah Ahmad, "Oil and Security in Brunei," _Contemporary Southeast Asia_ 2 (September 1980), p. 188.

128. K. Mulliner, "Brunei in 1984: Business as Usual After the Gala," _Asian Survey_ 25 (February 1985), p. 219.

CHAPTER 11

Regional Politics:
Fragmentation and Cooperation

At independence, the states of Southeast Asia found little to bind them together. Although many regional leaders spoke of the prominence of regional politics and the importance of cooperation among neighboring states, the bonds with Europe and the allure of global politics were stronger. Despite the strain in relations between London and Rangoon at the time of Burma's independence, and even though Burma did not join the British Commonwealth, Burmese Foreign Minister U. E. Maung suggested that his country might consider a defense pact with India or Pakistan, both Commonwealth members. The British also continued to supply arms to the Burmese for use against Karen and other rebels.[1] The nonaligned movement, a response to the global bipolar pressures exerted by the Soviet and U.S. superpowers, did little to draw together its regional proponents--Burma, Indonesia, and Cambodia--because its global perspective, established by Indian Prime Minister Nehru, was pursued by Premier U Nu of Burma, President Sukarno of Indonesia, and Prince Sihanouk of Cambodia. The United Nations (as opposed to a regional bloc of states) was seen as the primary organized supranational forum in which smaller states might exert leverage and seek redress against global powers.

Further, the traditional regional political system offered few models for interstate cooperation. A key element for such cooperation--acceptance of the concept of sovereign and equal states--had not been part of the traditional system. Subjugation by force had been the primary means for dealing with neighbors, and the standard interstate relationship was superior to vassal. Although the concept of their neighbors' sovereignty was readily accepted by all of these states at the end of the colonial

247

period (with a few polemical objections such as
Indonesia's reaction to the creation of Malaysia and
Singapore), their traditional and colonial experiences
left the Southeast Asian states a legacy of isolation and
ignorance of regional politics and problems.

BILATERAL RELATIONS IN THE REGION

Throughout their time since independence, the states
of Southeast Asia have maintained bilateral relations,
although there have been breaks between states and the two
Vietnams were not universally recognized throughout the
region. Bilateral relations have frequently been governed
by domestic political climates and reactions to the
foreign policy initiatives of neighbors. For example, the
common revolutionary experiences of Vietnam and Indonesia
drew them very close together at the height of Sukarno's
power and sustained an ambiguous but substantive elan
between them, despite Indonesia's dramatic shift to the
right. Indonesia had criticized Malaysia because the
latter's road to independence was "too easy" and lacked
revolutionary struggle, but their relations have now
shifted from hostile confrontation to intimate
friendship. Thailand and the Philippines were held at
arm's length by other regional states because of their
alliance relationship with the United States, yet
opposition to the presence of U.S. military bases in those
countries did not foil their cooperation in the
establishment of ASEAN.

Actual breaks in relations between two regional states
have occurred only rarely. In 1962, the Philippines
claimed the territory of North Borneo (Sabah) in
opposition to the British plan to make it part of
Malaysia.[2] Ambassadors were withdrawn for a time after
late 1963, but consular relations between the Philippines
and Malaysia were opened again in early 1964. The new
Federation of Malaysia and Indonesia did not establish
relations immediately upon Malaysia's formation, although
informal communications were maintained. In the period
when Vietnam was divided into two states, not all of their
neighbor's recognized both or either. Despite the general
continuity of bilateral relations within the region,
cooperative interactions were few: "All the Southeast
Asian countries more or less regularly consult with other
nations--mostly those outside Southeast Asia."[3]

REGIONAL ASSOCIATION AND COOPERATION

The historical experience of the Southeast Asian states explains much of the initial lack and subsequent slow evolution of regional cooperation. In fact, the propensity for conflict in the traditional system and the intraregional isolationism maintained by the colonial powers make it is somewhat surprising that cooperation has evolved as rapidly as it apparently has. Nevertheless, progress in regional cooperation has often been found "wanting" by Western analysts who argue, for example, that "the phrase 'regional cooperation' has already inspired so much high-sounding prose and so little action that it is naive to hope for some solid progress."[4] In the decade of the 1950s, regional cooperation was limited and "fragmentation and dependence on external influences [were] the result of absence of regional solidarity and lack of common culture and communications, and also a consequence of the dependence of the structures of resources on external assistance."[5]

Yet in less than four decades since independence, these states have developed a creditable record in cooperative ventures. Cooperative patterns of intraregional relations have developed both because and in spite of the traditional interstate system. Although little emphasis was placed on interstate cooperation in the traditional system, the time period during which the traditional system operated has been established as the politico-cultural base that defines the contemporary region.[6] Despite the great diversity in Southeast Asia, there is a sense of regional identity among Southeast Asians themselves that sets them apart from the rest of Asia and the world now more than at any time in the past.[7] It is this same sense of identity that was notably missing at the time of the first arrival of the European colonial powers.

Explanations for the development of regional cooperation are many. Certainly the fact that the elites (if not all the peoples) of Southeast Asia have accepted the concept of the "nation-state" from the Western international system has provided the framework for such cooperation. Then, too, the experience of coping with cold war politics in the early decades of independence gave Southeast Asians a sense of being exploited and manipulated from the "outside," thereby stimulating their sense of commonality and identity. Finally, geographic and cultural proximity have given added meaning to their feelings of togetherness.[8]

The similarities of views and experiences among the leadership elites of these countries have also been important in the development of regional cooperation. For the most part Western educated, they have apparently accepted Western concepts of international politics and cooperation. Although political leaders in Southeast Asia are sometimes thought to inhibit regionalism because "insecure national elites cannot risk compromising national goals,"[9] others believe that regionalism is enhanced because the elites "do not have to negotiate and bargain with an array of well-entrenched, politically organized popular interest groups prior to making decisions on regional affairs."[10] It seems increasingly clear that the governmental elites of Southeast Asia have found common interests not only in their backgrounds but also in the problems they face. They have not sought to compromise national independence in favor of regional integration but, quite the opposite, have sought to use regional cooperation to further national development and strength.

Regional cooperation has taken many organized forms to meet a wide range of economic, security, and general political objectives. Some organizations, such as SEATO, have been substantially controlled by outside forces, while others have been largely regional creations. Yet even those created by regional states have not always been successful: The MAPHILINDO experience demonstrated that regional organizations cannot survive if the member states do not have a common purpose for the organization. Some organizations have been more successful, and ASEAN, functioning now for nearly twenty years, appears to have demonstrated that a regional organization supported by a group of states having common objectives can not only survive but prosper.

There are other organizations in the region that have been successful as well, although most are special interest organizations or development agencies. The numerous economic organizations active in Southeast Asia include the Asian Development Bank (ADB), which receives its primary financing from the United States and Japan. The ADB makes loans to the countries of Southeast Asia (and beyond), and its resources are great enough to have a substantial impact on economic development in the region. The United Nations Economic Council for Asia and the Far East (ECAFE) and the Economic Council for Asia and the

Pacific (ECAP) have also provided funds for multinational as well as national development projects in Southeast Asia.

An unusual attempt at functional cooperation was undertaken in the Mekong project. With money from the United States channeled through ECAFE, the Mekong plan called for a series of dams, hydroelectric plants, locks, and navigation channels on the entire length of the Mekong River.[11] Although the principal advocate and financier was the United States, the project was acceptable to all the Meking riparian states because management was directly in the hands of the United Nations and ECAFE.[12] This complex project has proceeded despite conflict in the Mekong area through nearly all its years of activities.[13]

On the other hand, security organizations have been held in suspicion by some of the states of Southeast Asia because they required alignment, particularly in the years during the cold war, with one or the other of the superpowers. The policies of "active neutrality" pursued by these states has meant that security agreements and organizations are often not welcome. Most of the regional states have come to understand their principal security threat to be internal instability and subversion. Organizations such as the U.S.-sponsored Southeast Asian Treaty Organization (SEATO), aimed at countering expansionist goals of Soviet Union and China, carried too many strings and offered too few advantages.

Nevertheless, extraregional organizations and alliances have offered some states in Southeast Asia support and security they had not found in regional groupings. The United Nations has been one such organization. Various Islamic organizations have been of interest to Indonesia and Malaysia. Thailand and the Philippines participated in the U.S.-dominated SEATO alliance and still maintain bilateral agreements with the United States. Vietnam has recently signed a friendship treaty with the Soviet Union. Malaysia and Singapore have maintained security treaty ties to Britain, Australia, and New Zealand but rejected membership in ASPAC because of its ostensible anti-communist bias.

These extraregional linkages have provided a sense of community and strength where none existed before within the region. In some contexts, these external security organizations and agreements have strengthened certain states within the region, but most have been detrimental to the development of intraregional cooperation. The SEATO alliance, while focused primarily on China, also provided a real threat to North Vietnam. The British defense agreements with Singapore and Malaysia were once perceived as threats by Indonesia. The new Soviet-Vietnamese treaty of friendship and cooperation, while again primarily focused on China, also increases the potential Vietnamese threat to other states in the region, particularly Thailand, and has contributed to the polarization of the region.

There have been several attempts at creating organizations to serve the interests of member states that were not led by extraregional powers. These organizations were not, for the most part, specifically focused on security or economic integration; rather, they provided in broad terms learning mechanisms for cooperation that neither the traditional nor the colonial systems offered.

The first attempt at regional cooperation through a formal, locally created, and locally managed organization was the Association of Southeast Asia (ASA) among Malaya, the Philippines, and Thailand. Established in 1961 as the culmination of increasing sentiment from various regional leaders for some type of regional organization, it was the precursor of ASEAN. Though ASA was originally advocated by Malaya and the Philippines, Thailand's foreign minister, Thanat Khoman, became the principal force behind its founding.[14] ASA was successful in developing an infrastructure for regional cooperation consisting of annual foreign ministers' meetings, several high-level working parties, and a series of functional committees. But it suffered from its limited membership of only three states and sorely missed the participation of Indonesia and Burma.[15] Nevertheless, it cut across the major ethnic and religious divisions in Southeast Asia, bringing together Buddhist (Thailand), Muslim (Malaya), and Christian (Philippines) cultural streams while lacking only sinicized Vietnam of the region's major cultural groups.[16] ASA was also nearly immobile during the conflict between Malaya and the Philippines over North Borneo, and by the time it was revived for the foreign ministers' meeting in July 1966, the region, (especially Indonesia) was in the midst of a major reorientation that ultimately transformed ASA into a new organization with wider participation and a stronger mandate.

Another early attempt at regional cooperation in 1962 and 1963 was the creation of "politics of the moment." As proposed by Philippine President Macapagal, the confederation of ethnic Malay states known as MAPHILINDO was created to serve the immediate political goals of its members. Malaysia sought to assuage its confrontations with the Philippines and Indonesia. The Philippines hoped to prevent the incorporation of North Borneo in the new Malaysia, whereas Indonesia believed that its support of MAPHILINDO would strengthen Manila's support for Indonesia's confrontation against Malaysia.[17]

MAPHILINDO had a very brief history. The conflicting goals of its members ensured that very little could be achieved. When negotiations between Indonesia and Malaysia commenced, they took place in a bilateral framework sponsored by third parties such as Thailand, the United States, and Japan, and MAPHILINDO served no role in ending this confrontation.[18] Yet the potential of ethnic unity and the expanse of archipelagic territory under one organization captured the imagination of all of Asia and demonstrated the potential of any regional organization that included Indonesia.[19] Moreover, although MAPHILINDO left serious doubts within Malaysia's political elite about the cooperation with Indonesia, the previous commitment of Sukarno to MAPHILINDO made much easier Suharto's subsequent decision to join the Association of Southeast Asian Nations. In their commitment to MAPHILINDO, both Malaysia and the Philippines formally and publicly acknowledged that Western military bases were "temporary in nature"[20]--an important concept for the growth of regional cooperation. It is doubtful, however, that the idea of a united Malay peoples, espoused particularly by some in Indonesia,[21] has potential for political expression because the same clan and ethnic suspicions that inhibit national integration make regional integration even less probable.[22]

The formation of MAPHILINDO also had strong anti-Chinese overtones.[23] For Indonesia, in particular, regional cooperation offered possible protection against a "sellout" by the local Chinese.[24] Fear of the Chinese, whether local or mainland, had "the regional states sufficiently worried to talk frankly about collective security."[25] The formation of Malaysia was particularly threatening because of the expanded hinterland it would provide for the economically potent--and ethnically Chinese--Singapore.[26] This view was clearly articulated by one of Indonesia's leading elder statesmen who opposed the formation of Malaysia because "the new state . . . would inevitably become a second China. . . . The Singapore Chinese would then be able to extend their power through the entire area."[27]

With the end of Indonesia's confrontation policies against Malaysia as well as the Philippines' recognition that its North Borneo claims were not likely to succeed, the archipelagic area of Southeast Asia entered a new period of stability. A greater degree of cooperation than had been envisioned under either ASA or MAPHILINDO became possible. Although by 1967 Indonesia was under the leadership of Suharto, whose New Order government was dismantling most of the old Sukarno policies, the declaration of the Association of Southeast Asian Nations was drawn to include concepts not only from ASA but also from the politically inspired MAPHILINDO--particularly with respect to regional responsibility for regional security and stability and the presence of foreign bases in Southeast Asia.[28]

There were differing views at the time as to whether a new organization was necessary or whether ASA should be expanded, but much of the politics of this issue was a matter of domestic perspectives. President Ferdinand Marcos of the Philippines favored ASA and reportedly wanted a new organization only if it could somehow be shown to bear his "imprint." He supposedly wanted to establish his own position vis-a-vis previous Filipino Presidents Carlos P. Garcia and Diosdado Macapagal, who had been instrumental in forming ASA and MAPHILINDO, respectively.[29] Malaysia's Prime Minister Tunku Abdul Rahman also opposed a new organization at first, insisting that the ASA framework was sound and could be expanded if Indonesia wanted to join. Although he clearly remained suspicious of Indonesia's intentions, he also found it difficult to work with the Philippines to give continued support to ASA. Furthermore, it was domestically important that the Malaysian government not give the appearance of subservience to Indonesia. Indonesia, for its part, has always perceived itself as the leading state in the archipelago if not the entire region,[30] and the idea of humbling itself by applying for membership in an organization in which Malaysia and the Philippines would hold approval or rejection did not seem domestically advisable to the fledgling Suharto government. Singapore was not involved in early discussions about the development of ASEAN. But, once again, it was the strong commitment of Thailand's foreign minister, Thanat Khoman, to regional development, as well as the rapport between him and Malaysia's prime minister, Tunku Abdul Rahman, that made ASEAN possible. Also important was the work of Indonesia's new foreign minister, Adam Malik, in stressing the need for broader regional cooperation and giving sincere assurances of new directions for Indonesia.

The formation of ASEAN was said to herald a new era of regional cooperation for Southeast Asia, since it included most of the non-Communist states of the region and especially Indonesia.[31] More important, this step toward regional cooperation was adapted to Southeast Asian needs. In a manner historically similar to the borrowing of political concepts from outside the region and the molding of them to meet indigenous needs, the integrative tendencies pervasive in Western thinking on regionalism[32] were specifically rejected in favor of building a regional organization that would strengthen rather than diminish national identity and autonomy: "ASEAN is not a confederation, not to mention a federation, but simply an organization of sovereign states preserving their 'national identities,' all equal partners with no leaders (in theory), freely associating with one another."[33] This has clearly been the Indonesian view since ASEAN's beginning. A close adviser to President Suharto said that regional cooperation "is a diplomacy based on national interest, based fully on the condition and objective demands of the country concerned."[34] Put in its simplest terms, regional cooperation in Southeast Asia should be understood as the "collectivisation of interests aimed at national survival and the improvement of the international status quo."[35] Yet Western scholars, overlooking the Southeast Asians' desires, still insist that "meaningful economic integration . . . has yet to progress beyond a preliminary stage of economic regionalism."[36]

The first decade of ASEAN cooperation witnessed much discussion as the member states explored the problems and possibilities of cooperation through a formal, regional institution. Their progress was limited because of the lack of precedent for such cooperation and also because of the continuation of several bilateral conflicts among them. The continuing Sabah conflict between Malaysia and the Philippines during 1968 and 1969 made full cooperation impossible. Despite a personal appeal from President Suharto, relations between Singapore and Indonesia following Singapore's decision to execute two Indonesian marines captured during the Sukarno years were strained nearly to breaking.[37] The ability of the ASEAN member states to act collectively or bilaterally remained limited by the lack of cohesion and the growing ethnic fragmentation within the states among other factors.[38]

Analysts repeatedly expressed a mixture of hope and concern for ASEAN's potential,[39] but outside observers, ignoring the lack of historical precedent for cooperation, have probably established hopes that were premature and unattainable. The learning process in cooperation and the time needed to define problems in common terms have not been recognized in assessments of ASEAN. The traditional regional system clearly had considered conflict, not cooperation, to be the dominant mode of interaction.

There were substantive accomplishments in policies and programs during ASEAN's first ten years. For instance, in recognition of the vulnerability of the organization to political change, a system of meetings among foreign ministers or heads of state was set in place. Funding for ASEAN came through a joint account established in 1969 with contributions of US$1 million from each member state. These funds were used in projects subsequently approved by the foreign ministers in conference. Numerous agreements covered mostly uncontroversial issues such as tourism and educational exchange, and coordinated such activities as assistance for planes and ships in distress. A central ASEAN Secretariat was established to strengthen the organization's institutional character. In its external relations, ASEAN was not successful in attracting other regional states, particularly Burma, to join. South Vietnam's membership application was rebuffed, although South Vietnamese participants attended the meetings as observers.[40] ASEAN also played an important role in restoring diplomatic relations between Malaysia and the Philippines in 1969. In November 1971, the ASEAN foreign ministers approved the Kuala Lumpur Declaration stating that they would increase their solidarity and cooperation in order to have Southeast Asia universally recognized as a "zone of peace, freedom and neutrality" free from external manipulation, interference, and intervention. First articulated by Malaysia less than one year after ASEAN's founding and given varying degrees of support from other ASEAN members, ZOPFAN represented a measure of the level of strategic thinking within ASEAN. Although implementation strategies remain obscure, the doctrine gives coherence to several important concepts: (1) It acknowledged that the extraregional powers could not be removed from the region by the weaker regional powers, even acting collectively; and (2) neutrality in global struggles remains the only likely way for smaller states to avoid becoming pawns in superpower struggles.

The framework of ASEAN was obviously political in the sense that economics cannot be separated from politics, particularly for developing countries, although there appear to be only limited possibilities for intraregional economic cooperation within the ASEAN framework.[41] But politics in the sense of formal regional security or strategic policies were very limited from the beginning of ASEAN. The only military term included in the ASEAN Declaration is the reference to foreign bases. Ignoring the varying forms of member governments (with no reference to democracy), the declaration stresses regional linkages of history and culture, mutual interests, and common problems.[42] Much of ASEAN's first decade was spent defining these ties.

The Bali summit in 1976 was held in a "new" Southeast Asia, devoid of U.S. military power in Vietnam. Although the meeting revealed "much more public attention to political and security matters than usual," the five state leaders reconfirmed the belief that "economic rather than military cooperation was the key to stability in the region."[43] At Bali, the ASEAN heads of state also agreed to establish a permanent ASEAN secretariat and signed a Treaty of Amity and Cooperation for the settlement of disputes through processes established in the treaty, which among other goals became a framework for more effective policy coordination and formulation among ASEAN states at the regional level.[44]

ASEAN's tenth year (1977) proved to be its most substantive up to that time. Early in the year, a preferential trade agreement was signed. Several other agreements included a declaration of mutual assistance in natural disasters, as well as commodity-sharing agreements for oil products and rice. An ASEAN summit was held again in 1977, attended also by the prime ministers of Japan, New Zealand, and Australia, who participated in discussions concerning development assistance for ASEAN and its members. At that time, Japanese Prime Minister Fukuda added substance to Japan's efforts to rebuild its image in the region by pledging US$1 billion in credits for five regional industrial projects. Also in 1977, the first talks between ASEAN and the United States took place in Manila. It seemed that the world had begun to recognize more clearly the progress and prospect for regional cooperation in Southeast Asia: "ASEAN is a positive reality . . . an organic international organization, in the critical sense that like nations modify their interest in the regional collective cause."[45]

If ASEAN's first decade focused introspectively on defining areas of commonality, the second decade seems to have taken a dramatically different direction. Economic cooperation or integration through such agreements as an ASEAN free-trade zone has not developed. Nor have the five highly publicized, Japanese-funded regional industrial projects been successful. Low-level economic adjustments have been made, but Indonesia, which holds the weakest economic position of the ASEAN states, has blocked significant progress because of its sense of vulnerability, especially to Singapore.

Based on the recognition that "regional associations will afford bargaining power with foreign powers that individual governments lack,"[46] the ASEAN states have found the organization to be a useful mechanism for unified dealings with larger, extraregional, economic powers. In 1972, ASEAN ministers created the Special Coordinating Committee of ASEAN Nations (SCCAN) and, later, its subsidiary, the ASEAN Brussels Committee (ABC), both of which have coordinated activities and negotiated agreements among the members of the European Economic Community (EEC). In the years following, relations between ASEAN and the EEC have grown and joint ministerial meetings have been held, although the level of activity between them is comparatively low because ASEAN and Southeast Asia remain "relatively low in the European scale of global priorities."[47] In the time since the consolidation of Vietnam's control in Indochina, however, the EEC has taken a greater security interest in ASEAN.[48] ASEAN has also engaged in "active dialogue" with such organizations as the Economic and Social Commission for Asia and the Pacific (ESCAP) and the United Nations Development Program (UNDP).[49]

At other levels of external relations, ASEAN has dealt directly with such states as Japan, Australia, New Zealand, Canada, and the United States in an effort to negotiate more favorable economic positions. In some cases, such negotiations have focused on a specific commodity as in the Japan-ASEAN Forum on Synthetic Rubber, through which ASEAN has tried to protect the production levels of natural rubber (under pressure from increasing production of synthetic rubber).[50] However, despite the Fukuda Doctrine, Japan has been slow to deal directly with ASEAN, preferring separate bilateral agreements.[51] Negotiations with other bilateral partners, especially the

United States and Australia, have been difficult, but from the ASEAN perspective they have demonstrated that collective bargaining and action substantially strengthens the negotiating positions of these individually relatively weak states. To better deal with external organizations, ASEAN has formed a coordinated system of assignments for each member state to be responsible for relations with a particular state or organization.[52]

ASEAN will also play a key role in the development of the Pacific Community. In 1984, in fact, the ASEAN foreign ministers "strongly endorsed the so-called Pacific concept which calls for increased cooperation among littoral states of the Pacific Ocean."[53] Early considerations of the Pacific community concept, although acknowledging Southeast Asia's strategic position in the grouping, prompted concern that ASEAN's identity would be lost in the much larger Pacific arena.[54] However, the concept has grown: When the ASEAN foreign ministers met in Jakarta in July of 1984, they also met collectively for the third time with their counterparts from Australia, Canada, Japan, New Zealand, and the United States in what has been dubbed the "6+5."[55] ASEAN's confidence in acting decisively within the new Pacific community is important to both ASEAN and the larger community.

The primary value of ASEAN, despite repeated statements to the contrary, would appear to be strategic and security-related management of regional order.[56] It has been observed that "from the outset ASEAN helped provide an intangible yet quite significant security function by creating a sense of solidarity among like-minded governments keenly aware of their delicate internal power bases."[57] Although the ASEAN member states have felt economically vulnerable owing to their varying degrees of underdevelopment, it is the potential for internal political manipulation of their underdevelopment by external forces that they most fear because the international environment is viewed as "predatory, hazardous, even brutish in nature."[58] Initially, the concept of security was articulated in terms of national and later regional "resilience," meaning the development of sufficient levels of domestic stability so as to eliminate the potential bases for Communist or other insurgency. To enhance security, joint border patrols and information exchanges were begun on a bilateral basis. Particularly from the Indonesian perspective, China was the principal threat, not in terms of direct invasion but because of its willingness and ability to support internal insurgencies led by local Communist groups.[59] This view of China became an ASEAN version of the old "domino theory."[60]

The security role of ASEAN remains an indirect one. Various member states, both before and since the formation of ASEAN, conducted joint military exercises and numerous joint border patrol operations, but these continue outside the ASEAN framework. ASEAN is not a formal military alliance, nor is it linked directly to external alliance with the British through Malaysia or Singapore or the United States through Thailand or the Philippines. Such security as it offers is derived from the ·collective strength gained from internal harmony and stability, thus precluding opportunities for external penetration and disruption. Nevertheless, while an alliance is out of the question, ASEAN is a security organization because of the "shared sense of priorities of its member governments"--even though its primary function is limited to giving "attention to apprehensions which they hold in common through displays of political solidarity and attempts at harmonization of policy as well as through economic cooperation."[61]

With the fall of South Vietnam and Cambodia to North Vietnamese control, the security picture for ASEAN changed dramatically.[62] Although views within ASEAN differ as to whether the current principal threat to national and regional resilience arises from Vietnam or China, ASEAN has shown itself to be rather skillful in managing politically the regional and global aspects of its growing confrontation with Vietnam. Beginning in 1975, the ASEAN states confronted the reality of the U.S. retreat from Vietnam and that country's unification, as well as the collapse of the conservative military government in Cambodia. Although not previously outspoken in support of U.S. involvement in Vietnam (despite participation in the war by two ASEAN members), the group was unprepared initially to deal with a fully Communist Indochina.

Vietnam's invasion of Cambodia and its installation of a client government there brought ASEAN to a united opposition position.[63] The ASEAN governments were unable to meet this invasion with a military response and could do little to undermine the growing Soviet support of Vietnam and its policies, but they have succeeded at the global level in inducing a much greater degree of rejection of Vietnam's actions and isolation of its

position. The most obvious manifestation of this
isolation has surfaced at the UN, where Vietnam first
sought to have its client government recognized and
seated. As ASEAN lobbying in each successive year proved
successful in defeating recognition by substantial
margins, Vietnam eventually dropped its initiative to have
the Heng Samrin regime seated in the UN. ASEAN also
successfully guided resolutions through the UN General
Assembly calling on Vietnam to withdraw its troops from
Cambodia and to allow Cambodians to select their own
government. Finally, to head off waning support for the
ASEAN position because it seemed to legitimize the vicious
Khmer Rouge, ASEAN brought together the coalition of
Cambodian opposition groups, which, though very weak,
enabled ASEAN to gloss over Khmer Rouge atrocities. The
issues themselves may not soon be resolved, but both the
political and global nature of these ASEAN policy
initiatives have great significance for the future of
ASEAN.

There are important differences among ASEAN members in
their respective bilateral approaches to Vietnam.
Thailand, as the "frontline" state confronting the
expanded Communist threat and with substantial ethnic
linkage across its borders, reacted as expected with the
greatest concern. The Philippines, at the other end of
the spectrum, did not see the changed situation in
Indochina as much of a threat. Indonesia and Malaysia,
still viewing China and the Chinese as the primary
regional threat, have been conciliatory toward Vietnam.
Indonesia, initially cautious in remembering its common
revolutionary heritage with the Vietnamese but also
distrusting their Communist ideology, has made serious
bilateral overtures toward Vietnam in seeking a solution
outside of the ASEAN framework. By the mid-1980s,
Indonesia was aggressively seeking solutions through
bilateral action, although still not rejecting the ASEAN
strategy. Singapore supported the Thai position but
raised concerns about the increasing bipolarization of the
region.[64] While recognizing these different bilateral
policies, ASEAN has nonetheless been able to maintain a
common regional policy in opposition to Vietnam.

As with most previous ASEAN ventures, its Indochina
initiatives have succeeded not because national goals were
subjugated to a greater regional goal, but because a
regional policy was shaped that took into account the
critical need of one state (in this case, Thailand) while
leaving room for others (Malaysia and Indonesia) to play

out their own policy initiatives. The seriousness of the Cambodian crisis and its direct threat to Thai security make the entire Indochina crisis a formidable challenge for the ASEAN decisional processes. The bilateral initiatives by ASEAN member states cannot ignore Thai sensitivities without threatening the fabric of the organization. On the other hand, as the ASEAN position has become caught up in global politics, the regional focus can be more readily maintained through bilateral contact. Although the strategy of mixing bilateral initiatives with the joint ASEAN approach may be confusing and appear weak in integrative terms, the reality of the matter for Southeast Asia and ASEAN is that integration is not now and perhaps never will be the critical issue.

Regional cooperation in Southeast Asia, which during the early post-World War II years had been singularly "in response to outside leadership,"[65] has increasingly followed indigenous initiatives. The Thais, sensing by the early 1960s that U.S. support would not last forever, moved toward regional cooperation through ASA. The successive withdrawals of the French, British, and Americans left primary control of security in the hands of the regional states. With the temporary relaxation of global confrontation in Southeast Asia, the regional states focused more directly on their principal security concern--internal subversion.

The decline of cold war bipolarity in Southeast Asia and the cuts in U.S. support may have given the regional states a broader range of foreign policy options and a greater measure of security. Although this apparent latitude would appear to contradict the view that for states such as those in Southeast Asia, "an increase in security almost always meant some loss of autonomy."[66] The breakdown of the U.S. alliance system in Southeast Asia did not stimulate new threats to the security of most of the regional states. Except for Thailand, the ASEAN states have experienced a greater measure of stability, particularly in their relations with China. Vietnam, on the other hand, has entered an alliance with the USSR but still feels a major threat to its security from China.

Interstate cooperation in Southeast Asia, however, must be understood in the context of the traditional regional system. There is no historical precedent for intense political cooperation, as the chronicles and oral traditions of the region give value to aggrandizement of the individual state at the expense of neighbors. Neither did the colonial experience provide positive reinforcement for cooperative policies. Yet, also in the traditional style of the region, cooperation has been the role of personalized leadership, as exemplified in the decisional importance of summit diplomacy in development of ASEAN.[67]

The contemporary states of Southeast Asia, beginning from this base, have had to define the very terms of cooperative politics, build a knowledge base of interests and peculiarities of each neighboring state, and seek out strands of commonality among themselves. That they have succeeded in such organizations as ASEAN is more than remarkable, given their individual problems of national identity and cohesion, the contemporary instability throughout the region, and the propensity for external penetration and interference.

RESPONSES TO REGIONAL POLITICS

Regional cooperation among Southeast Asian states can be divided into three periods: 1945 to 1959, when most political initiatives originated with powers outside the region; 1960 to 1967, when the states within the region began to experiment with regional organization directly; and after 1967 when regional cooperation became entrenched in the foreign policies of a majority of the states in Southeast Asia.[68] Parallel with this increasing regional cooperation are several other trends that have characterized regional politics since the states of Southeast Asia gained independence. First, over a similar period of time, there has been a trend toward diminishing relationships with former colonial metropoles. Second, the limits of superpower intervention have been defined, and the regional states themselves have taken a greater role in defining the agenda for regional politics. And, third, that regional agenda is increasingly being defined in terms of cultural and historical understandings of the region itself.

Regional cooperation in Southeast Asia has from the beginning been constructed around concepts of the exclusiveness of the region. All of the internally founded organizations--ASA, MAPHILINDO, and ASEAN--have accentuated the theme of Asian solidarity and the "Asian way" for management of interstate relations. MAPHILINDO, in particular, had peculiarly racial and geographic connotations given its ethnic Malay and archipelagic Southeast Asian composition. The concepts underlying this "Asian way"--such as ASEAN's consensus-style decisionmaking processes and the ability of the group to think in terms of regional cooperation to strengthen national rather than integrative capacities--remain somewhat obscure. All have focused some of their regional exclusiveness on China and, to a lesser extent, on other extraregional powers. This exclusiveness has heightened regional consciousness. Although the concept of a regional culture seems an exaggeration,[69] it is apparent that the commonality of culture throughout the region has enhanced the development of a regional identity; to the extent that this regional identity is developed, so the likelihood of regional cooperation is strengthened.

NOTES

1. John F. Cady, A History of Modern Burma (Ithaca: Cornell University Press, 1958), pp. 597-598.
2. Bernard K. Gordon, The Dimensions of Conflict in Southeast Asia (Englewood Cliffs, N.J.: Prentice-Hall, 1966), pp. 9-40.
3. Richard Butwell, Southeast Asia, Today-and Tomorrow (New York: Praeger Publishers, 1961), p. 163.
4. Far Eastern Economic Review (December 18, 1969), p. 593.
5. George Modelski, "Indonesia and the Malaysia Issue," The Yearbook of World Affairs, 1964 (London: Sweet and Maxwell Stevens Journals, for the London Institute of World Affairs, 1965), p. 130.
6. Sharon Siddique, "Cultural Development in ASEAN: The Need for an Historical Perspective," in ASEAN Identity, Development and Culture, edited by R. P. Anand and Purificacion V. Quisumbing (Quezon City and Honolulu: University of the Philippines and the East-West Center, Culture Learning Institute, 1981), pp. 68-85.
7. J.D.B. Miller, "How Many Asias Are There?" Asia Pacific Community 3 (Winter 1978-1979), pp. 70-72.
8. For the converse of this point, see Fred R. von der Mehden, "Southeast Asian Relations with Africa," Asian Survey 5 (July 1965), p. 341, where the author describes these relations as "sparce and seemingly haphazard"--a description that still applies. Some Southeast Asian states have found common bonds in Islamic organizations, although the differences between Middle Eastern and Southeast Asian Islam seem to lessen the potential for these groups to supplant the region as a primary focal point.

9. Pauker, "Geographic Abstraction or Political Reality," in Diversity and Development in Southeast Asia, edited by Guy J. Pauker, Frank H. Golay, and Cynthia Enloe (New York: McGraw-Hill, 1977), p. 20.

10. H. Wriggins, "The Asian State System in the 1970's," in Asia and the International System, edited by Wayne Wilcox, Leo E. Rose, and Gavin Boyd (Cambridge, Mass.: Winthrop Publishers, 1972), p. 367, citing Ernest Haas, "The Challenge of Regionalism," in Contemporary Theory in International Relations, edited by Stanley Hoffman (Englewood Cliffs, N.J.: Prentice-Hall, 1961), p. 236.

11. C. Hart Schaaf and Russell H. Fifield, The Lower Mekong: Challenge to Cooperation in Southeast Asia (Princeton, N.J.: Van Nostrand Company, 1963), pp. 100-118. See also Prachoom Chomchai, "The Mekong Development Plan: Its Problems and Prospects," Asia Pacific Community 1 (Summer 1978), pp. 43-56.

12. Donald G. McCloud, "The United States Toward Regional Organizations in Southeast Asia," World Affairs 133 (September 1970), pp. 137-140.

13. See the report of the Committee for Coordination of Investigations of the Lower Mekong Basin, Annual Report 1984 (Bangkok: ESCAP, 1985).

14. Bernard K. Gordon, East Asian Regionalism and United States Security (McLean, Va.: Research Analysis Corporation, 1968), p. 42.

15. North Vietnam was not invited to join, and it was generally understood that neither Laos nor Cambodia would participate.

16. Charles A. Fisher, South-East Asia: Social, Economic and Political Geography (London: Methuen, 1964), p. 773.

17. Gordon, East Asian Regionalism, pp. 47-48.

18. Ibid., pp. 48-49.

19. Frances L. Starner, "Mysteries of MAPHILINDO," Far Eastern Economic Review (May 14, 1964), pp. 335-337; Albert Ravenhold, "MAPHILINDO: Dream or Achievable Reality?" (Manila: American University Field Staff, Inc., 1964); and George McT. Kahin, "Malaysia and Indonesia," Pacific Affairs 37 (Fall 1964), pp. 266-267.

20. Guy J. Pauker, "Indonesia in 1963: The Year of Wasted Opportunities," Asian Survey 4 (February 1964), p. 689.

21. See Alejandro M. Fernandez, "The Greater Malayan Confederation Proposal: Cultural, Economic and Political Consideration," in "Proposed Outlines of a Greater Malayan

Confederation" (Manila: unpublished document of the University of the Philippines), cited in Gordon, The Dimensions of Conflict, pp. 22-23; see also Muhammad Yamin, "Unity of Our Country and Our People," in Indonesian Political Thinking, 1945 to 1965, edited by Herbert Feith and Lance Castles (Ithaca: Cornell University Press, 1970), p. 438.

22. In Arnold Brackman, Southeast Asia's Second Front: The Power Struggle in the Malay Archipelago (Singapore: Donald Moore Press, Ltd., 1966), the author argues that the "Malay triangle formed a second barrier--after Indochina--against Communist expansion."

23. Kahin, "Malaysia and Indonesia," pp. 254, 264-265.

24. Michael Leifer, "Trends in Regional Association in Southeast Asia," Asian Studies 2 (August 1964), p. 196.

25. Werner Levi, "The Future of Southeast Asia," Asian Survey 10 (April 1970), p. 350.

26. John O. Sutter, "Two Faces of Konfrontasi: 'Crush Malaysia' and the GESTAPU," Asian Survey 6 (October 1966), p. 527.

27. Mohammad Hatta, "One Indonesian View of the Malaysia Issue," Asian Survey 5 (March 1965), p. 140.

28. See Gordon, East Asian Regionalism, pp. 52-54. Gordon presents a chart showing nearly verbatim transposition of parts of the MAPHILINDO text to the ASEAN declaration.

29. Ibid., pp. 55, 63.

30. Numerous analysts have pointed to Indonesia's desire for regional leadership. For example, George Modelski identified three Indonesian goals: (1) regional hegemony, (2) leadership of a regional association, or (3) dynamic leadership of all regional states when participating in the global system. See Modelski, "Indonesia and the Malaysia Issue," pp. 141-143. See also George McT. Kahin who, in "Malaysia and Indonesia," p. 263, says that the Indonesians assume a "moral right" to regional leadership; or L. Edward Shuck, Jr., who, in "The Outward Reach of Indonesia," Current History 63 (December 1972), p. 258, argues that Indonesia "covets" regional leadership; or John O. Sutter who, in "Two Faces of Konfrontasi," contends that Indonesia has always sought to maintain a regional leadership role and has reacted negatively to events that might threaten their regional role.

31. Gordon, The Dimensions of Conflict, pp. 191-193, and East Asian Regionalism, passim; as well as Sheldon Simon, "East Asia," in World Politics, edited by James N.

Rosenau, Kenneth W. Thompson, and Gavin Boyd (New York: Free Press, 1976), p. 530; and Donald C. Hellmann, Japan and East Asia: The New International Order (New York: Praeger Publishers, 1972), pp. 33-34. See also Tan Sok Joo, ASEAN: A Bibliography (Singapore: Institute of Southeast Asian Studies, Library Bulletin No. 11, 1977); and Ikuo Iwasaki, Japan and Southeast Asia, A Bibliography of Historical, Economic, and Political Relations (Tokyo: Institute of Developing Economies, 1983).

32. William R. Thompson, "The Regional Subsystem: A Conceptual Explication and a Propositional Inventory," International Studies Quarterly 17 (March 1973), pp. 89-117. This article contains a summary of the major characteristics of regional systems; yet it leaves little room for regional development based on non-Western cultural and historic experience.

33. Russell H. Fifield, National and Regional Interests in ASEAN: Competition and Cooperation in International Politics (Singapore: Institute of Southeast Asian Studies, Occasional Paper no. 57, 1979), p. 7.

34. Ali Moertopo, Indonesia in Regional and International Cooperation: Principles of Implementation and Construction (Jakarta: Yayasan Proklamasi, 1973), p. 3.

35. Fuad Hassan, "Notes on the Prospects of Regionalism in Southeast Asia," (Jakarta: Institute of Strategic Studies, 1973), mimeographed.

36. Frank H. Golay, "The Potential for Regionalism," in Pauker et al., Diversity and Development in Southeast Asia, p. 117.

37. Donald G. McCloud, "Indonesia in Southeast Asia: An Events Data Assessment of Indonesia's Primary Foreign Policy Environment," Asian Forum 9 (Winter/Spring 1976-1977), pp. 67, 78-79.

38. Arnfinn Jorgensen-Dahl, Regional Organization and Order in South-East Asia (London: Macmillan Press, 1982), pp. 212-221.

39. Asia 1975 Yearbook (Hong Kong: Far Eastern Economic Review, 1975), p. 64.

40. Asia 1974 Yearbook, p. 289.

41. Bernard K. Gordon, "Economic Impediments to Regionalism in Southeast Asia," in The International Politics of Asia, edited by George P. Jan (Belmont, Calif.: Wadsworth Publishing Co., 1969), p. 371.

42. Fifield, National and Regional Interests in ASEAN, p. 7.

43. Ibid., p. 15.

44. Agerico O. Lacanlale, "Community Formation in ASEAN's External Relations," in Anand and Purificacion, ASEAN, Identity, Development and Culture, p. 381. The full text of the ASEAN Treaty of Amity and Cooperation can be found in the Asia 1977 Yearbook, pp. 58-59.

45. "Relationships," Asia 1977 Yearbook, p. 57.

46. Sudershan Chawla, Melvin Gurtov, and Alain-Gerard Marsot, eds., Southeast Asia Under the New Balance of Power (New York: Praeger Publishers, 1974), p. 114.

47. Stuart Harris and Brian Bridges, European Interests in ASEAN (London: Routledge & Kegan Paul, for the Royal Institute of International Affairs, 1983), p. 72. See also M. Rajendran, ASEAN's Foreign Relations: The Shift to Collective Action (Kuala Lumpur: Arenabuku, 1985), pp. 61-62, 147.

48. Robert Hull, "European Community-ASEAN Relations: A Model for International Partnership?" Asian Affairs: Journal of the Royal Society for Asian Affairs 15 (February 1984), p. 24.

49. Jun Nishikawa, ASEAN and the United Nations System (New York: United Nations Institute for Training and Research, 1983).

50. Rajendran, ASEAN's Foreign Relations, pp. 147-149.

51. Frances Lai Fung-wai, "Without a Vision: Japan's Not Playing a Greater Role in ASEAN's Solidarity and Development," in Anand and Purificacion, ASEAN Identity, Development and Culture, pp. 342-344. See also Chee Peng Lim, "International Rivalry: U.S.-Japanese Competition in the ASEAN Countries," Contemporary Southeast Asia 4 (June 1982), pp. 35-57.

52. Lacanlale, "Formation of ASEAN's External Relations," in Anand and Purificacion, ASEAN Identity, Development and Culture, pp. 385-387.

53. Asia 1985 Yearbook, p. 235.

54. Zakaria Haji Ahmad, "The Pacific Basin and ASEAN: Problems and Prospects," Contemporary Southeast Asia 2 (March 1981), pp. 339-340.

55. Sean Randolph, "Pacific Overtures," Foreign Policy 57 (Winter 1984/1985), p. 138.

56. Michael Leifer, "The Paradox of ASEAN, A Security Organization Without the Structure of an Alliance," The Round Table 271 (July 1978), p. 261.

57. Charles E. Morrison and Astri Suhrke, "ASEAN in Regional Defense and Development," in Changing Patterns of Security and Stability in Asia, edited by Sudershan Chawla and D. R. Saedesai (New York: Praeger Publishers, 1980), p. 201.

58. Jorgensen-Dahl, Regional Organization and Order in South-East Asia, p. 72.

59. Ibid., pp. 99-104.

60. Leifer, Indonesia's Foreign Policy (London: Allen & Unwin, for the Royal Institue of International Affairs, 1983), pp. 132, 179-180.

61. Leifer, "The Paradox of ASEAN," p. 264.

62. See K. K. Nair, ASEAN-Indochina Relations Since 1975: The Politics of Accommodation (Canberra: Australian National University Press, Canberra Papers on Strategy and Defense, No. 30, 1984).

63. Lau Teik Soon, "ASEAN and the Cambodian Problem," Asian Survey 22(June 1982), pp. 548-560.

64. Chan Heng Chee, "The Interests and Role of ASEAN in the Indochina Conflict," in Indochina and Problems of Security and Stability in Southeast Asia, edited by Khien Theeravit and MacAlister Brown (Bangkok: Chulalongkorn University Press, 1981), pp. 184-187.

65. William Henderson, "The Development of Regionalism in Southeast Asia," International Organization 9 (November 1955), p. 476.

66. Marshall R. Singer, "The Foreign Policies of Small Developing States," in Rosenau et al., World Politics, p. 289.

67. Jorgensen-Dahl, Regional Organization and Order in South-East Asia, pp. 186-189.

68. Ibid., pp. 9-14.

69. See Raul A. Boncan, "ASEAN, The Natural Community," Asia Pacific Community 2 (Fall 1978), pp. 46-47; and, in entirety, Anand and Purificacion, ASEAN Identity, Development and Culture.

CHAPTER 12

The Interstate System of Contemporary Southeast Asia

Southeast Asia has historically been and still remains a subordinate state system. Nevertheless, its traditional cultures were vibrant and economically diverse, and as the region has reestablished its identity in the contemporary global system, its traditional vibrance, originality, and independence have reappeared, despite its subordinance to the global and greater Asian systems. At independence these states began a process of accommodation and adjustment to a global system built on values and institutions from the old European regional system. At the same time the values and institutional concepts from their own traditional system were reawakened and reasserted. As the states have gained cohesion and strength internally as well as experience in the international field, the Southeast Asian system has shown a growing measure of independence and creativity in responding to its subordinate position. This trend will continue. Although Southeast Asia will not lose its subordinate status, it will increase its effectiveness in dealing with that status.

The foreign policies of the states of the region demonstrate, in particular, the trend toward more effective relationships. During the 1950s and early 1960s, the more influential regional leaders devoted much effort to the global politics of alignment and non-alignment. In the late 1960s and throughout the 1970s, however, Southeast Asian political leaders focused instead on national cohesion and regional cooperation. Most Southeast Asian states were still closely tied to their former colonial power in the early decades of independence, but by the 1970s the declining global status of those powers forced Southeast Asian leaders to reevaluate their policies. The regional states, in the process of these transitions, have grown to understand each other in ways never possible under the traditional or colonial systems.

The principal needs of the state have not changed over the several centuries between traditional and postcolonial times: (1) to control conflict; (2) to improve resource management as population densities increase; and (3) to organize and manage domestic and international commerce. However, the domestic and international environments in which these states must meet these needs has changed tremendously. No longer can the government presume that the autonomous village will provide sufficient economic opportunities or adequate social welfare. The economic and social disruption of Southeast Asian society in the colonial period broke down many traditional social relationships, especially at the village and clan levels, without providing alternative social or public service philosophies. Both at independence and at present, the governments of Southeast Asia have found that they must deliver to their constituencies a range of programs and opportunities that clearly are beyond the traditional capacities and responsibilities of the old Southeast Asian states.

Since the 1500s, when the state system of Europe began colonial expansion, the string of regional subsystems that made up the global system were at first economically and eventually politically eliminated, and the international system was transformed into a truly global system. Crucial to this transformation was the global acceptance of the concept of a multistate system of sovereign and equal states. The traditional Southeast Asian system, in contrast, was based on the primacy of a single state with various subordinate states arranged around this central actor, usually in a system corresponding roughly to geographic distance from the primary state.[1] It has become increasingly evident, however, that adoption of the Western European model has not everywhere been complete, given the weight of cultural difference and historic experience. A concept such as neotraditionalization, usually applied to the bureaucratic, political, and economic behavior of individuals, also has explanatory power for interstate behavior. This appears to be particularly true of Southeast Asia, where, as the newness of independence has worn away, the traditional dimensions of state structures and behavior have resurfaced.

The present regional system in Southeast Asia differs in many fundamental ways, of course, from the traditional system that preceded the colonial intrusion. Yet in other respects the traditional values and patterns of behavior, safely sheltered in the cultural totality that is Southeast Asia, have begun to reemerge as the states of the region individually and collectively define with greater vigor and confidence their own unique identities. The process of neotraditionalization in interstate behavior has not meant the reassertion of precolonial behavior patterns in an original and unfettered form. Instead, the leaders of states in Southeast Asia, finding themselves participants in a multistate system based on Western international law, have pursued their own ends and sought to provide for the security of their own states through whatever means were at their disposal. These leaders have been conditioned by the entire cultural and political experience of Southeast Asia--by the rules and behavior patterns of traditional Southeast Asia as well as by the colonial and contemporary systems of government and international relations. Although the form of the Western interstate system has been accepted globally, within Asia and particularly in Southeast Asia there remain manifestations of the traditional system in the daily functioning of interstate relations.

The states of Southeast Asia have become members of the global multistate system and, in the main, follow its prescriptions for interactions. All maintain formal embassies in the leading capitals of the world. The volume and range of interstate contacts far exceed those of any previous period, given the degree to which diplomatic form is followed as well as the many educational, economic, sporting and other exchanges that reinforce the concept of sovereign equality among states. The ways in which the states of Southeast Asia have adapted to this system, while simultaneously restoring many of the familiar values and patterns of behavior of their traditional interstate system, can be understood if the region is again divided into subsystems.

THE CULTURAL AND RELIGIOUS SUBSYSTEMS

In the traditional system, Indian religions and political concepts provided for all of Southeast Asia (except Vietnam) a modicum of cultural homogeneity, particularly among the royal elites in the region. These concepts in particular underlaid the political legitimacy of the king, and they were understood and accepted by the population as the rationale for the state and for life itself.

In the current system, however, no such homogeneity can be found. Government in the region, having lost its divinity, has not found another basis for its legitimacy. The Thai monarchy does play an important role in maintenance of political legitimacy, but the bureaucratic polity in Thailand also must maintain legitimacy as the decisionmaking arm of the government.[2] Buddhism has been a factor in contemporary politics in Burma, Thailand, and, at times, Vietnam, but it has not provided a firm base for political legitimacy. As premier in Burma, U Nu gave strong support to Buddhism and "became the link between the Burmese people, whose religious faith he shared and whose folk tales he knew, and the sophisticated Westernized Socialists who dominated much of the thinking" in the government.[3] Buddhist monks have been active in political protests in Vietnam but have not offered an organized alternative to communism there.

Islam also became a strong religious force in the traditional system, preceding the Europeans in the region and supplanting Indian kingship in most of the archipelagic states. However, even in the traditional period, Islam was adapted by the Southeast Asians to the preexisting political concepts of Hinduism; they changed names and terms but seldom the substance or functions of royalty.[4] Moreover, although Islam may have spread through archipelagic Southeast Asia in response to the Christianizing efforts of the Portuguese, it was not successful politically in drawing the region's sultanates together to combat the European penetration. In its more conservative political forms, Islam has at times been so reactionary that progress in cooperation with nonbelieving states proved difficult.

In the present system, professions of support for democratic principles of government, in one form or another, have replaced religion as the legitimizing force behind government. Democratic practices in government may be no more real than was the traditional king's interaction with Vishnu, but even the most autocratic or dictatorial governments in Southeast Asia, whether Right or Left ideologically, govern in the name of the people.

One of the imponderable questions of the current age is whether the people understand the implications of this shift in the basis of legitimacy or whether they expect the same responsiveness from government as they had received under the traditional system. There are no reliable answers, but it would appear (if we exclude the experience of some students and some of the urban elite) that expectations of governmental support and services have changed very little, despite the radically different base for governmental legitimacy.

THE ECONOMIC SUBSYSTEM

The current economic system of Southeast Asia has also changed from that of its traditional predecessor insofar as its dependence on the global economic system, although great during the traditional period, is more complete now. The subsistence base of village agriculture has been largely destroyed in an economic sense, while the social fabric and independent welfare system of the village has been broken in economic change and disruption of landholding patterns as well as by dramatic population growth and migration to cities. The remnants of village economic and social systems may offer some measure of insulation for a percentage of Southeast Asia's population, but they cannot provide a subsistence security base against the rises and falls of the global economic system.

Other aspects of Southeast Asia's present economic system more nearly resemble the traditional system. Much of the trading sector at all levels is controlled by foreigners (especially the Chinese, at present) although Indians also play a significant role in some states. The distaste that Southeast Asians, especially ethnic Malays, traditionally displayed for commerce remains prevalent. There is some evidence that during the traditional period indigenous Southeast Asians played a more active role in commerce,[5] and that these groups were eliminated during the colonial period.[6] The historical situation may be in doubt, but in the contemporary system all of the economies of the Southeast Asian states have been influenced by nonindigenous ethnic groups. The Malaysian economy is largely controlled by Chinese and, to a lesser extent, by Indians, and government policies designed to assist ethnic Malays increasingly produce friction. In Indonesia, the Chinese community is numerically much smaller than in Malaysia but has held substantial control in the economy, although in recent years the government and the army have taken a much larger role in the economy. The most sophisticated economic entity in the region--Singapore--is almost wholly Chinese in character. Burma and, more recently, Vietnam have driven out many of the Chinese (as well as the Indian, in Burma) business community, and the governments have taken control of most commercial activities. Among the countries of Southeast Asia, only in Thailand has the Chinese business community been more effectively assimilated.

The present economic system also resembles the traditional system in terms of the lack of clear separation of commercial and state activities. The traditional role of the wealthy merchant classes in supporting the kings of Southeast Asia, as well as the traditional state's direct participation in commerce by collecting taxes and levies in kind and marketing these surpluses, finds parallel activities in contemporary Southeast Asia. The close relationships between government officials and major commercial interests, interpreted as matters of corruption in Western eyes, find easy historical precedent in traditional Southeast Asia. Government participation in the economic sector has also been formalized in state monopolies such as the state petroleum organizations of Indonesia, Malaysia, Burma, the Philippines, and Thailand. There are other state-run economic organizations such as Burma's agricultural corporation, an appendage of the ministry of agriculture that plans, supervises, and markets major crops.

In the traditional economic system, government intervention was limited both by the weakness of the state's bureaucratic apparatus and by the power of the wealthy merchants as a counter to the power of the king. In the current system, both of these old restraints appear to have been reduced. Bureaucratic effectiveness, however scant at the outset of independence, has improved greatly in recent decades. A high level of governmental economic control also exists at present. Although wealthy merchants still have the ability to obtain favors and to influence policy, they cannot replace the government at their will.

Finally, although the subsistence economic structure of the village has been broken, no alternative has been found. The core of the former peasant society has been separated from its social and economic base, but the economies of the states have not developed sufficiently to sustain these people as producer/consumers. In an economic sense, large segments of the population in all of the states of Southeast Asia exist in economic limbo--somewhere between starvation and ad hoc subsistence. Governments have yet to develop the will or the resource base to provide the social welfare that these people could have expected from the traditional village.

THE POLITICAL AND DIPLOMATIC SUBSYSTEM

At independence, the states of Southeast Asia were brought into the global diplomatic system and such international organizations as the United Nations. In this respect, the international system accepted and confirmed the sovereignty of each state, a status that was not universally accepted domestically for most of these states. There is no historical precedent for a sovereign territorial state. Sovereignty in the traditional Southeast Asian state was held in the person of the ruler and extended through space (i.e., territory) to a limit that, in effect, became the perimeter of the kingdom. The concept of territorial sovereignty was externally imposed during the colonial period and did not represent, as territorial sovereignty had in Europe, a growing recognition among the general population of a national and territorial identity. Tan Sri Ghazali Shafie, Malaysian minister of home affairs, has said that "one of the unpleasant realities of Southeast Asia is that many of its states are mere territorial entities in search of national identities."[7]

Responses to their new sovereign status differed among the regional states, depending on their experience in attaining independence, their longer-term · relationships with the colonial power, and the perceptions of their national leaders as to the critical issues facing the new nation. One of the few relatively consistent positions among the new regional states was the propensity of each of them to ignore its regional neighbors in favor of relations with former colonial powers and major donors of economic or military assistance. Thailand, the most experienced in foreign affairs among the Southeast Asian states, had by 1954 established a full embassy within the region only in Burma and the Philippines, although Cambodia, Laos, Indonesia, and Vietnam were accredited with lower-level legations. In the same year, Indonesia had full embassies within the region only in Burma and the Philippines, although it maintained embassies in fourteen countries outside the region, including not only such major countries as the United States but also a number of Islamic states. Burma and the Philippines did not establish relations until 1956, when they accredited their respective ambassadors already in place in Bangkok rather than establish embassies in Rangoon and Manila.[8]

For several states, diplomacy offered a way of enhancing weak domestic political legitimacy. The Southeast Asian state was defined, increasingly, as the vanguard of a new global system in opposition to superpower politics. Burma and Cambodia sometimes used this policy in the nonaligned movement, but it was Indonesia's Sukarno who molded antiglobal themes for national as well as international purposes.[9] Given Burma's geographic vulnerability vis-a-vis China, particularly, and Cambodia's position in the midst of territory under dispute by global powers, nonalignment became the only policy offering some hope of continued independence for these states. In terms at least of the maintenance of independence (a primary fear for small states in contention with global powers), this policy strategy has been successful for Burma but ultimately not for Cambodia. Indonesia, on the other hand, initially formulated its nonaligned policies to minimize domestic criticism that it leaned too much to the Left or the Right,[10] although Sukarno later would align with Peking and Hanoi.

Since independence, all of the states have been involved with neighbors in an effort to define and control disputed or otherwise uncertain borders. As a corollary to their newly acquired territorial sovereignty, all of these states have had some difficulty in controlling border areas. Burma was among the most active in settling border disputes, especially with China and India, although many of Burma's problems stem from ethnic divisions existing within Burma and extending across the internationally recognized borders. Thailand has had similar border problems with Burma, Cambodia, and especially Laos, where Lao-speaking peoples have lived for centuries on both sides of the Mekong River. Historically, the Mekong has been an artery for communication and commerce, not a border line. The archipelagic states, too, have had problems with ethnic minorities who historically held separate and sovereign status. Because Southeast Asian statehood has most often been built around the values and religion of a dominant ethnic group while other ethnic groups equal in historic experience were passed over during the colonial age, the sense of sovereign legitimacy gained from global recognition was critical for the newly independent states of the region.

The transition from this extraregional focus to a more intimate set of relations within the region did not begin until the Southeast Asian states had gained experience in the international system and developed a more complete sense of their independent status. Not only the utility of the global system for providing political legitimacy but also the need to rely on global mentors for security guarantees lessened. A new regional context emerged in which these states recognized that their own future could be controlled internally. At about the same time, the global powers, particularly those in the West, perhaps began to understand that "assumptions concerning the possibility of transforming Southeast Asian states into some copy, or at least approximation, of nations in the West were illusory."[11]

By the mid-1960s, diplomacy in Southeast Asia had entered a new phase in which regional relations were gradually strengthened. As the identity of the states individually solidified, so the Southeast Asian region, too, took on an image of its own. As the residue of colonial influence diminished and the pressures of the cold war diminished, it became more obvious that within Southeast Asia itself there exist subregional areas of spheres of influence. One analyst has concluded that the "Southeast Asian islands clearly represent a sphere of influence within which historical forces have contested for prominence."[12] Events in Indochina have created a second sphere controlled from Hanoi.

THE MILITARY SUBSYSTEM: SECURITY AND REGIONAL CONFLICT

It is clear that in traditional times the states of Southeast Asia used force to good advantage. It is also clear that the role of military force is now radically different, not only in the obvious areas of modern equipment but, perhaps more importantly, in the military's value as an instrument of state power. In the traditional system, the power of the military depended on the continued support of semi-independent chieftains, leaders, and lords, but after World War II and independence, the hierarchical command structure of the modern military as adopted in Southeast Asia has made it the most efficient and effective bureaucratic structure in these countries: From one perspective, "a military establishment comes as close as any human organization can to the ideal type for an industrialized and secularized enterprise."[13] In all of the countries of Southeast Asia, the military has played an important role in supressing rebellions and insurgencies. In all of the countries except Vietnam, Malaysia, and Singapore, the military has extended that influence directly into the political sphere, at one time or another taking direct control of government in Indonesia, Burma, Thailand, and Cambodia.[14]

A lack of internal cohesion still characterizes the present system in Southeast Asia. Challenges come from ethnic minorities seeking greater autonomy or independence, or from ideological competitors seeking revolutionary change. Gone is the traditional role of Southeast Asian states as masters of the international sea-lanes and providers of entrepot services for international commerce. In a sense, Singapore still plays this role, but the naval complement no longer exists. In virtually every country in Southeast Asia it is the army that is paramount among the military services in both size and political influence.[15]

Although Southeast Asia has often been the arena for confrontation between the superpowers, most of the violence in the region since the breakdown of the U.S. containment policy has been domestic in character, as governments have tried to quash revolutionary insurgencies. The use of force in the traditional system was the primary tool for securing new territorial limits of the kingdom. In the present system, the territory of the state has been defined and, with very few exceptions, agreed upon by all actors in the international system, but force has remained a principal means for securing control within the territory.

Interstate violence continues also. Although the level of this violence has been reduced, it has not been eliminated as an acceptable means of interaction. Force remains a potent tool in the range of interstate contacts within Southeast Asia. In his study of Japan in East Asia, Hellmann argues that the continuing use of violence in Asian regional relations will eventually force Japan to expand its military capacities.[16] Vietnam's occupation of Cambodia may be the most conspicuous recent example, but others abound: Indonesia in Timor, and earlier in the Irian and Malaysian campaigns; the Philippines in the Malaysia dispute and in conflict with its Islamic minorities; Malaysia and Thailand on their common border; and Burma in the border regions with China and Thailand.

Despite the international conflicts involved in the recent invasion of Cambodia and Indonesia's takeover of East Timor, the states of Southeast Asia have compounded their declining diplomatic concern for global strategizing with an increasing concern for issues of internal stability and security. States such as China are still feared for their potential as fomentors of insurgency, but governments have realized that the best counter to potential insurgencies is a strong, stable, and growing domestic economy. Early paranoia associated with the departure of U.S. ground forces from the region has given way to more realistic planning, not only in the military field but also in such areas as rural development and agricultural production policies.

The states of Southeast Asia have eschewed formal military alliances among themselves, although many have established security agreements with extraregional powers. However, as the regional states have intensified bilateral relations among themselves since the mid-1960s, and as regional associations such as ASEAN have gained strength, they have found it easier to "talk frankly about collective security."[17] A wide variety of military interchanges such as joint maneuvers, training exchanges, intelligence exchanges, and joint planning exercises have been carried out bilaterally among ASEAN members. And in Indochina, of course, Vietnam has signed treaties of friendship and cooperation with both Laos and Cambodia.

EXTRAREGIONAL POWERS

As in the traditional Southeast Asian system, and as should be expected in any subordinate system, extraregional powers have been active in the post-World War II era in Southeast Asia. The configuration of powers has expanded, but, following an initial period of near-domination, especially by the United States, the regional states have nevertheless asserted their independence and taken more effective control of regional as well as national politics. Although this does not imply that Southeast Asia's subordinate status will end, it does suggest that external power can be contained and that the regional states, as they develop their international skills, will find more opportunities for independent action.

Traditional extraregional power roles have changed. India, which provided much of the cultural and philosophical underpinnings for the traditional system, has lost most of its influence, although Buddhism remains strong among the mainland Southeast Asian states and Burma has kept close relations with India. In the early years of independence, Jawaharlal Nehru was one of the truly global spokesmen for neutralism and nonalignment, and Sukarno, U Nu, and Sihanouk were closely associated with him as leaders of the newly independent nations of Asia. But this collegial relationship did not spread beyond the nonaligned movement, and in the modern era India has not played the leadership role ascribed to it by early scholars.[18]

The role of China as an extraregional power has followed very closely its traditional patterns, particularly with regard to political interaction. Its traditional economic role as the principal source for goods traveling through Southeast Asia has ended, and, as a result of the great increase in Chinese population now residing in Southeast Asian countries, its current role is less well understood. China's recent political activities in the region have been indirect, coming largely through relations with fraternal Communist parties. At different times, China has maintained strong government-to-government relations with Indonesia (1960-1965), Cambodia (1975-1979), and Vietnam (until 1975). China's relations with Burma have been stable and friendly but not intimate.

The Chinese approach to Southeast Asia has been low-key, not unlike its traditional foreign policy strategy. China has made much of the hydraulic agrarian nature of its society in trying to assert its influence over Communist ideological thought in Asia. The Chinese policy toward Southeast Asia as a regional whole has not been well formulated, although on the mainland the Chinese sought to limit Soviet involvement in Indochina and, failing to succeed there, have expanded relations with Thailand and Burma in addition to providing support to Cambodian insurgents. At the same time, the Chinese military incursion into Vietnam could be considered a manifestation of the tradition of punishing an ungrateful vassal.

However, China as well as the other superpowers have recognized that the nature of the global system puts the present Southeast Asian system in a new position. No longer one of a series of loosely linked and semi-independent regional systems, Southeast Asia has instead become an area of direct global involvement and confrontation. The United States strategy of containment of the Communist Asian heartland was challenged and broken on Southeast Asian soil. Moreover, China's opposition to Vietnam's control of Cambodia stems not from a fear of a powerful Vietnam but from the recognition that the Soviet alliance with the Vietnamese introduces a new form of containment, with the Soviet Union now militarily entrenched on China's southern flank.

For the United States and the USSR, there appear to be few vital issues pertaining to Southeast Asia that require direct intervention. It is only when and if the global powers confront one another on a global issue in the region that some form of superpower conflict is likely. The United States might consider it vital to protect the sea-lanes that connect Japan to Middle Eastern oil, but Southeast Asia cannot claim the same vital position that Europe, for example, holds for U.S. interests. If the Soviet Union should "deglobalize" its foreign policy, as has been suggested,[19] the importance of its relationship with Vietnam may diminish; particularly, should the Soviet Union and China reach a rapprochement in their bilateral relations, Vietnam's strategic importance in the regional context would further diminish. For China, on the other hand, Southeast Asia, whether Communist or non-Communist, remains strategically vital and will become increasingly vital in economic terms.

Economic competition for the Chinese will come not from the Soviet Union or the United States, but from Japan. Through the end of this century, as Chinese economic capabilities expand, Southeast Asia will be important for raw materials and markets. In the meantime, Southeast Asia itself will increase its own productivity and seek Chinese markets. With Japanese technological and managerial leadership the economic future should be bright, although any conflict in Southeast Asia could undermine this potential.

CHARACTERISTICS OF THE SYSTEM

This study has outlined in broad terms the interstate system of southeast Asia from its historical base to its present configuration. The level of generalization necessary for such an overview becomes both its strength and its weakness: The themes and generalities used to describe the region systemically can often be challenged with specific examples that vary dramatically from the norms. Yet it is the norms that provide the framework against which the exceptions can be more readily understood. That the norms constitute a working and unique system appears beyond doubt; moreover, the system's unique characteristics will become more evident as the individual state actors find in their contemporary policies that elusive mix of cultural interpretation and adaptation to meet external challenges and threats, as these cultures have done so effectively for two millenia or more.

Institutional Strength. The current states of Southeast Asia exhibit many of the same weaknesses as their traditional predecessors. These states did not evolve, historically, through common undertakings of the mass of the population. The modern state has been unable to build broad-based support, especially among religious and ethnic minorities. Even among states that experienced a common revolutionary struggle against former colonial masters, unity was lost once the common goal of expelling the colonial power was accomplished. This became immediately apparent after Indonesia gained its independence, and it explains in large part the failure of parliamentary democracy there.[20] Similar problems appear to be overtaking Vietnam, particularly as it has tried to impose new policies in the south.[21]

The centrist nature of the current Southeast Asian state also resembles that of its traditional predecessor. Revolutionary movements in the region have been led by Western-educated urban elites, many of whom have demonstrated little understanding of the rural regions of their countries. Political parties have rarely been mass organizations and often are little more than small cliques of politicians. There have been exceptions, such as some of the region's Communist parties, but most of the government controlled organizations that have extended into rural areas, such as Indonesia's GOLKAR[22] or Burma's BSPP after 1981,[23] have remained extensions of outward control from the urban center to the rural fringes. None has had notable success in engendering strong political support among the rural populations.

Although the boundaries of the Southeast Asian states were, for the most part, clearly demarcated at independence, most of these countries have had difficulty extending effective power throughout their territorial limits. This has been a problem in the archipelago, but separatist movements in Sumatra and in Eastern Indonesia

have been supressed and the Muslim rebels in the
Philippines have so far been unable to bring their fight
to any great success. Border regions in mainland
Southeast Asia tend to resemble the "no-man's land" that
separated the traditional states. For years, Vietnam made
free use of the border territories in Laos and Cambodia
for military purposes. The Lao population on both sides
of the Thai-Laotian border sees itself as a separate
people, and the Shan, Karen, and other areas technically
within Burma are administered largely as independent
states, primarily lacking international recognitions.[24]
Not only have borders on land been difficult to protect,
but coastal shipping has suffered from the piracy that has
escalated in recent years, taking advantage of refugees
fleeing Indochina.[25]

Against these institutional weaknesses in the state
must be balanced the general improvement in bureaucratic
efficiency and management. At independence, poorly
trained political appointees filled the bureaucracies.
However, some three decades of training and education
(much of the advanced training being done internationally)
have meant a greater capacity for planning,
decisionmaking, and implementing government policy,
although perhaps in a neotraditional style.

Interstate Exchange. On the basis of their experience
before and during the colonial period, the newly
independent states of Southeast Asia initially found
little in common. At first they sought their closest
political and economic relations outside the region,
despite many public flourishes about the importance of
good relations among their more immediate neighbors.
However, the nonaligned and Western-aligned states (except
Burma) have discovered that there is a certain safety in
numbers and that their common developmental and political
plights have given them much in common. Their capacities
for cooperative interchange are still limited by lack of
resources as well as the fragile nature of their political
institutions. Nevertheless, cooperation among a
significant group of regional states has developed beyond
levels anticipated only a few years ago. Southeast Asia
has been "characterized by an imbalance of 'power,' which
the region's governments, determined to control their own
fate, may prefer to any balance system dominated by major
military powers."[26]

Conflict remains a common component of regional
interactions. With the Vietnamese control of Indochina,

the region seems poised for a period of bipolar conflict between the ASEAN group and the Communist group. Because the sovereignty and territorial integrity of these states are "soft," the extension of power into the frontier zones has been a valid option in the range of interstate behavior. In short, the regional multistate system has in some situations taken on the complexion of an imperial or hegemonic system.

The traditional Southeast Asian system gave a strong position to hegemonic relations between states. The propensity toward monopoly control of commercial sea-lanes, commodity ports, and entrepot centers, especially in the archipelago, reinforced this unequal relational structure. Throughout traditional Southeast Asia, ethnic suspicions reinforced by Hindu/Buddhist and Confucian political concepts of the state legitimized superior-vassal interstate relations in the regional system. These superior-vassal elements of hegemonistic relations have found expression in the present system: "From a security perspective, the past decade has witnessed the development of two Southeast Asias. One, centered on the membership of the Association of Southeast Asian Nations . . . the other, centering on a Vietnamese-dominated Indochina."[27]

Although seeming to contradict the tenets of independence and self-determination, both leading regional powers--Vietnam and Indonesia--have sought control of the full colonial territory from which they sprang. With the consolidation of its hold on Indochina, Vietnam fulfilled an objective stated at least as early as the 1930s for the Indochinese Communist party. In addition, the process of Vietnamese expansionism dates back several hundred years. A paranoia for security, developed from decades of foreign hostility emanating from neighboring states, may have strengthened the ideological resolve to consolidate Indochina, but Vietnam's success engenders the expansion of a major ethnic group in a manner almost endemic to Southeast Asian history. Indonesia fought doggedly to claim all of the former Dutch territory despite a paucity of historical or cultural ties to such areas as West Irian, but, while long harboring desires for regional leadership,[28] it has had less success in imposing its will on any neighboring states. Sukarno's bombastic policies of confrontation have given way to more subdued position, but, particularly since the formation of ASEAN, Indonesia has consolidated its influence within the archipelagic subregion of Southeast Asia. Some see

Indonesia as the paramount but not dominant state in the region.[29]

The Vietnam/Indochina and Indonesia/ASEAN subsystems can be seen as analogues to the traditional imperial systems of traditional Southeast Asia, although imperialism must be viewed less in Hobson's economic terms (i.e., as a function of expansion of excess capital) and more, as Schumpeter has argued, in terms of the inherent propensity of states to expand.[30] Nationalist, ethnic, and cultural motivations for Vietnamese and Indonesian expansion are plausible and have solid historical precedents. And to the extent that "regional organization corresponds to countries falling within that sphere, then the nature of a successful grouping will likely be hegemonial."[31] The obvious differences between the strategies and structures of the two hegemonic subsystems can be explained in terms of available, usable power in which security is not perceived "solely as a military matter in the conventional sense" but can be envisioned as including "sources of domestic instability--political, economic, social, cultural, and ideological."[32] In the East Timor situation, Indonesia did not hesitate to use military force to consolidate its position, but its role in ASEAN has grown without military power. Since 1967 Indonesia has also developed substantial influence with Malaysia and Singapore,[33] in a relationship described as the "eldest brother" role among the three.[34] Indonesia and Vietnam have been identified as two "core members" of the larger East Asian system and "the two most important states of Southeast Asia, Indonesia for the insular archipelago and North Vietnam for the mainland."[35]

In this regional analysis, Thailand sits in a particularly difficult position on the frontier between two imperial subsystems, whereas both Burma and the Philippines are, for the present, in more peripheral positions. If these hegemonic subsystems collide, it will be along the Thai border with Cambodia or Laos. Following age-old regional patterns for the extension of power from competing centers toward the frontier under challenge, it appears likely that the Thai-Cambodian borders as recognized internationally may change.

One such possible scenario may be the erosion of the north and northeastern border of Thailand. Should this happen, the frontier between Thailand and Indochina would drift westward as refugees, ethnic Lao, and other peoples are reabsorbed under Indochinese control while the Thai peoples are constricted to the west and south.

Reportedly, Thai military sources received from a Lao defector documents that outlined plans to develop an "autonomous zone" in five Thai provinces to ensure Communist control of the Mekong hydroelectric system.[36] Vietnamese troops have entered Thai territory on several occasions, and recent actions, especially the planting of land mines,[37] may signal their intent to more permanently defend this territory. Under this scenario, equilibrium of a new frontier would in all likelihood be reestablished before Thailand collapsed completely. Should Indonesian forces be used to preserve some element of an independent Thai state, the configuration of imperial power would again shift. It is also possible that intensified pressure on its Indochinese border would leave Thailand unable to control its southern border with Malaysia, thus opening further possibilities for expansion of Indonesian influence through Malaysia or, more directly, through the use of Indonesian troops.

Alternatively, certain of the Thai military leaders are known to favor extending Thai control into the western provinces of Cambodia. Rumors of the weakness of Vietnam's military position could make such a Thai military offensive more plausible. However, the positions taken by other ASEAN states to support any such major military offensive would be critical, especially for Thailand's long-term abilities to sustain control of this added territory. The end result of this campaign would be the partition of Cambodia and its effective demise as a state.

The unfolding of imperial power in Southeast Asia has polarized the region. This new polarization may jeopardize regional stability and increase the possibilities for conflict by focusing for the first time nearly all of the region's power resources at one point--the Thai-Indochina border. However, both Vietnam and ASEAN also have a common interest in limiting and controlling regional involvement of extraregional states--an interest that could lead to some type of regional accommodation.[38] Most of the regional states in both groups view possible Chinese intervention as the most critical threat to the region. Thailand, the single important exception to this view, fears further Vietnamese expansion. But a series of Vietnamese actions and assurances coupled with ASEAN guarantees could mitigate, if not eliminate, this fear. The possibility for conflict between the two regional groupings is high, but there is little evidence to suggest that Indonesia can or will seek to expand its imperial zone, although pressures on Thailand could force Indonesian action. Vietnam appears to control the future in its choice to push further or to hold and regroup, whereas Thailand will play a prominent role to the extent that it can secure itself as a stable and strong buffer between the two imperial poles.

System Dependence. A principal characteristic of a subordinate system is its relatively greater dependence on the larger system rather than the reverse. This was true for the traditional Southeast Asian system, and it remains true today. Southeast Asia did demonstrate that it can influence and even overcome the dominant global system when nationalist movements defeated the returning colonial powers, when the North Vietnamese defeated the United States, and when the ASEAN states martialed UN support against the Soviet Union and Vietnam on questions of Cambodia. But despite these specific incidents, Southeast Asia remains limited in its ability to influence the global system.

Nonetheless, clear limits have been found in the ability of global actors to influence the region. The United States was unable to achieve its goal in Vietnam; the Soviet Union was careful to remain aloof when China attacked its Vietnamese ally; and even the Chinese did not attempt a serious military conflict with Vietnam. Thailand, the Philippines and others, fearing the worst when U.S. troops withdrew from the region, have found that alternative arrangements and linkages with regional neighbors may be more effective and dependable than fickle relationships with globally-oriented superpowers.

As a consequence, Southeast Asia's dependence has lessened and its regional states have found greater latitude in opening new relations with former enemies and developing closer working relationships among themselves. Dependence will certainly continue, but regional states will find more opportunities to shape the nature of global interventions to fit their own regional and national needs. The current level of dependence should continue for some time. Vietnam must somehow resolve the political situation in Indochina and address its very considerable economic development problems. Indonesia, if it is to provide strong regional leadership, must scale back its financial dependence on the West, deal with the Soviet-Vietnamese presence in Indochina, establish stable working relationships for itself and the region with China, and find a balance against the Japanese economic

domination in Southeast Asia.[39] When each of the key
regional power blocs has stabilized its own group, better
relationships between the two will be possible. At that
point, Southeast Asia will move again toward further
regional autonomy.

A CONCLUSION

There are many who have argued that Southeast Asia
does not, in fact, exist as more than a geographic place
requiring external molding,[40] whereas others have
searched for evidence of regional unity.[41] One critic
has maintained that no group of states should be
considered a true region unless the states there show (1)
a "common institutional structure," (2) some "common
cementing experience," or (3) distinctive and intensive
interstate actions.[42] The evidence reported in this
book meets these criteria. Of course, the Southeast Asian
system may not be as tidy as that of Europe. It must also
be acknowledged that "Southeast Asia" as a contemporary
term and in its historical context is still in the early
stages of definition. But, at this point in time, it is
already clear that Southeast Asia's common historic
experience is leading to similar state and now regional
institutional structures unique to the region. Both
historically and currently, Southeast Asians have
"abundantly demonstrated their capacity to absorb and,
more important, to descriminate in what they absorb"[43]
in the process of creating a system suitable to their
circumstance.

NOTES

1. See, for example, the study edited by John King
Fairbank, The Chinese World Order: Traditional China's
Foreign Relations (Cambridge: Harvard University Press,
1968).
2. Fred W. Riggs, Thailand: Modernization of a
Bureaucratic Polity (Honolulu: East-West Center Press,
1966), pp. 91-109.
3. John F. Cady, A History of Modern Burma (Ithaca:
Cornell University Press, 1958), p. 597.
4. L. F. Brakel, "State and Statecraft in 17th
Century Aceh," in Pre-Colonial State Systems in Southeast
Asia, edited by Anthony Reid and Lance Castles (Kuala

Lumpur: Malaysian Branch of the Royal Asiatic Society, Monograph no. 6, 1975), pp. 56-66. The author provides an excellent analysis of the continuing Hindu substance of ritual and practice in Aceh under the sultans, despite their conversion to Islam and their adoption of Islamic terms, titles, and labels at the court.

5. John K. Whitmore, "The Opening of Southeast Asia: Trading Patterns Through the Centuries," in Economic Exchange and Social Interaction in Southeast Asia, edited by Karl L. Hutter (Ann Arbor: Michigan Papers on South and Southeast Asia, no. 13, 1977), pp. 73-96.

6. J. C. van Leur, Indonesian Trade and Society (The Hague: W. van Hoeve, Ltd., 1955); and L. A. Peter Gosling, "Contemporary Malay Traders in the Gulf of Thailand," in Hutter, Economic Exchange and Social Interaction in Southeast Asia, pp. 73-96.

7. Asia 1975 Yearbook (Hong Kong: Far Eastern Economic Review, 1975), p. 217.

8. Russell H. Fifield, Diplomacy of Southeast Asia (New York: Praeger Publishers, 1958), pp. 49-52, 219.

9. Jon M. Reinhardt, Foreign Policy and National Integration: The Case of Indonesia (New Haven, Conn.: Yale University, Southeast Asian Studies Monograph Series, no. 17, 1971), pp. 122-124. The author provides a brief account of how Sukarno turned a confrontation with the International Olympic Committee to great domestic political advantage.

10. Franklin B. Weinstein, Indonesian Foreign Policy and the Dilemma of Dependence (Ithaca: Cornell University Press, 1976).

11. Milton Osborne, Region in Revolt: Focus on Southeast Asia (Victoria: Penguin Books, 1971), p. 184.

12. Reinhardt, Foreign Policy and National Integration, p. 149.

13. Lucian W. Pye, "Armies in the Process of Political Modernization," in The Role of the Military in Underdeveloped Countries, edited by John J. Johnson (Princeton, N.J.: Princeton University Press, 1962), p. 75.

14. J. Stephen Hoadley, Soldiers and Politics in Southeast Asia: Civil-Military Relations in Comparative Perspective (Cambridge, Mass.: Schenkman Publishing Co., 1975).

15. Ibid., p. 153.

16. Donald C. Hellmann, Japan and East Asia: The New International Order (New York: Praeger Publishers, 1972).

17. Werner Levi, "The Future of Southeast Asia," Asian Survey 10 (April 1970), p. 350.

18. See K. M. Panikkar, The Future of South-East Asia (London: Allen & Unwin, 1943), cited in Peter Lyon, War and Peace in South-East Asia (London: Oxford University Press, 1969), p. 25. Panikkar prescribed an Indian-Chinese partnership for the economic development and collective defense of Southeast Asia.

19. Vernon V. Aspaturian, "The Foreign Policy of the Soviet Union," in World Politics, edited by James N. Rosenau, Kenneth W. Thompson, and Gavin Boyd (New York: Free Press, 1976), p. 93.

20. Herbert Feith, The Decline of Constitutional Democracy in Indonesia (Ithaca: Cornell University Press, 1962).

21. Edmund McWilliams, "Vietnam in 1982: Onward into the Quagmire," Asian Survey 23 (January 1983), pp. 71-72.

22. R. William Liddle, "Evolution from Above: National Leadership and Local Development in Indonesia," Journal of Asian Studies 32 (February 1973), pp. 287-309.

23. David J. Steinberg, Burma: A Socialist Nation in Southeast Asia (Boulder, Colo.: Westview Press, 1982), pp. 80-82.

24. "Burma--The Wars that Will Not Stop," Time (Asian edition, May 31, 1982), p. 23.

25. One of the factors that make these attacks so lucrative is that many Asians, who traditionally are cautious of political regimes and of the value of currency, would be carrying or wearing all of their wealth in the form of gold jewelry.

26. Melvin Gurtov, China and Southeast Asia--The Politics of Survival (Lexington, Mass.: Heath Lexington Books, 1971), p. 177.

27. Sheldon W. Simon, "The Two Southeast Asias and China: Security Perspectives," Asian Survey 24 (May 1984), p. 519.

28. Bernard K. Gordon, "The Potential for Indonesian Expansionism," Pacific Affairs 36 (Winter 1963-1964).

29. Robert A. Scalapino, Asia and the Road Ahead: Issues for the Major Powers (Berkeley: University of California Press, 1975), p. 147. The study concludes with an excellent bibliographic essay on the current and future international relations of Asia.

30. J. A. Hobson, Imperialism: A Study (Ann Arbor: University of Michigan Press, 1965); and Joseph A. Schumpeter, "Imperialism and Social Classes," in The Imperialism Reader, edited by Louis L. Snyder (Princeton, N.J.: D. Van Nostrand, 1962).

31. Reinhardt, Foreign Policy and National Integration, p. 149.

32. Peter Polomka, "Intra-Regional Dynamics: ASEAN and Indochina," in International Security in Southeast Asia and the Southwest Pacific Region, edited by T. B. Millar (St. Lucia: University of Queensland Press, 1983), p. 117, citing Jusuf Wanandi, "The International Implications of Third World Conflict: A Third World Perspective," in Third World Conflict and International Security, Part I (London: International Institute for Strategic Studies, Adelphi Papers No. 166, Summer 1981).

33. Donald G. McCloud, "Indonesia in Southeast Asia: An Events Data Assessment of Her Foreign Policy Environment," Asian Forum 9 (Winter/Spring 1976-1977), p. 74.

34. Benedikt N. Marban, "Posisi Indonesia di Asia Tenggara," in Kejakinan dan Perdjuangan, edited by P. D. Laluthamallo (Jakarta: BPK Gunung Malia, 1971).

35. Sheldon Simon, "East Asia," in Rosenau et al., World Politics, p. 530.

36. The Bangkok Post (March 30, 1975), cited in Robert E. Zimmerman, "Thailand 1975: Transition to Constitutional Democracy Continues," Asian Survey 16 (February 1976), p. 170.

37. Associated Press (Bangkok), May 6, 1985.

38. Polomka, "Intra-Regional Dynamics," in Millar, International Security in Southeast Asia and the Southwest Pacific Region, p. 138.

39. Simon, "East Asia," in Rosenau et al., World Politics, p. 538.

40. William Henderson, "The Development of Regionalism in Southeast Asia," International Organization 9 (November 1955); Michael Leifer, "Trends in Regional Association in Southeast Asia," Asian Studies 2 (August 1964); and Lyon, War and Peace in South-East Asia.

41. Michael Brecher, New States of Asia (London: Oxford University Press, 1963); Bernard K. Gordon, The Dimensions of Conflict in Southeast Asia (Englewood Cliffs, N.J.: Prentice-Hall, 1966).

42. Lyon, War and Peace in South-East Asia, p. 3.

43. Charles A. Fisher, South-East Asia: A Social, Economic and Political Geography (London: Methuen, 1964), p. 776.

Acronyms

ABC   ASEAN Brussels Committee

ADB   Asian Development Bank (Manila)

ANZUS   Defence pact that includes Australia, New Zealand, and the United States

ASA   Association of Southeast Asia

ASEAN   Association of Southeast Asian Nations

ASPAC   Asian and Pacific Council

CENTO   Central Treaty Organization

ECAFE   Economic Commission for Asia and the Far East

EEC   European Economic Community

ESCAP   Economic and Social Commission for Asia and the Pacific

IGGI   Inter-Governmental Group on Indonesia

MAPHILINDO Regional organization that included Malaysia, the Philippines, and Indonesia

NATO   North Atlantic Treaty Organization

OPEC   Organization of Petroleum Exporting Countries

PKI   Indonesian Communist Party

PRC   People's Republic of China

PRG   Provisional Revolutionary Government (of South Vietnam)

SSCAN	Special Coordinating Committee on ASEAN
SEATO	Southeast Asia Treaty Organization
UNCTAD	United Nations Conference on Trade and Development
VOC	Dutch (or United) East Indies Company
ZOPFAN	Zone of Peace, Freedom, and Neutrality

Index